THE VIEW FROM CASA CHEPITOS

THE VIEW FROM CASA CHEPITOS

A Journey Beyond the Border

JUDITH GILLE

Davis Bay
Press

SEATTLE | 2013

Several of the stories in this book have appeared in online magazines and anthologies. "*La Madrina*" originally appeared in the Hugo House News under the title "The Wedding Dress." Chapter 22, "*El Diablo y la Virgen*," is scheduled to be published as "The Devil and the Virgin" in *Not Somewhere Else but Here: A Contemporary Anthology of Women and Place* published by Sundress Publications, 2014.

Library of Congress Cataloging-in-Publication Data
Gille, Judith
The view from Casa Chepitos: a journey beyond the border /
Judith Gille. — 1st edition.

    p. cm.

1. Mexico — Description and travel 2. Mexico — social life and customs
3. Title

Cover design by Dorit Ely.
Cover photograph by Bob Weil, co-author of "*The Art of iPhone Photography: Creating Great Photos and Art on Your iPhone*."

Book design by John D. Berry.
Text typeface: MVB Verdigris

NOTE TO THE READER:
The names of many people in this story have been changed. Some for obvious reasons, and a few for reasons that are not so obvious. — JG

Printed in the United States

Davis Bay Press
1420 East Pine Street, E502
Seattle, WA 98122
davisbaypress@gmail.com

For the people of Callejón de Chepito,
con mucho cariño.

CONTENTS

*The real voyage of discovery
consists not in seeking new landscapes,
but in having new eyes.*

MARCEL PROUST

Prologue

IT WASN'T A QUEST FOR LOVE that propelled me back to Mexico. At least, not love in any conventional sense. It wasn't the end of a tumultuous affair or a messy divorce.

It was the closing of a store. A store named City People's. A store I'd founded years before in a burst of youthful idealism.

And the dreary Seattle weather. Twenty-three years of low-hung clouds, pissing gray skies, and meager hours of thickly filtered daylight had worn a hole, fathoms deep, in my psyche.

Finally, there was a dusty memory. One I had filed away, a long time ago.

February 1974. I am walking up a cobblestone street in San Miguel de Allende wearing a pair of Earth Shoes. My toes are numb from hiking uphill in the weirdly designed soles. Yet I feel happier than I've ever felt before. The air is light and clear. The sky, a brilliant blue.

I arrive at the home of a woman in her seventies, a retired friend from my textile design class at the Instituto Allende. She has invited another student and me for *comida*, the Mexican midday meal.

Entering my friend's living room, I am overwhelmed by a sense of déjà vu. I feel as if I have dreamt of the small *sala*, with its walls the color of papaya flesh and its whimsical collection of folk art. Masks of fantastic creatures and cutouts of dancing skeletons leap from walls; striped serapes drape leather *icapali* chairs; intricately patterned Oaxacan rugs are scattered about the terracotta parquet; a giant clay corn goddess, glazed in deep green, graces a corner table.

Enchanted by the colorful cacophony, I think: *I could retire like this.* But the thought passes quickly. I am only twenty years old. Retirement is a lifetime away.

Years later, for no apparent reason, the memory began to migrate toward the front of my brain. To the place where longing resides.

Part One | *La Casa*

Any given moment can change your life …
you just have to BE there.

LEIGH STANDLEY

1 | *Skating*

O N A COLD AND RAINY EVENING in early January 2002, I went to the front hall closet and dug out my Rollerblades. Then I walked two blocks to City People's Mercantile, the store I had opened twenty-two years, two months, and seven days before, and let myself in the back door, one last time. The following day my business partners and I would hand the keys over to a pair of real estate developers, who had bought the building.

Standing in the blue-green glow of a few remaining fluorescent fixtures, I barely recognized the cavernous, empty space where I'd worked for most of my adult life. The inventory had been sold off or donated; the cinder block walls stripped bare of display cases, fixtures, and racks; the cash register stands and offices cleared out. All that remained were the dark green and white signs hung with fishing line from the ceiling identifying the store's various departments: Hardware, Garden, Cookshop, Lifestyles, Clothing, Toys, and Office and Art. I leaned down beneath Office and Art and snapped on my skates.

As I glided onto the smooth terrazzo floor — something I'd yearned to do ever since we'd moved in — years of memories began looping through my mind. With each circle I made, the stressful days, the sleepless nights, the long hours, the clogged drains and backed-up sewers, the leaky roof, the grumpy customers, the interminable lines at holiday time came flooding back.

Still, like the 8 mm home movies of my early childhood, happier images also flickered by.

There was our first meeting with Corr, the clerk for the Pacific Marine Schwabacher hardware company who spent hours helping my partners and me put together our first hardware order. There was purchasing our first cash register and ringing up our first sale. Securing a business loan when the odds were stacked against us. Blowing past our sales projections.

There was our hardware manager Verna Wells and her all-women hardware staff. There were employee rafting trips on the Wenatchee River, bowling competitions at Village Lanes, and holiday parties at my house.

There were the faces of loyal customers, our "regulars," for whom the store provided a daily refuge. There was Mary, a gray-haired anti-nuclear activist, and cranky old Clayton, an eighty-year-old widower who shuffled in each day for a handful of nails or a bit of small talk. There was Big Ed, who did odd jobs for Mr. Lindsey at the Capitola Apartments and wore the same dark-green work shirt and trousers every day for seven years. There was Mrs. Postie, a character straight out of Faulkner, who lived alone behind shuttered windows in a pale pink mansion on the corner of Thirteenth and Mercer. She phoned her orders in and we hand-delivered them.

There were young parents who came in seeking a morning's diversion. Like the pretty blonde with the towheaded Irish twins perched like fledglings in their English pram. As college students, the boys would return to reminisce about roaming our toy department as toddlers.

As I circled the store, the voices of countless customers haunted me:

"City People's is my favorite place to shop."

"I love City People's, they've got everything."

"City People's is such an important part of the neighborhood."

I skated until my trembling legs would go no farther.

Then I walked back down the alley in darkness as freezing rain nipped at my face.

If it hadn't been for Seattle's gloomy winters, I might have been able to bear the psychic burden of shutting down one of the city's most beloved retail destinations and laying off thirty-nine employees, including one who was battling breast cancer, only three months after 9/11.

But with little more than seven hours of light each day and the forecast alternating between rain turning to showers, rain turning to sleet, and wind with rain and sleet, I began to bottom out.

I couldn't sleep. I lost my appetite. When the new owners of our building announced that a Walgreens would be replacing City People's, demonstrations broke out in the parking lot. My house was egged. My car was vandalized. I began to avoid going out in public because everywhere I went the question *why* hovered in conversations. Why did we close the store? Why couldn't we find a way to keep it open?

I answered the questions over and over, as much to convince myself that we'd made the right decision as to respond to the queries.

Then one afternoon, on my way to the grocery store, I spotted an ex-employee walking toward me. It was the man who'd been our bookkeeper for the last six years. He and I had always gotten along well, and it cheered me up to see him again. I smiled as he approached.

"Hi, Sean, how are you doing?" I said.

He ignored my greeting and just kept walking. When I broke down sobbing in the middle of the sidewalk a minute later, passersby made a point of steering clear. As if my misery was somehow contagious.

Weeks went by with little relief from my tears, mood swings, weight loss, and sleeplessness. Eventually, my husband, Paul, suggested I see a doctor. Though resistant at first, I finally made an appointment with my family doc, who referred me to

mental health services. The psychiatrist I eventually met with —
a ruddy-cheeked man with an excruciatingly upbeat manner —
handed me a questionnaire to fill out. Amid the questions about
my eating and sleeping habits were others, such as "Do you
feel excessively guilty?" and "Do you feel life is meaningless?"
Answering them only depressed me more.

I assumed I'd flunked the man's quiz when he diagnosed the
shadowy pit in my brain as depression brought on by seasonal
affective disorder. He, rather cheerfully I thought, wrote out a
prescription for antidepressants and handed it to me.

I slogged across a rain-slicked parking lot to the pharmacy
and had the prescription filled. I took the medication home, set
the small brown cylinder filled with tiny white pills on my desk,
and stared at it for a long time.

Then I decided to take matters into my own hands. I went
online and searched for San Miguel de Allende — a place from
my youth I remembered as being full of light, full of color, full of
life. Full of everything currently missing in my life. That evening
I sent an email to a San Miguel real estate agency inquiring about
a house for rent, and, unwittingly, set a whole new life in motion.

2 | *Reunion*

I T WAS EARLY FEBRUARY 2002 when I called to invite my three older sisters and mother to join me for a reunion at the house I'd rented in San Miguel. My sisters Margaret and Rachel, who had spent the summer of 1972 there, had provided the inspiration for me to move there a year later, by myself, to study art and Spanish at the Instituto Allende.

We all looked forward to revisiting the charming Mexican hill town, but I privately hoped that the bright light of Mexico's central plateau would break the emotional spiral I'd been on for months and free me from reliance on antidepressants. I was equally desperate to escape the media's obsession with 9/11 and our president's fixation on catching the "evildoers."

However, in hindsight, I realize that I was searching for something more than just clear skies, warmer temperatures, and an escape from the depressing news. I was looking for something I'd lost over the last twenty-five years.

AT THE LAST MINUTE Rachel couldn't make it, but my sisters Frances and Margaret and I flew into Del Bajío International Airport, sixty miles northwest of San Miguel, where we were to meet our mother, who'd spent the prior three weeks in the state of Guanajuato on an Elderhostel. The three of us had barely cleared customs when we heard a familiar warble echo across the terminal.

"*¡Hola! ¡Hola!*" Our mother, a tiny, bird-like woman with

straw-colored hair and pale, papery skin, was a whirlwind of energy, even at eighty-two. Her manic hand-waving made it easy to spot her in the crowd of placid Mexicans.

Standing beside her was the man she'd hired to drive us to San Miguel.

"Girls, this is Elee-AY-zar," she said, seriously botching the pronunciation of his name. I looked at Eleazar, to see if he seemed amused or offended, but he gave no indication. The mild-mannered man with the pencil-thin mustache simply gathered our bags and waved us toward the parking lot.

Having just finished the Elderhostel course in Mexican history, my mother was our resident expert on colonial Mexico. We'd barely closed the doors on Eleazar's Chevy Suburban when the lecture began.

"This area is known as the birthplace of the Mexican revolution," she said, beginning a ten-minute dissertation that ended with the severed heads of Mexico's revolutionary fathers being hung from iron cages on the corners of a granary in the city of Guanajuato. During the hour-plus drive from the airport to San Miguel, the conversation droned on between my mother, my sisters, and Eleazar. I rolled down the car window and soaked up the clear luminescence of Mexico's high desert. The undulating gray-green foothills of the Sierra de Guanajuato were scrubbed with a mixture of mesquite and *huizache* trees, agave, and cactus. Small herds of lean cattle and goats ambled along the fenceless roadway. The air was filled with the scent of burning mesquite, which brought back a memory of my very first night in San Miguel.

December 1973. I step off a bus from Mexico City as afternoon is turning into evening. After a mad rush through the smog-shrouded city and six hours on a dilapidated second-class bus crowded with people, poultry, and one ornery pig, San Miguel's crisp, thin air, with its incense of mesquite, is a welcome relief.

I survey the scene around me as the bus rumbles away down Calle Insurgentes. The town appears desolate in the fading light: a sea of crumbling whitewashed walls punctuated by wooden doors and windows interned behind heavy iron grilles. The film-noir essence of the landscape fills me with a stark loneliness. A loneliness exacerbated by the awareness that, with my pale pink skin, hazel eyes, and shaggy blonde hair, I'm an alien among the stoic indigenous faces flowing silently by.

In the light of a solitary streetlamp, I consult my *People's Guide to Mexico* for directions to the cheap hotel where I've booked a room for the night. I fumble with a hand-me-down map — a gift from my sisters — then make my way through a maze of narrow streets until I find the dreary little bargain hotel I'm looking for.

A sleepy-eyed clerk rouses himself long enough to lead me, staggering under the weight of an overstuffed backpack, up the hotel's steep, narrow staircase to a guest room barely larger than a walk-in closet. It's depressingly spare: white stucco walls, a terracotta tile floor, and a simple wood-frame bed covered with a thin cotton spread. The sole window is shuttered and bolted. When the clerk nods and closes the door, I loosen the belt on my backpack and let it slide to the floor. Then I collapse on the bed and lie staring at the ceiling, exhausted from the twelve-hour journey and consumed with uncertainty about my decision to come to Mexico.

I've left behind a cozy apartment at the top of a lovely brownstone in a leafy East Coast city; a sweet-tempered, long-haired boyfriend; and a handful of moderately interesting professors teaching moderately engaging courses. I've left behind friends and family, and the safety of all that is familiar, to come live in this ancient, dusty country whose language I can barely understand.

Questions hover over me like anguished spirits: What if my Spanish doesn't improve and I can't make myself understood? What if I don't get into school? What if I make no friends? What if I contract amoebic dysentery like my sister did? What if someone rips off all my money? What if I'm attacked, molested, or raped? Who would know? Who would care? It suddenly, and a bit belatedly, occurs to me — I don't even know how to phone home.

THE MEMORY SLIPPED AWAY as Eleazar rounded a steep curve and turned down a long, two-lane highway leading into the city. A gleaming new sign beside the road welcomed us: "*Bienvenidos a San Miguel de Allende.*"

Welcome *back* to San Miguel, I thought, feeling smugly nostalgic.

Near the entrance to the town, we made a sharp left and bumped up a deeply rutted dirt lane. It was reminiscent of many roads I'd been on in Mexico and gave me the happy impression that little had changed since I'd left San Miguel years ago. But then Eleazar explained — this washed-out dirt road was only a temporary diversion.

"The new entrance to San Miguel will be finished soon," he said. "There will be a new *glorieta*, with a statue of El Pípila in the center." While he lectured on El Pípila, an indigenous hero of the revolution of 1810, I found myself wondering what changes, other than this glorious new roundabout, had taken place in San Miguel.

It didn't take long to find out. As we crested the hill and I caught sight of the town, my heart sank. The town's perimeter appeared to have expanded exponentially. The hills surrounding San Miguel, once cloaked in nopal and maguey, wild sage and mesquite, were now layered with hundreds, maybe thousands, of brightly colored houses. New neighborhoods cascaded down every hillside, in every direction. Streets existed where none had been before. Streets lined with cable companies, auto-supply stores, furniture retailers, OXXO convenience stores, and Pemex gas stations. It was as if real estate developers had been working overtime since I'd left nearly three decades before. I was afraid the sleepy town I'd fallen in love with in 1973 no longer existed.

3 | *Fall from Grace*

I LEFT SAN MIGUEL DE ALLENDE — the first time — the day after my twenty-first birthday. Broke and bleary-eyed, I climbed into the back seat of a Chevy Suburban belonging to a guy I barely knew and headed north across the Sonoran Desert for the thirty-hour trip to Albuquerque.

The previous night, friends and I had celebrated my nascent adulthood with White Russians in a bar named for a flat, brown bug. We were a mismatched bunch gathered at La Cucaracha that night — artists, musicians, writers, a Vietnam vet, an accidental drug runner. For some of us Mexico had provided refuge, for others she had revealed new artistic possibilities. San Miguel had been a revelation for me. In my innocent twenty-one-year-old mind I'd imagined myself settling there, making art in that colorful context, creating an exotic life that reached beyond the suburban predictability I'd grown up with.

When my rowdy crowd of *compañeros* encouraged me to make a birthday toast, I climbed up on a rickety chair and, above an itinerant musician's sorry rendition of "Brokedown Palace," I raised a glass of milky liqueur and shouted out a promise. A promise that I'd soon be back in San Miguel.

But then life and reality intervened. An art history degree from a university in Virginia, a year in France, a retail store in Seattle, moving in with my future husband, purchasing a house, the birth of my son, two more stores, the arrival of my daughter, another store, numerous cats, and a golden retriever named

Katy all colluded to postpone my return to San Miguel.

By the time I finally made it back, twenty-eight years later, I could barely remember the adventurous young woman who'd once roamed Mexico in Earth Shoes. While I'd been busy achieving things, a stressed-out, middle-aged, menopausal woman had laid claim to my body and my soul. A woman too often provoked to rages by her intractable teenage son, and too easily reduced to tears by a straight-shooting, disapproving mother.

Since leaving home at eighteen, I'd earned a college degree, traveled the world, learned two languages, taught myself an array of business skills, built a mini retail empire in Seattle, and raised two kids. But the one thing I'd never been able to do was win my mother's approval.

Though small in stature — she's five foot two and shrinking — my mother possesses a persona three times her actual size. She's witty, well-informed, gregarious, and a great storyteller. She can be expressive and supportive with total strangers, yet rarely with her own children. It is difficult for her to demonstrate affection, and she's never been comfortable expressing pride in our successes. "Tooting your own horn," as she called it, was frowned upon in our family. On the handful of occasions she's visited me in Seattle, she's offered few words of praise for my family or our accomplishments.

On one particular visit, I remember bringing her to see our store on Sand Point Way. It was fairly new at the time and filled with goods that were beautifully displayed by our talented merchandiser. My mother had loaned us money to construct the garden center there, so I thought surely she'd feel compelled to, at least, say something positive about her investment. But when I brought her there, she wandered around the entrance for a few minutes, then turned around and walked out. I had to run to catch up with her in the parking lot.

"Mom, where are you going?" My voice cracked as I struggled

to keep years of accumulated disappointment in check. "What did you think of the store?"

"I'm sure you'll do well here," she said, looking around. "This appears to be a very affluent neighborhood."

It was the closest thing to praise for my business accomplishments I would ever receive from her.

But the problem wasn't really her. It was me. I'd somehow reached middle age and still needed my mother's approval to feel okay about myself. Without it, nothing I had accomplished in life seemed good enough.

So I kept striving away — adding more stores, remodeling the first ones, expanding product lines, employing more people, improving our neighborhood, volunteering in classrooms or for school auctions and fundraising committees, serving on nonprofit boards, and organizing community projects — in hopes of proving something to myself, if not to my mother.

Then, one day, everything changed.

Our loan officer at Bank of America called to say he'd like to meet with my business partner Dianne and me. Something he rarely did.

"My supervisor will be joining us," John said. The forced enthusiasm in his naturally mellow voice put me on edge.

"What's this about?" I asked, though I already knew the answer. For months I'd been hoping to avoid the conversation altogether.

"There's concern about your debt-to-equity ratio, and the fact you've paid nothing on the line of credit for the new store in two years."

He rambled on for a while, making it sound as if no one in particular at Bank of America was questioning our financial solvency. It seemed there was just this giant amorphous concern, like some phantom 1950s sci-fi creature, lurking in the corners of their downtown offices.

In all honesty, they had good reason to be worried. We *were* in trouble. Like so many others caught up in Seattle's exuberant business climate in the late '90s, my four business partners and I had become overextended. By the year 2000, we had four ten-thousand-square-foot stores, 140 employees on the payroll, and owed nearly $1 million to Bank of America. We'd maxed out the credit lines at three of our four stores when the newest one sucked the others dry by losing a record $350,000 in its first two years. To further complicate matters, my partners and I had risked everything — our homes, our cars, our bank accounts, our investments — to secure the financing we needed to grow.

It was all on the line, and John knew it.

"You'd better come up with a plan soon," he said. "They're talking about calling in the loans."

IT WAS IN THE FALL OF 1979 that I took the $8,000 inheritance my maternal grandfather had left me, found a couple of willing women partners, and launched Seattle's first worker-owned general store, City People's Mercantile. Customers could find almost anything at City People's: beeswax candles, barbecue grills, cotton socks, clay pots, duct tape, dog food, faucet washers, flip-flops, garlic presses, hammers, houseplants, space heaters, lily bulbs, lightbulbs, muffin tins, Miracle-Gro, paint rollers, reading glasses, shower curtains, Silly Putty, silk scarves, toilet plungers, patio umbrellas, wool mittens. After we merged with The Woodstove Store, we even sold Jøtul stoves.

For the first five years, we limped along, peddling our oddball mix of merchandise in a tiny storefront on a sleepy Capitol Hill side street. My partners and I slaved away, putting in long hours but gaining little, other than sweat equity, to show for it. Our prospects for profitability began to improve when our offer to purchase a building that had once housed an old grocery store on the corner of Fifteenth Avenue and East Republican was accepted.

Armed with a ream of spreadsheets, sales projections, and a ninety-page market survey created on my boyfriend's Commodore 64 computer, we went in search of our first commercial loan. After ten months of bouncing from one unwilling male banker to the next, we finally found a sympathetic woman, the president of Olympic Savings, who was willing to make the loan.

We bought the building, gutted and remodeled it inside and out, and opened for business three weeks before Christmas in 1984.

The new store was an instant success. It began turning a profit almost immediately. When the staff grew sevenfold in two years, we abandoned the idea that all the workers should be owners, but continued to share profits with our employees. My original partners moved on; new ones bought in.

City People's became the anchor for Capitol Hill's deteriorated Fifteenth Avenue business district. After it opened, other new businesses began to sprout up and thrive — flower shops, restaurants, hair salons, bookstores. Over the years, the store grew to be more than just a neighborhood retail outlet; it became a local gathering spot and community center. Customers stopped in, not only to pick up plumber's putty or potted plants, but to meet and connect with others. City People's was a place to see and be seen. A place where lifelong friendships were formed in the aisles, and a few romantic alliances too. Some of the relationships between employees ended noisily in the stockroom or in our offices, but others turned into long-term relationships that resulted in marriage and families.

WITHIN DAYS of my conversation with our loan officer, John, Dianne and I were on the phone with a crusty Baltimore business consultant named Alan Gallant. We thought Alan, with his years of experience in retail co-ops, was just the person we needed to review our business and help our partners and us formulate a plan to save our stores — and our assets.

It was late July when he flew out to Seattle. For four days the heavyset man lumbered up the narrow stairs to our sweltering offices. With his shirtsleeves rolled up, he sweated over stacks of financial records, studying them through bottle-thick glasses. At the end of the week, he gathered the five of us together to announce his prognosis.

"You've got too many stores and not enough skilled people to manage 'em." Alan was direct to the point of bluntness. "Either you hand over management to an experienced CEO, which will cost upwards of $150K a year, or you go back to a two-store model and manage 'em yourselves. Those are your options."

My partners and I quickly reached consensus on not hiring a CEO. We weren't about to pay someone else nearly three times what we made to homogenize our unique stores. But our other choice, closing two stores, wasn't something we were eager to do either. Then there was the bigger question — which stores would we close? Since all of the partners, except one, worked in one or another of the stores, the choice affected each of us differently. I finally posed the question no one else dared to ask.

"If we did close two stores, which ones would you suggest?"

"Fremont first," Alan said without hesitation. Then he paused for a moment, anticipating our reaction. "Then Capitol Hill."

"Capitol Hill!?" I said, nearly shouting at him. I was stunned at the idea of closing our flagship store, *my* neighborhood store, the first one I'd opened.

It was my baby. The thought of losing it was inconceivable.

"But Sand Point's the one that's bleeding cash. Capitol Hill's been profitable for years!"

I suddenly felt like I couldn't breathe in the hot, airless room.

"The problem is twofold. Number one, you've got a long-term lease on the Sand Point store and it would cost you a bundle to get out of. Number two, the profitability of the Capitol Hill store has shrunk significantly in the last couple of years. Your labor costs are killing you.

"Plus, selling the real estate would allow you to generate some working capital again."

My heart beat faster with every word he spoke. I felt like Abraham, being asked by God to sacrifice Isaac, his firstborn son. Only unlike God, I knew Alan wasn't bluffing.

OVER THE YEARS, our stores had received all kinds of awards and commendations. We'd been awarded the Mayor's Small Business Award, featured on every "Best of Seattle" list, and named — along with Nordstrom, REI, and Fran's Chocolates — one of the "Top Ten Quintessential Seattle Shopping Experiences."

Yet far more important to my partners and me was that people from all over Seattle, not only those who lived on Capitol Hill, thought of the store as their store. Many mistakenly thought it was a co-op. We took pride in the fact that our customers and staff often used possessive pronouns when they talked about City People's.

Our Capitol Hill store manager, a woman with a heart the size of Montana and more integrity than anyone I've ever known, always spoke of the store as if it were hers. The day we had to break the news to her that she and her staff were being laid off the week before Christmas was the worst in my thirty-eight-year retail career.

Because of the steadfast attachment our staff and so many Seattleites had to the Capitol Hill store, it seemed the entire city felt betrayed when we announced the closing. And as with any betrayal, real or imagined, emotions ran high. They ranged from tearful soliloquies at the cash registers to violent rants in the aisles as we liquidated merchandise, cleared fixtures, and sold off the real estate.

FOR YEARS I HAD A RECURRING DREAM about our Capitol Hill store, one that haunted me each time I awoke from it. In it, the store was always open for business and filled with customers, but no one had turned on the lights. Everyone was shopping in the dark. I would run to the electrical panel and madly flip the switches, but it was no use. I never could get the lights to come on. I tried analyzing the persistent nightmare; I even bought a book on how to interpret dreams. After reading it, I began to think that the darkness in the dream signified a secret, or something that was out of my control. But I stopped having the dream after the store was gone and have since come to believe it was an omen. The work of my subconscious mind predicting a darkened future for our store.

More than ten years have passed since the lights went out for good at our iconic Capitol Hill store, and the city still mourns its loss. I still mourn its loss. But as with all endings, a new beginning would emerge from the darkness.

One unlike anything I could have imagined at the time.

4 | *La Casa*

S OMETHING I'VE LEARNED about myself over the years is that my subconscious has a mind of its own. One that is often at odds with my conscious mind. My conscious mind will often say no, but my subconscious will insist on yes, and then, because it thinks it knows best, it will drag us along for the ride. Like it did one night, just before I left for the reunion in San Miguel, when my husband found me browsing Mexican real estate ads online.

"You're not thinking of buying property in Mexico, are you?" Paul asked.

"Of course not!" I assured him. "It's just fun to look."

While visiting friends and family in New Orleans, Santa Fe, San Antonio, and Laguna Beach in recent years, I'd scanned real estate ads and toured open houses for properties I could never afford, trying to imagine a future with a brighter climate. Each time I did, it made my husband nervous.

"Promise you won't make any offers?" he said.

"I promise," I said, and returned to my browsing.

BUT THERE I WAS, mid-morning on the first Monday of my return to San Miguel, being dragged uphill from the house I'd rented to the offices of Allende Properties by a subconscious mind that knew something I didn't.

At the appointed time, I stepped through an arched portico into a cream-colored oasis. The empty office, a light, airy room decorated with an array of sleek desks and Pentium computers, exuded the feeling of money and upper-class America. The place transcended the "old" San Miguel I was familiar with — one filled with exposed brick and stucco walls crowned with shards of glass stuck into concrete. I studied the real estate display boards and noted that home prices in San Miguel were somewhat transcendent too.

The office manager, a young man I'd traded emails with for the last couple of weeks, arrived within minutes. In an apologetic tone he explained that Claudius, the agent who would be working with me, was running late. He assured me that he'd be along shortly.

While I waited, I explored the newly remodeled office complex. Like many of San Miguel's colonial buildings, this one was being rescued from a state of noble decay. I wandered around the inner courtyard, admiring the *cantera*, the beautiful hand-chiseled stonework still done in Mexico for about two dollars and fifty cents an hour. A collection of shops typical of the "new" San Miguel were tucked behind walls of windows built into the stone: a gourmet cookware store; a gallery with an eclectic mix of contemporary and folk art, jewelry and clothing; and a tidy office housing one of the town's two insurance agencies.

Forty-five minutes later, a tall Mexican man resembling a youthful Julio Iglesias burst through the front door. The office manager nodded in my direction.

"I'm Claudius. Sorry I'm late," he said, flashing me an alarmingly perfect smile.

I forgave him his trespasses immediately.

"Come with me. My driver is waiting." We headed out the door toward a white Toyota Corolla parked at the curb. Claudius held the door open while I climbed into the back; then he slammed it shut and hopped in up front next to another, equally handsome, young man.

"This is Octavio. He's learning about selling real estate and will be our driver today."

It turned out the two of them, with their Shakespearean monikers, had been friends since childhood. And our real estate tour was really just an excuse for a boyish joyride. As we negotiated San Miguel's mid-morning congestion, they entertained me with infantile jokes, slapstick routines, and stories of growing up in San Miguel.

"There was no minimum driving age in San Miguel when we were kids. I started driving when I was twelve," Claudius told me.

Terror rose up inside me thinking of my own son — now sixteen and driving — behind the wheel at age twelve. I'd be afraid not only for his life, but for the lives of others in his path. When I mentioned this to Claudius, he only laughed.

"There weren't so many cars in San Miguel back then. Fewer things to hit!"

"How about the police? What did they do?"

"The cops used to pull me over once in a while. But they only wanted to know if my dad knew I had his car. Of course, I always told them yes!" He and Octavio shot knowing glances at each other and cracked up again.

The three of us spent the next several hours driving from one end of town to the other, wandering through one uninspiring house after another. All were owned by expatriates who had dragged the trappings of suburban America with them to Mexico. The houses were laden with faux French provincial furniture, heavy velvet curtains, ornate wrought-iron patio furniture, incongruous Oriental carpets, crocheted or quilted bedspreads. I recognized much of the décor from my childhood in the sixties: gilded plastic wall clocks, pastel bedroom furniture, art objects made from marbles, chairs upholstered in white Naugahyde. Claudius explained that houses listed for sale by Americans in

San Miguel typically came fully furnished. He was enthusiastic about every house we entered.

"Think of the potential!" he exclaimed. All I could think of was how much work it would take to dispose of the entire interior design scheme.

By two in the afternoon I was tired and hungry and ready to quit my quest to see behind San Miguel's famous, photogenic doors. But Claudius had one more house to show me.

"You've got to see this one! Fantastic views! You'll love it!"

I mulled it over. I was intrigued by the idea of touring a "house with a view." Nothing he'd shown me that morning had had much of a view. I checked my watch.

"Okay. One more. But then I need to get back." I had promised to meet my sisters and mother for lunch.

In order to reach this last house on our tour, Claudius instructed Octavio to take a sharp right up a hill into a neighborhood east of the Ignacio Ramirez market. I could tell from the lack of remodeled houses that this was more of a Mexican neighborhood, not an expat enclave like the other parts of San Miguel we'd seen that morning. Mangy dogs chased us up a steep hill as the car's wheels bounced through deep potholes where cobblestones were missing. We turned up a narrow lane marked with a hand-painted street sign at the corner. Certain letters in the street's name had been crossed out and replaced with others by a graffiti artist. Seeing it, Claudius and Octavio broke into a fit of laughter. The meaning eluded my limited, book-learned Spanish. But I knew it was slang, and I was sure it was gross.

Halfway up the hill, Claudius signaled Octavio to pull over. We climbed out and he led me across the street to an opening, barely six feet wide, between two houses. I had to concentrate to avoid stepping in the dog poop and broken glass littering the walkway.

"The house is here?" I asked. "Where's the street?"

"It's a *callejón*. There are lots of these alleys in San Miguel. They are great little walking streets. You don't need a car here." When I looked at him doubtfully he added, "Walking is good for you!"

I should have skipped this and gone to lunch, I thought. Except for the abundance of magenta bougainvillea and a lovely cerulean wall, little appealed to me along the odd little alleyway. But like a well-trained pup, I obediently followed Claudius down it anyway.

Midway through the alley, he turned left between two houses. We passed through a ten-foot-tall iron gate and climbed a series of steps. On the first landing, a pretty Mexican woman with long hair pulled back in a ponytail and wearing a red-checkered apron stood in the doorway of a *tienda*. The store was small and dark, with racks of Bimbo snacks, a bin of dried beans, and a display cooler filled with beer. As we passed, I turned and smiled at the woman.

She offered me a curious Mona Lisa half-smile in return.

I trailed Claudius up another set of stairs until he stopped in front of an ornate wooden door interned behind an iron gate. He pulled out a crowded ring of keys and inserted one into the gate's lock. It didn't work. He tried another. That one didn't work either. He spent the next five minutes trying one key after the other, with no luck. My stomach growled.

He walked back down to the *tienda* and had a brief conversation with the woman in the checkered apron.

"I'll be right back," he hollered up to me and disappeared down the alley.

The woman fixed her large brown eyes on me, and I suddenly felt like an intruder. Few Americans, it seemed, lived along the narrow alley. I wondered how she felt about having a gringa looking at a house for sale in her mostly Mexican neighborhood.

"¡Hola, Gracia!" another woman below called out to her. I was relieved when the two of them disappeared into the store.

TEN MINUTES PASSED before Claudius came jogging back down the alleyway. He was out of breath, but clutching a new set of keys.

"We're not going to visit this house," he said matter-of-factly. "I have a better one to show you. It's right across the alley." I shrugged, figuring we'd come all this way, I might as well see *something*. So I followed him back down the steps and across the alley to a house painted the color of goldenrod above and forest green below.

He pulled open the exterior gate and inserted a key in the lock of a massive metal door. This time the key worked. The heavy door groaned as he pushed it open. He stepped in and leaned against the door to keep it from slamming shut in the warm afternoon breeze.

I stepped through the doorway into a courtyard filled with foliage from the jungles of Oaxaca: passionflower and trumpet vines, fifteen-foot ficus trees and giant split-leaf philodendron. An abundance of sword fern, tradescantia, spathaphyllum, and spider plants spilled onto the tile floor. There was even a banana tree with tiny green bananas in a giant cobalt pot nestled against a fuchsia-colored wall. I felt drawn to the house's hot pink façade, like a magpie to a shiny jewel.

Claudius led me from the verdant entryway into a spacious blue and yellow tiled kitchen. A handsome pine table sat squarely in the center. A playful collection of Mexican folk toys — brightly painted merry-go-rounds, wooden Ferris wheels, horse-drawn carts — lined the shelves above the sink. Up a few steps was a living room that opened onto a second courtyard, shaded by a magnificent thirty-foot Peruvian pepper tree. A stone and tile fountain, flanked by pots of ruby hibiscus, bubbled cheerfully.

I eagerly followed Claudius up a spiral staircase to the bedrooms. The first was awash in deep carmine. The feathery branches of the pepper tree floated beyond a window seat, giving it the air of a tree house. Hand-painted flowers decorated a brick fireplace in the corner and hand-loomed woolen spreads from Michoacán covered twin beds. A vision of my eight-year-old daughter Hannah ensconced in that bedroom flitted through my mind.

Down a short hallway was a large, luminous master bedroom. Claudius threw open the curtains to expose a miraculous westward view. Distant purple hills stretched across the horizon; the silvery waters of a faraway lake glistened in the afternoon sun; the radiant spires, domes, and bell towers of San Miguel's many churches emanated from the landscape below. The coo of a mourning dove floated up through the open window.

"Let's check out the terrace," Claudius said with an impish grin. We continued up the steep spiral stairway to a rooftop terrace where we were treated to an even more astonishing view.

A view that extended 180 degrees.

I stood perfectly still, unable to move, I was so awed by the exquisite panorama below.

But my heart raced ahead, and the two disparate parts of my mind became fixated on one undeniable feeling: *I'm in love.*

I looked at Claudius, who already knew.

"How much do they want for it?" I asked, completely forgetting the promise I'd made my husband.

He hesitated.

"Well … I'm not sure."

I suddenly felt like an adolescent with a mad crush whose best friend has just told her that someone likes her, but she can't say who.

"What do you mean you're not sure?!"

"I will find out and let you know," he said.

But my subconscious mind wasn't about to let him off the hook. It knew this was a house I was meant to come home to for the rest of my life, and couldn't wait a minute longer.

It especially didn't want to play games with a real estate agent. All it wanted was the facts, right there and right then.

I continued to try and pry the information out of him, but eventually realized he wasn't holding out on me. Claudius didn't seem to know much of anything about the house.

"We can talk later this afternoon. I'll have more information for you then," he promised.

Later seemed like forever. I didn't want to leave. I wasn't hungry anymore. I just wanted to keep wandering around the wonderful house, pretending it could be mine. Then I realized I was over an hour late to meet my mother and sisters for lunch. Reluctantly, I agreed to call him at his office later that afternoon.

5 | Complications

I CAUGHT UP WITH MY MOTHER AND SISTERS in the court-yard of the Posada Carmina. Sitting in the sweet-scented shade of orange trees, I yammered nonstop about the house.

"It's amazing!" I said. "There's absolutely nothing that needs to be repaired or redone or even redecorated. It's perfect just as it is!"

I was aware, even then, that many Americans moved to San Miguel in order to build their dream houses on the cheap, but the idea repulsed me.

For good reason.

My sisters and mother were well-acquainted with the fixer-upper Paul and I bought in 1982, when our Seattle neighborhood was still affordable. A realtor friend once described our 1906 classic four-square as having "lots of potential." Over the years, we'd spent hundreds of thousands of dollars and the majority of our free time trying to realize that potential. We became slaves to the process and our lives a never-ending chain of remodeling projects.

To make matters worse, my talented but detail-oriented husband insisted on doing all the work himself. In old houses like ours, what you think is going to be a weeklong project often turns into an epic saga. Paul would start out planning to patch and paint the living room walls, and before I knew it, he'd be soaking and peeling six layers of old wallpaper. The project would turn into a three-month-long battle with crumbling plaster and recalcitrant lathe.

Nothing was ever completely finished before my husband would launch into his next project. In our thirty years in the house, he remodeled nearly every room in the house — the kitchen, two bathrooms, all four bedrooms, the front porch, and back deck. Twice.

Hence, I was smitten by the idea of owning the completely finished and beautifully decorated Mexican house. I'd already envisioned a whole new life there — one full of sunshine, blue skies, and blissful, colorful orderliness. Two thousand miles away from the construction debris, fiberglass bats, and basement buried in building materials that I normally lived with. And light-years away from the winter depressions and guilty feelings I was eager to leave behind in Seattle.

WHEN I ANNOUNCED MY INTENTION to buy the house with the view, my sisters were thrilled. They wanted to hear every detail. By the time the waiter arrived with my lunch, Frances, an avid traveler, was setting a date for our next reunion at my new house. My mother, however, was less enthusiastic. At eighty-two, she still possessed an astute business mind and critical voice, and she was soon drilling me with questions.

"I didn't think Americans could hold title to Mexican property. Don't the banks hold title to properties down here? And how do you know the house is structurally sound? Do they have housing inspectors or building codes in Mexico? Who'll watch over the house when you're not here? Second homes are expensive to keep up. How do you plan to pay for it?"

"I'll rent it out when we're not here," I replied, though I knew nothing about the particulars of renting houses in Mexico or what the rental market in San Miguel was like.

Nor could I answer any of her other questions. Still I didn't want to listen to what I thought of as her "negativity."

I did, however, know what compelled her to pose those questions — her insistence on battling my impulsive tendencies. She had rushed to the altar at age twenty-one, desperate to get away from her imperious and hypercritical mother, and to snag my father before he was conscripted into World War II.

My mother was initially drawn to my father because of his charm and sociability. He was handsome and dapper in the exquisitely tailored suits he bought for himself at Jack Henry or Brooks Brothers. He drove expensive cars that his mother gave him, and he appreciated good food and dinner parties, as long as someone else was picking up the tab. He was a great bartender and made an excellent gin and tonic.

But in private, he was a self-absorbed man who often complained about the burden of supporting his wife and six children. Neurotic about his health and money, he was miserly and uninvolved in our lives. He was neither curious nor intellectual, which made him a poor match for my bright, ambitious, adventuresome mother with her can-do spirit. But being a woman who adheres to a strict "You make your bed, you sleep in it" philosophy, she stuck with him until the day he died.

The problem is, she has held up that old adage as a model for her children to live by too. For years she'd been battling my predisposition toward rashness, which runs deep, in an effort to keep me from making my own mistakes in life. But that day at Posada Carmina, I didn't want her, or anyone else, throwing cold water on my Mexican home fantasy, so I shrugged off her pesky questions.

After lunch we returned to the rental house, where I immediately phoned Allende Properties in search of Claudius. I was desperate to find out the price of the house. But he wasn't there. I left a message for him with my number and waited near the phone for an hour. But he didn't call.

When I realized that I'd just have to be patient — a trait I've always appreciated in others but never developed myself — I decided to walk off my jitters. I wandered San Miguel's cobble-stone streets, imagining the worst. That my gorgeous dream house was far too expensive or that it had slipped into the hands of some other, less-deserving gringo, before I'd even been able to make an offer.

OUR PLAN FOR THAT EVENING was to dine with friends of my mother's, a couple who'd recently moved to San Miguel from Missouri. But I wasn't in the mood. I didn't want to leave the rental house in case Claudius called. I eventually agreed to go along, if only to please my mother.

Our would-be hostess had emailed the month before about a house some friends of hers were selling, and Mother thought, out of courtesy to the woman, I should at least look at it. But I wasn't interested anymore. I'd already found the perfect house.

We took a taxi across town, up into an area where new houses with grass lawns had replaced cactus-covered hills. The couple's rambling, adobe-style house and two acres were surrounded by a six-foot wall with a gated driveway. We rang an intercom buzzer at the gate and our hostess remotely beamed us through. A tall, sturdy woman with a big smile and short-cropped salt-and-pepper hair, she stepped out onto the veranda and waved us toward the front door after we were through the gate. The house's interior was cavernous; the kitchen alone had an acre of granite countertop.

Our host, a friendly man who looked significantly older than his wife, filled six oversized wine goblets with red and white wine, and we settled onto a pair of oversized leather couches in the living room. It overlooked a swimming pool and garden area where the couple's two pet burros were busy mowing the lawn.

"Your mother tells me you're thinking of buying a house in San Miguel," our hostess said with a broad smile.

"Well, I thought I was only looking. But today I actually found a house that I love."

She asked me about the location and what the house was like. As I described the details of what I remembered about it, her face lit up.

"Good heavens!" she exclaimed, clapping her hands together as if I'd just delivered the best news. "That's my friend's house! The one I emailed your mother about!"

She jumped and ran to the phone to dial her friend. After a brief explanation, she handed me the receiver.

"Hello," I said, still stunned by the coincidence. The house's owner greeted me, but her voice sounded frosty.

"I understand you were in my house this afternoon," she said. "How did you get in?"

"A real estate agent from Allende Properties showed it to me. Actually, we went up there to look at a house on the other side of the alley, but the keys didn't work, so we ended up taking a tour of yours instead. I love your house; you've done a great job decorating it," I said. I thought a little flattery might warm her up a bit.

"That agent had no business taking you into our house," she snapped. "He did not have our permission."

"Oh my God, I am *so* sorry! I didn't know. He never said anything. Believe me, if I'd known that, I would never have gone in." I felt like crawling under one of the enormous leather sofas.

Despite her fury, the woman told me the house was, indeed, still for sale. When she finally revealed the asking price, I wanted to burst into song and dance around the room like one of those madcap stars in a Broadway musical. I managed to keep from singing but immediately forgot Rule Number One for the buyer in a real estate transaction: Exhibit Restraint.

"I'd like to make an offer on your house!" It nearly burst out of me. Then I did something even worse: I offered the full asking price.

We arranged for her husband to meet me at the house a few days later to discuss it further.

As I was about to say good-bye, she added one last thing.

"Just make sure you don't bring the real estate agent," she said sternly, and hung up.

6 | *House of My Dreams*

AFTER WE CLOSED THE STORE and I fell into depression, the past took on an inflated sense of importance. Like someone suffering from a terminal illness, I felt I had little reason to look forward and every reason to look back. I began thinking of the innocent, youthful days I'd spent traversing the globe as the epitome of all that had been worthwhile and enlightening in my life. Of course, it was an illusion. But it persisted nonetheless. I could not, at that moment, imagine what the future might hold, and I'd never been any good at living in the present. Reminiscing about the past seemed my best option.

The reunion in San Miguel provided an opportunity for me to indulge in memories of my lost youth, which spurred me to embark on a mission to unearth the remaining vestiges of my student days there. While searching for my old haunts, I was dismayed to discover that La Cucaracha, the bar where I'd celebrated my twenty-first birthday, had been replaced with a Banamex, and that vanilla lattes, not White Russians, were now being served in the cafés beneath San Miguel's *portales*.

The jail on San Francisco Street, where I'd spent time bribing officials to release my miscreant friends and buying sweaters knitted by inmates, had been moved to the outskirts of town. The humble *casita* I'd called home in 1973 was now a cluster of gated villas with an elaborate security system intended to keep out the kind of people my friends and I had once been.

The hills of Atascadero, Los Balcones, and Ojo de Agua, hacienda lands where I'd hiked thirty years before, had once been home to coyotes, jackrabbits, wildcats, and an amazing array of birds and butterflies. But the wealthy *hacendados* had sold their lands to developers who divided it into lots for the multicolored mansions crowding the hills surrounding San Miguel's historic center. Only *el chan*, the spring at El Charco—where I remember downing a bottle of mescal with my buddy Enrique, who choked on the worm—and the surrounding acreage, had been rescued from developers and turned into a botanical garden and bio-reserve.

The French Park, now referred to as the Parque Juárez, was a profusion of tropical vegetation and interesting birds. As a neo-phyte birdwatcher in the '70s, I spent hours there, eagerly spot-ting my first vermillion flycatchers, Wilson's warblers, rufous hummingbirds, and snowy egrets. On my return I discovered that the neighborhood surrounding the park was still a popular nesting place, but for a new species of bird—the richly plumed from New York, Montreal, Los Angeles, and Dallas.

Despite the changes to the town's periphery, San Miguel's *centro* was nearly exactly as I remembered. More importantly, the town's culture and small-town feeling had not changed. Wander-ing through the *jardín*, San Miguel's central gathering spot, was reassuring: it was still one of the prettiest plazas in Mexico. The flagstone square, shaded by twenty-foot Indian laurels, bustled with life from early morning until late at night with the majestic, apricot-colored Parroquia looming in dramatic backdrop, as it has for more than two centuries. Fragments of *ranchera*, the music of love and longing strummed by mariachis in silver-studded costumes, drifted on the evening air. Families filled wrought-iron benches, snacking on *elote*, a souped-up ver-sion of corn-on-the-cob, while boisterous teenagers eyed each other as they promenaded around the square in the same court-ship ritual I remembered watching when I was young. Only the white, collared blouses and pleated skirts worn by the girls had been replaced with Gap jeans and Old Navy T-shirts.

ON THE FATEFUL MORNING that I was to meet with the owner of my dream house, I got up early and strolled through San Miguel as it unfurled toward the new day. A golden light cast by the rising sun highlighted the beauty of the colonial city: its striking spires and intricately tiled domes; its rustic, cobbled streets and plazas; its walls drenched in the colors of exotic spices — nutmeg, turmeric, saffron.

The streets were tranquil, and few people were out at the early hour. I watched the town's shopkeepers sweeping the cobbles clear of debris from the prior evening's revelry, and opening their doors, once again, to the world.

As I wandered down Hernandez Macias Street, I spied the lovely courtyard garden of the Bellas Artes. After a fretful night spent obsessing about my upcoming rendezvous, the graceful arches of the art school were an invitation to sit quietly and reflect. Again, my thoughts drifted back to that first lonely night in the dismal bargain hotel.

December 1973. I've been traveling since dawn with nothing to eat but a breakfast of watery omelet and dehydrated sausage on the flight from Houston. I force myself to shed my self-pity long enough to wander downstairs to the dining room, where I find a handful of carefully arranged square tables covered with white linen tablecloths. Each table has four straight-backed wooden chairs but no guests to fill them.

I feel awkward as the handsome, dark-skinned waiter in a crisp white shirt approaches. My junior high school Spanish seems woefully inadequate as we fumble through the exercise of finding just the right table for me in the empty dining room.

I attempt to read the menu. The only word I recognize is *sopa*, so I order the soup.

I feel conspicuous as I wait for it to come, as if there's a spotlight highlighting my lack of companionship. In my twenty years, I've never dined alone in a restaurant, only in the company of my large, boisterous family or with friends. The silence and solitude make my chest hurt. By the time the soup arrives, I'm no longer able to curb my emotions. Tears flow freely into the greasy broth the waiter has set before me.

My one relief is that he seems to be ignoring me as he stands at attention in the corner of the dining room. But my emotions soon get the best of him, and he returns to the table.

"*¿No le gusta la sopa?*" he asks, thinking it's the soup that's troubling me.

I shake my head. A giant lump forms in my throat and I can't speak. My eyes and nose are running freely. I reach for a napkin to wipe them, but realizing it's linen, I return to my room to search for a Kleenex. I crawl into bed, fully clothed, cover myself with the thin blanket, and fall into a deep sleep.

The next morning I awake late. Sun streams through the cracks of the shuttered window. I climb from the bed, unlatch the bolt, yank open the heavy shutters, and lean out. The scene below teems with texture and color and life — cobbled streets, whitewashed walls, apricot church spires. Crimson bougainvillea tumbles over rustic stone walls. A flock of swallows, in perfect formation, circles the bell tower of an ancient chapel. The new day, with its brilliant colors and sun-soaked landscape, feels like a much-needed embrace.

AS I SAT IN THE QUIET SANCTUARY of the Bellas Artes, with the trill of a Mexican house finch filling the air, I felt a psychological shift taking place inside me. With it came a sense of relief, the kind one feels on arriving home after a long and arduous journey. A buoyancy filled my soul, and a feeling of optimism that I hadn't felt for months. When I suddenly burst out laughing, a woman sweeping the far side of the courtyard overheard my exuberant cackling and looked up. *La pobrecita gringa está loca en la cabeza*, I imagined her thinking.

But after everything I'd been through — losing the store; my place in the community; the trust of my employees, neighbors, and customers; my sense of purpose and direction — after battling endless questions, depression, and guilt, San Miguel seemed like a second chance in life.

A chance for a new beginning, in a new community. A community filled with sunlight, new people, and new possibilities. A chance to rediscover the sense of wonder and openness and curiosity that comes naturally in youth, but for me had waned with age, responsibility, and a preoccupation with proving myself. As I stood up to leave, I felt more determined than ever.

I *had* to make the house deal work out.

7 | The Deal

JERRY PUTZ SAT OPPOSITE ME at the large pine dining table in the kitchen of my dream house.

A man in his mid-sixties, he had thinning gray hair and a quiet, decisive voice that suggested he was a serious kind of guy. He described the house's short history, sharing details that made me love it even more — like the fact that a woman architect had designed it.

He then recounted the story of a couple who, not long before, had also fallen in love with the house. They seemed intent on buying it, he told me, but for some unexplained reason, they'd backed out at the last minute.

"Down here everything's done on a cash basis, and I don't think they had the money to close," he said. "My wife was extremely disappointed."

I was certain that the reason they'd backed out was because the house was destined to be mine, but I didn't dare say this to Jerry, whose eyes had suddenly narrowed behind his rimless glasses.

"My wife is very upset that you were in here with that agent," he said in a tone more often used with a problem child than with another adult making a full-price offer on your house.

Normally I bristle when men speak down to me, and can respond quite curtly. But desperate to make a deal, I silently pleaded with my ego: *For once in your life, just let it go!*

Plus there *was* the trespassing issue. Though I knew next to nothing about Mexican real estate law, I knew that in the United States it's illegal for agents to enter a house without the owner's permission. So, instead of getting uppity, I groveled. Just a bit.

"I want to say, again, how sorry I am. I honestly didn't know that Claudius didn't have permission to bring me in here." Then I got to the point.

"I made your wife an offer on the phone the other night, and I want to reassure you that I'm quite serious about it. Unlike the people who backed out on you, I do have the cash in the bank." Which was only the *tiniest* little white lie.

My words cheered Jerry right up. We moved forward, discussing earnest money, closing costs, where and how I should transfer money to their account in the States. By the time we were finished, he was practically beaming. It was now my turn to ask for something.

"I think Claudius deserves something for his time," I said. "I'd like to set aside $5,000 from the proceeds for him."

Jerry frowned. "I'll mention that to my wife."

With that, the meeting abruptly ended.

I returned to the rental house and hadn't been back for five minutes when the phone rang. It was Jerry's wife. She had a problem with me withholding the money to pay Claudius's fee.

"It's our responsibility to pay the agent, you know. You need to pay us the full amount. We'll make sure Claudius gets what he's due," she assured me.

I knew from past real estate transactions that sales commissions are normally the seller's responsibility, so I agreed.

"Okay, but I'd like to be sure that he gets something," I told her. "I think he deserves it."

"We'll make sure he's taken care of," she said. "And by the way, we've got a closing date."

She told me when and where I needed to sign the purchase and sale agreement and where I should send the excessive earnest money deposit she and her husband required. The closing, she said, was to take place three weeks later at an attorney's office on San Francisco Street.

"Fine. I'll be there," I told her. But as I hung up the phone, I felt my chest tighten. I hadn't told my husband, and, contrary to what I'd told Jerry Putz, I didn't really have the required cash on hand. Yet there I was, arranging to close on a house in Mexico.

THE DAY BEFORE I RETURNED TO SEATTLE, I stopped by the offices of Allende Properties.

I'd never heard back from Claudius. Then again, there was no answering machine at the rental house, nor had I been sitting by the phone awaiting his call. Still, I wanted to find out if Jerry had contacted him to let him know about our agreement. But Claudius wasn't there, and I didn't leave a message. I was leaving the next day.

I'd stayed several days longer than planned in order to complete the earnest money transaction. My mother and sisters had already left, so I was alone when Eleazar returned to drive me to the airport. As we drove out of town, he asked if I'd enjoyed my time in San Miguel. I confessed that I'd liked it so much I'd put a profligate amount of money down as a deposit on a house. He asked where the house was located.

"Callejón de Chepito," I said.

"Chiquito or Chepito?" he asked, trying to figure out if the house was on Chiquito, a tony little street in *el centro* where a number of expatriates lived, or on Chepito, the narrow alleyway in a Mexican neighborhood, uphill from the artisan's market.

"Callejón de *Chepito*," I said, pronouncing it clearly this time.

The frown on his face was not reassuring.

"Is there something the matter with Chepito?" I asked.

"No. Not ... really. It's just that there's been a little trouble up there."

"What kind of trouble?"

"I heard somebody was stabbed in Chepito a few weeks ago.

But they caught the guy who did it, and he went to jail ... I think," he said, looking as if he was concentrating a little too hard on his driving.

During the flight back to Seattle, I turned Eleazar's words over and over in my mind, worrying that I'd made an egregious error putting more than a quarter of my retirement account down as earnest money on the house. I knew so little about it, or the neighborhood, or San Miguel for that matter. In my fervor to buy the house, I'd chosen to ignore all those little details.

I'd heard people refer to the impulsive purchase of Mexican real estate by intoxicated Americans as a "tequila buy." But I didn't even have drunkenness as an excuse. I was totally sober when I saw the house and made the offer.

Part Two | *El Barrio*

Nobody has ever before asked the nuclear family
to live all by itself in a box the way we do.
With no relatives, no support, we've put it in
an impossible situation.

MARGARET MEAD

8 | *The View from Casa Chepitos*

W HEN THE YOUNGEST OF HER SIX CHILDREN went off
to kindergarten, my mother decided it was time she
too went back to school to complete her undergraduate degree.
While the other mothers on our block — the "normal" ones in my
adolescent opinion — coffee-klatched their way through languid
suburban days, mine spent hers racing back and forth between
our house and downtown Kansas City to attend classes at the
University of Missouri. It was there that she discovered her passion for anthropology, archaeology, and ancient cultures. In particular, the Mayan civilization of Mexico and Central America.

In 1967, inspired by a professor's lectures on the Mayans, she
arranged our first trip to Mexico, to the ruins of the great Mayan
cities of Chichén-Itzá and Uxmal on the Yucatán Peninsula. For
reasons unclear to us, my mother thought visiting ancient ruins
in the remote jungles of Mexico in August, one of the hottest,
most humid months of the year in the Yucatán, would be interesting for her three teenage daughters, eight-year-old son, and
hypochondriac husband. My older brother refused to come
to Mexico with us and our father put up a fight, but as always,
Mother managed to cajole him into coming.

The trip turned out to be the worst, best vacation ever. We all
suffered from miserable bouts of Montezuma's revenge. We battled mosquitoes and sand fleas, poisonous scorpions, and taran-
tulas the size of newborn kittens. Our pale skins burned horribly
in the August sun. I developed sunstroke; my mother passed out

in a parking lot; and Daddy wrecked the car in Mississippi on the way home. Yet I remember that trip as one of the best our family ever took together.

While I still can remember watching in horror as my mother collapsed from dehydration in the parking lot of a cheap motel in Mississippi, I also remember tasting my first Spanish tapas with her in the ancient bar of the Hotel Mérida. I remember Mérida's colorful market: the piles of mangoes, papaya, pineapple, and guava; the sweet scent of freesia, tuberose, and calla lilies; the vibrant piñatas, brightly glazed ceramics, and delicately embroidered cotton blouses.

I remember being the only tourists at Chichén-Itzá the day my sister Rachel fainted after climbing the seventy-five steps of El Castillo in the noonday sun. And our tour guide, Señor Escalante, threatening to throw my sisters and me into the yawning chasm of the Cenote Sagrado, the sacred spring where Mayan virgins had routinely been sacrificed twelve centuries before.

I remember the white sand beaches and startling aqua-blue waters off Isla Mujeres, where we swam with giant sea turtles and bronze-skinned Mexican boys. We ate fresh conch soaked in lime juice right from the shell, but protested loudly when Daddy ate our turtle friends for dinner that night.

I remember singing and dancing with a group of timid Mayan girls at the only motel in Piste. They sang indigenous songs and performed traditional dances, and in the spirit of cultural exchange, my sisters and I harmonized on a gospel tune and taught the Mayan girls to do "The Loco-Motion."

I don't know how my siblings remember it, but for me that introduction to the exotic culture and colorful messiness of Mexico provided an antidote to the sheltered life I led in Kansas.

A few years later it would serve an even greater purpose — the memory of it would impel me to return to Mexico, a place I would revisit, again and again, to educate myself and replenish my soul.

It wasn't surprising that I looked to Mexico as the cure-all for my seasonal melancholies and midlife crisis, since it was my mother's own disenchantment with domestic life and desire for fulfillment that led me there in the first place. She was the one who taught me that looking past things as they are for a new set of variables is "just what you do when the chips are down."

What did come as a surprise, however, was that I faced the same problem she had thirty-five years before. Because I, too, had to convince my husband and kids that Mexico was going to be as interesting for them as it was for me.

BACK IN SEATTLE I began draining bank accounts and siphoning off stock funds to come up with the cash needed to close. I was also strategizing on how to get my husband and kids to return to San Miguel with me.

I'd fully expected Paul to give me grief when I finally admitted I'd broken my promise, but he actually wasn't such a bad sport about it. However, there is something I need to explain.

The relationship I have with my husband is by no means perfect. Temperamentally we're very different people, our styles strikingly divergent — mine's a raving Sarah Bernhardt; his is more the stoic Olivier — but that's what drew us to each other in the first place.

I'm a planner, a schemer, an optimist, and a risk taker. Paul, on the other hand, takes life one day at a time, insists on seeing the cup as half-empty, and offers sober assessments of my wackier ideas — like buying a bankrupt lumber store on a remote island off the coast of Washington state or investing my life savings in tech stocks in the fall of 1999.

Like most couples, we've struggled through the years to make our marriage work. We're both scarred by the traumas in our birth families, and have done plenty of time in couples therapy as a consequence. The primary result of our many hours on the couch has been a lot of receipts and a slightly more civil attitude toward each other. But there are three things we have learned through the years that have helped preserve our marriage, and our sanity. First, we allow each other the room to explore new possibilities; second, we still enjoy making each other laugh; and last, but in no way least, we maintain separate bank accounts.

As divorce attorneys will confirm, money is one of the top three issues driving couples apart today (the other two are sex and meddling outsiders, such as in-laws). Since the beginning of our relationship I've earned my own living, paid my own way, and kept my money in a separate account. Paul and I discovered early on that not hassling over each other's line-item expenditures frees us up to argue about more important things. Like who last cleaned the fridge (me, to be sure).

So when I announced to him that we were soon to be the lucky owners of a beautiful house on a run-down alleyway in Mexico, he simply shrugged and replied, "It's your money."

However, convincing him and my two kids that they wanted to spend time there was somewhat more problematic. Spring break was coming, and it coincided nicely with the dates I needed to be in San Miguel for the closing. Anxious to share my wonderful new house and the future I imagined for my unsuspecting family, I began checking airfares and was thrilled when I found a discounted fare to León through Zacatecas, Mexico. But neither my husband nor my kids were excited about the idea, especially sixteen-year-old Will, who was alarmed at the prospect of missing the first weeks of spring training with his high school baseball team. He'd begun finagling to stay home alone the minute I brought up the idea. But I wasn't going for it, and he was furious. One afternoon our disagreement culminated in a showdown in our Seattle kitchen.

"I'm not going!" he screamed.

"Sorry, Buster, you *are* going!" I said.

"You can't make me!"

"Oh yes, I can and I will!" I hollered back.

He grabbed his old Louisville slugger, stomped down the stairs into the backyard and began furiously swinging at what I suspected was an imaginary me.

"I hope you realize you're ruining my life!" he yelled a few minutes later, broadcasting our argument to the entire neighborhood. I sank into a kitchen chair, deflated.

It wasn't the first time I'd been told I was ruining his life — more like the millionth. But it was the first time I wondered if it might really be true.

I still cling to the naïve belief that things happen for a reason. I like to think that if you can just hang in there, everything will unfold as it should — a holdover ideology from what my mother calls my "flower-child days." This time, however, I was more than a little worried that the crash course with destiny I seemed to be on really *could* screw up my kids. After all, I'd left for a family reunion in Mexico and returned the soon-to-be owner of a house in a sketchy neighborhood where people were being stabbed. I suspected that if Will, Paul, or my daughter Hannah knew the unsavory details, they would all think I was trying to ruin their lives.

I had friends for whom this kind of midlife crisis had had big upsides — one friend and her daughter spent a memorable year in China, and the result of another friend's "crisis" turned out to be a new, more flexible career. But other people I'd known hadn't been so lucky. What had started out as discontentment, dysthymia, or depression in one spouse or the other ended up taking more malignant forms that tore those families apart.

I didn't want my search for happiness to ruin my son's life, or wreak havoc on my mostly happy family. Isn't every mother's worst fear that her children will one day blame her for everything that has gone wrong in their lives? I wondered if mine would have reason to.

IT TOOK A GREAT DEAL OF COAXING and the bribe of a new metal bat, but Will and the rest of the family finally acquiesced to coming to San Miguel for two weeks. The day we left, he dragged his duffel, stuffed with his new bat and a surplus of baseball equipment, to the airport and grew testy when the security agent at American Airlines required him to check it.

However, things were looking up.

The Putzes, feeling generous with their supersized down payment in hand, offered to let us stay in the house prior to closing, and when Eleazar arrived at the airport in León and cheerfully welcomed me back, I felt as if I already had an old friend in Mexico.

"I didn't realize it was quite so narrow," Paul said, looking down the alley for the first time. "It can't be more than six or seven feet wide."

A hush fell over the callejón's busy midday life as the four of us dragged our suitcases over broken concrete and loose gravel, past piles of dog poop and shattered glass. Children dressed in plaid Catholic school uniforms, on their way home for *comida*, pressed themselves against the walls and stared wide-eyed at my six-foot-tall, blond-haired husband and son. I could tell from the look on my own kids' faces — especially eight-year-old Hannah's — that they were disgusted by the dog-doo, but nobody said a word.

Luckily, when we made it to the house, at least Hannah was happily surprised. "Gee, Mom, this house is nicer than our house in Seattle. Can we afford it?" she asked.

"Looks like the skylight leaks," Paul said, pointing to water stains on the wall beneath it.

I looked at Will, whose lanky body was thrown over an upholstered chair like an old coat, but he only raised a tentative eyebrow at me.

After a brief tour, the conversation turned to what we were going to call our new Mexican home. I tossed out a suggestion my mother had made after she realized she wasn't going to talk me out of buying it: Casa Bella Vista, after the Hacienda Bella Vista, a citrus ranch on the Rio Grande that my great-grandfather owned in the 1930s. But none of us felt it was quite right. We ended up settling on a simpler name: Casa Chepitos. Though no one, even the people who had lived on Callejón de Chepito all of their lives, could ever tell me exactly what *chepito* meant.

LATER THAT NIGHT, in the master bedroom of the newly christened Casa Chepitos, I lounged in the dark in the Putzes' king-size bed, enjoying the view. I'd flung the bedroom windows open wide and was gazing down upon the lighted domes, bell towers, and spires of San Miguel's many churches. Paul, who was busy filling jugs with purified water and distributing them to the bathrooms while cautioning the kids to be sure to use it when they brushed their teeth, eventually joined me.

"I've always envied people who live in houses with beautiful views," I admitted to him, as if it were some dirty little secret.

"Well, you don't have to envy anyone anymore. You've got a pretty amazing view here."

Growing up in Kansas had made me yearn for what was beyond the relentlessly monotonous horizon. When I moved to Seattle, it was, at least in part, for its breathtaking and abundant vistas. There are city views and mountain views; views of Puget Sound, Mount Rainier, and Lake Washington; views of bridges and ferryboats and the Space Needle, of Queen Anne and Capitol Hill, Lake Union and the Ballard Locks. But I'd never lived in a house with a view in Seattle.

Now that I was soon to be the owner of this beautiful house with its fabulous view, I felt a bit greedy.

But I rationalized the feeling away. Who wouldn't covet this sumptuous visual tableau laid out below us? This perch from

where we could watch yellow Wilson's warblers and scarlet tana-
gers flock to the lavender jacaranda trees in spring, silver moons
rise over the distant shimmering lake at the Presa de Allende,
and the sky at sunset turn from aqua to scarlet, then to purple
with the deepening of dusk.

I lay back on the bed and squeezed my eyes partially shut until
the lights of the Parroquia church became the flames of a thousand candles burning within its lacy spires, like a dreamy illus-
tration of a castle in a children's book. I ruminated on the idea
of fairy tales and myths, and how much our lives are shaped by
them, for better or for worse. Deep inside I knew that, contrary
to all those happy-ever-after endings, love at first sight can often
end disastrously — even if the object of one's affection is a house.
But on that first night in my beautiful new house, I turned off my
inner critic (who is undoubtedly related to my mother) in order
to silence any doubts she might want to dredge up. All I wanted
at that moment was to figure out a way to spend as much time as
possible in my new fairy-tale castle with its breathtaking views.

I turned to Paul, who'd grown quiet.

"What would you think about taking a year off from work to
come live here? Or maybe we could retire and live here full-time
when Hannah goes to college?"

The sound of his soft, even breathing was his only response.

9 | *Los Bravos de San Miguel*

OUR TINY ALLEYWAY, too narrow for cars to drive down, was the perfect playfield for pickup soccer and baseball games. Late into the night, the persistent *thunk* of balls bouncing off the windowless stucco walls and the exuberant cries of kids echoed down the callejón.

By the second day of our first visit to Casa Chepitos, Will too was using it as his surrogate backyard. I was sitting on the concrete bench across from our front door that day, watching him take practice swings with his shiny new bat, when two Mexican girls, one short, the other tall, and both dressed in snug-fitting jeans and T-shirts, came walking down the alley. The shorter one smiled at my son as they approached.

"My brother plays baseball," she said to him in Spanish. Her thick, shiny black hair was pulled back tightly. Two wavy, carefully gelled strands hung over faintly familiar dark-brown eyes.

"What's your name?" Will asked. His Spanish accent was not half-bad.

"I'm Lupe," she said. Then she turned to her taller, copper-haired companion. "And this is my cousin, Paola." Paola offered Will a shy, toothy smile.

Lupe ran up the steps and ducked into her mother's store. She soon returned with her skinny, eleven-year-old brother Marcos in tow. It seemed that all of Gracia's children had her eyes: gorgeous, liquidy, deep-brown pools surrounded by thick, dark lashes.

Marcos and Will hit it off immediately. Despite his resistance to coming, it wasn't long before my son had befriended half the neighborhood kids and joined their nightly games in the alley.

But after a few days, he grew tired of playing baseball with eleven- and twelve-year-olds.

When he learned that San Miguel had a team of sixteen- to twenty-year-olds called Los Bravos, he asked Marcos to take him to see the coach.

Marcos led him up to the man's auto-repair shop, where a pack of pit bulls paced and snarled at the boys from behind a razor-wire fence. The coach, whose overalls were covered in motor oil and gear grease, proved more amiable than his dogs. He told Will that as long as he brought his own gear up to the stadium the following Tuesday at five in the afternoon, he was welcome to join their practice.

ON TUESDAY, WILL BEGAN TO FIDGET as soon as lunch was over. Eager to join a real team, he wandered around the house pestering me about the time every half hour, since there were no clocks in our new house.

"Here, just take my watch," I said, handing him my Timex. I was relieved when he packed up his duffel and left for the mile-long hike uphill to the stadium, though I suspected he would be the first person there.

Sure enough, when he arrived at exactly five o'clock, he found the place deserted except for a couple of sleepy burros that stood grazing in the outfield. He surveyed the field while he waited. He noticed there were no bases on the diamond or chalk lines defining the base paths. On the pitcher's mound, in lieu of the standard rubber, a splintered scrap of plywood was staked to the ground. Walls of concrete block covered with ads for Bimbo snacks, Bardahl motor oil, and Dos Equis beer encircled the dusty field, separating it from the cactus-covered desert beyond.

Forty-five minutes passed with no sign of a team or the coach.

Will had given up and was repacking his gear when a battered late-model Chevy pickup with a pile of boys in the back rolled up. The auto mechanic/coach hopped out of the cab, tossed some bases around the field, and, shortly after six o'clock, practice was finally under way.

Using a mix of Spanish and hand gestures, Will and the coach agreed that he should start at center field, just to the left of the somnolent burros. But the numerous raised eyebrows and conspiratorial glances between the other players put Will on edge. During batting practice, a kid from the callejón, whose nickname was El Gato, intentionally hit him with the first pitch.

Subtle resistance to working out with a gringo persisted for the first couple of days. But it wasn't long before Will's friendly nature and good humor were rewarded with inclusion into the group. His teammates even honored him with his own *apodo*. They called him Güero Palma, after a notorious Sinaloan drug-runner.

The boys began letting him in on their jokes. They taught him the meaning of *¡buey!*, *¡qué chingadera!*, and *¡aye, cabrón!* For Will, learning the meaning and correct pronunciation of Mexican slang was almost as much fun as playing ball. His teammates were amused by my son and they encouraged him to hang out and drink beer with them after practice. All of them, that is, except the team's star player, Ángel.

Ángel was the second-youngest child of Señora Rosa, our neighbor to the north. Though barely old enough to grow a mustache, he already had a young wife and a tiny six-month-old son, Ángelito. He was tall for a Mexican — nearly a head taller than his brothers — and he sported a mullet with a cluster of long black curls that hung down his back. His natural athletic ability and caustic wit made him popular with the neighborhood kids and his Bravo teammates.

Ángel loved baseball, but was a completely undisciplined player. He paid little attention to the coach's instructions, bat-ted with a lit cigarette between his lips, swigged shots of tequila before going on deck during games. Like a used-up boxer who doesn't know when to quit, he swung like a madman at outrageously bad pitches.

Unlike the other players, he had no interest in befriending the new gringo. He made his feelings clear one day in the callejón when Will stopped to say hi. Ángel responded by snorting and turning his back. My son shrugged it off, but it made me nervous.

"*Es un joven enojado,*" a kid with a bad temper, Gracia told me when I asked her about Ángel. He was part of the group of young men who sat on the stone bench in front of our house on weekends, drinking beer until they were red-eyed, barely able to stand, and often quite loud and raucous. Ángel appeared to be a big, volatile kid, just like Will, and the potentially incendiary combination scared me. Remembering Eleazar's story about the stabbings on the callejón, I warned my son to steer clear.

10 | *The Game*

A T PRACTICE ONE AFTERNOON, the coach asked Will if he'd like to start at center field in a game the following Sunday at noon against the Bravos' archrivals, the Guerreros of Dolores Hidalgo.

"*¡Sí, claro!*" Will said, jumping at the chance to play in a real game.

When Sunday arrived, Paul, Hannah and I trudged uphill to the Stirling Dickinson stadium. By the time we arrived, half the neighborhood was already assembled in the concrete bleachers. A bevy of nubile teenage girls that I recognized were clustered together in the stands, dressed in scanty tank tops and low-slung jeans. I suspected they were there to check out the ball players, including the cute new gringo on the block.

Spectators straggled in, filling the bleachers where a corrugated tin overhang provided the only protection from a searing midday sun. The atmosphere in the sweltering stadium was more like a county fair than a baseball game. Children and stray dogs raced around the infield. The burros, still out at center, grazed unperturbed by the burst of activity. Blue-bottle flies circled vendors selling everything from sliced melon to *jícama con chile* and icy-cold *cerveza*.

Bottles of cheap tequila were being raffled off, ostensibly to raise money for new uniforms.

My husband bought a handful of raffle tickets to support the cause and ended up winning a bottle of Jose Cuervo.

The Bravos were clad in an array of mismatched uniforms, making it hard to distinguish players from bystanders. Will, wearing a faded Bravos jersey two sizes too large, mingled with the players in the dugout. The coaches and other men gathered outside it, talking and downing bottles of beer or shots of tequila, as they waited for the Guerreros to show. Noon was long past. One o'clock came and went, and still no one seemed to know or care where the other team was.

Finally, around quarter past one, two truckloads of Guerreros rolled up. As the players filed into their dugout, I noticed that few of them were in their teens. Many of the team's muscular *campesinos* appeared to be well past thirty.

With the Guerreros' arrival, the atmosphere in the stadium took on a more serious tone. Kids and dogs were rounded up and chased off the field. Players began to take their positions, but no one bothered to remove the burros in center field. As Will took his place out there, a man sitting behind us inquired loudly: "*¿Quien es el pendejo en center?*" I considered telling him that the asshole in center field was my son, but thought better of it.

The game's only umpire, a small, wiry man who'd spent the last hour and a half chugging tequila with the coaches, staggered out to his position behind the pitcher. Dressed in an oversized, bright red button-down shirt, the man looked more like the target for a bull than the umpire of a baseball game. He called out something that I assumed meant "play ball" in slurred Spanish, and the game finally got under way.

The Bravos' ace pitcher, a handsome, light-skinned twenty-year-old with the nickname El Gringo, was on the mound. The lanky, long-legged kid resembled Satchel Paige in his windup and delivered a first pitch that dropped in at the plate. With a few solid strikes, he easily retired the side.

As the Bravos came up to bat, the stands came alive. First up was the first baseman, a heavyset kid with the nickname El Gordo. "Gordo, Gordo, Gordo," chanted the crowd as El Gordo smacked a fastball. The hard-hit ball dropped in just left of the center fielder. El Gordo lumbered toward first base, making it with seconds to spare. Will, batting second, struck out swinging on four pitches. He slammed down the bat and stomped back to the dugout.

Ángel was up next. After settling into position at the plate, he took two wild swings at even wilder pitches. He looked to be aiming for the fences with every swing. Jumping on the third pitch, he juiced a fastball as it crossed the plate. It flew away and bounced against the cinder block wall beyond center field. "Home run!" the ump called. As Ángel skipped across home base, he waved his arms triumphantly and grinned at the applauding crowd.

After a brief chewing out by the coach, the Guerreros' pitcher settled down and struck out the next two batters. Over the next few innings, they managed to pick up a couple of runs while holding the Bravos to two. By the top of the ninth, the score was tied. As the Bravos took the field, Will headed out to center field again.

El Gringo, having pitched the entire game, appeared tired as the number two batter for the Guerreros took the plate. On the first play of the inning, the Bravos' right fielder bobbled a pop-up, allowing the batter to safely reach first. Things went downhill from there when the next batter sent the first one home on an error by Popeye, the bug-eyed third baseman.

"¡Cabrón!" yelled Ángel, who was playing shortstop. He angrily charged Popeye, who fought right back. Like a couple of roosters in a Mexican cockpit, they hissed and spit and kicked dirt at each other.

The umpire, reeling from the quantity of tequila he'd consumed throughout the game, seemed uninterested in restoring order on the field. Things eventually settled down when the coaches intervened. But with the afternoon heat, the misplays, and suddenly being down by one, the atmosphere in the stadium began to feel like the inside of a pressure cooker.

The cleanup batter for the Guerreros, a stocky *campesino* with biceps the size of small melons, stepped up to the plate. He bore a striking resemblance to Edgar Martinez, all-time batting champion for the Seattle Mariners. On the first pitch, the man hit the ball hard, sending it to the right of center field.

Dodging a burro, Will ran toward right field, but the ball was clearly beyond his reach. I wondered what colorful expletive the Bravos fans would lob at a gringo who lost the game for them and thanked God the ancient Mexican ritual of sacrificing members of the losing ball team had ended in the ninth century. Surely the gringo would have been nominated to go first.

But then, in the midst of my lament, a minor miracle occurred. Perhaps it was fear of rebuke from his teammates, or an eagerness to impress the girls from the callejón, but Will's adrenaline kicked into overdrive. In a play reminiscent of a young Ken Griffey Jr., he leapt into the air and snagged the ball.

A handsome man dressed in a crisp, white guayabera sitting beside me turned and asked,

"*¿Es su hijo?*" Being that we were the only fair-haired people in the entire stadium, I was faintly amused by his question, but I answered him with a straight face.

"*Sí, es mi hijo,*" I said.

"*¿Como se llama?*"

"Guillermo," I told him, Spanish for William. We chatted for a few minutes and I learned that he came to all of the Bravos' home games. Not only for the love of baseball, but also because he liked tequila, and his wife wouldn't allow him to drink at home. My husband, being a guy who prefers a glass of red wine to a shot of tequila, donated our raffle prize to the man.

The Bravos, now up to bat again, were down by one. The leadoff hitter reached first on a ball that dropped into the outfield. Then El Gordo struck out. With one man on and one out, Will stepped up to the plate. My heart began to race.

In a low, guttural voice, the man in the guayabera began chanting, "Guillermo, Guillermo, Guillermo." Soon the entire crowd had joined in, including the girls from the callejón. With one inspired swing, Will drilled a line drive straight at the Guerreros' pitcher. But instead of hitting the pitcher, who ducked, the ball smacked the umpire, who was standing behind him, squarely in the chest and knocked him to the ground. As the ball bounced off the ump, the pitcher grabbed it and threw Will out at first. But in all the chaos, the player on first had made it to third base. The man behind us who'd called Will a *pendejo* stood up and screamed, "Guillermo!" I turned around in time to see him pump a victory fist in the air.

Paul suddenly jumped up and elbowed his way through the celebrating crowd to the fence. He signaled for Will to come over, and they had a brief conversation. Afterward, Will headed out to the mound and wrapped his arm around the shoulder of the diminutive ump. A roar of laughter swept the stadium as Will leaned over and offered the man his sincerest apology in broken Spanish.

The Bravos were now down by one with one man on, two men out, and Ángel was up to bat. Aware that the fate of the game rested squarely on his shoulders, he burst onto the field like a young bull turned loose in the bullring. He pawed at the dirt around home plate with his sneakers. He waved the bat wildly in the air over his head. He choked back a smile as fans jumped to their feet, chanting and clapping and screaming his name.

When the first pitch crossed the plate, Ángel swung so hard he spun round like a top, completely missing the ball. This only increased the crowd's intensity. The following pitch was fouled into the stands. The next one, too. In both dugouts, anxious players leaned forward, heads turning in unison, straining to see where the ball went each time.

Ángel swung at seven consecutive pitches. Each went foul behind the stands. The fans had worked themselves into a frenzy when, suddenly, the battle between pitcher and batter abruptly ended. Ángel crushed a ball that traveled so far beyond the wall in left field that the Guerreros' outfielder never did find it.

The fans at a World Cup soccer game could not have matched the enthusiasm of the Bravos' fans that day. Only the annual reading of El Grito, the historic, impassioned cry for Mexican independence from Spanish rule, gets a reception in San Miguel as exuberant as Ángel got rounding the bases. He beamed as he crossed home plate and was rushed by his teammates, who pounced on him, slapping his back and smacking hands with him in midair. As we filed out of the stadium along with the exuberant crowd, I turned back to the field and saw Will, in the middle of it all, exchanging high fives with Ángel.

A FEW DAYS LATER, I ran into Ángel hanging out in the callejón. He was cradling his infant son in the crook of his arm.

"That was a great game on Sunday," I said.

"Yeah, it was pretty cool," he said with a smile. We rehashed the game for a few minutes, savoring its highlights together. He told me a little about his life, about his wife, and his baby son, whom he seemed very proud of. That brief, but sweet, conversation allowed me to see how badly I'd misjudged Ángel. Beneath his unruly, tough-guy exterior was a devoted father and a genuinely nice guy.

The morning we were to leave San Miguel to return to Seattle, Will wandered into my room. He hovered close as I stuffed the few last things into my suitcase and zipped it up. Then he leaned over and gave me a quick hug.

"Thanks for buying the house and making me come down here, Mom. I'm really glad I did."

Then he headed out the door to say good-bye to his new friends in Callejón de Chepito.

11 | *El Barrio*

WITHIN DAYS OF CLOSING ON THE HOUSE, I headed over to Allende Properties to look for Claudius. I wanted to make sure Jerry Putz had paid his commission. He was there, sitting at a computer, when I walked in. He looked up at me, but this time no movie-star smile flashed my way. In place of his charming, comic persona was a sullen, skeptical one.

"Come over here," he said. "I want to show you something."

On his screen saver was a photo of a happy toddler, a pretty little girl with brown eyes and dark-blonde hair.

"This is my baby. I want you to know that you have taken food out of her mouth, doing what you did."

He told me that the Putzes had given him nothing. Not a penny in commission. Plus they were threatening to sue him for trespassing.

I explained everything: How they turned out to be friends of friends, how I'd wanted to withhold his commission but they'd guaranteed me they would pay him. He softened slightly after hearing my side of the story. I promised him I would talk to the Putzes and remind them of their obligation.

I called their house but didn't get an answer. I left a message but they didn't return my call.

I sent them a long email reminding them of our conversation and how they had assured me Claudius would get paid.

By the time I got an answer, I was back in Seattle. Their email defended their position and reiterated their fury at our trespassing in the house. They claimed an attorney friend of theirs from Mexico City had advised them to pursue legal action against both of us and suggested that if we didn't back off, they would do just that.

The owner of Allende Properties called me in Seattle and we had a long conversation. He was clearly unhappy about the situation but understood that I'd acted in good faith. Still, I felt bad that Claudius hadn't received anything for his time. So I called my friend Sam, a Seattle land-use attorney, and asked what he thought about me paying Claudius a thousand dollars as a finder's fee.

"Don't do it," he said. "If you do, you could open up a can of worms. You might be held liable for the entire commission all over again. It's not your responsibility. You did your part. Claudius and his boss need to go after the sellers for the commission."

A few more emails went back and forth but to no avail. In the end, the Putzes didn't pursue a lawsuit, but Claudius got nothing. I blamed myself for not having thought to put it in the closing contract, but later learned that even when it's written into a contract, there's no assurance that real estate commissions in Mexico, especially finder's fees, will get paid.

The following June, as soon as school was out, the kids and I headed back to San Miguel. Will was anxious to see his new friends again and rejoin the Bravos. Hannah too was eager to return to her new nest at Casa Chepitos and see the friends she'd made in the callejón. Eleazar wasn't available the day we arrived, so he arranged for another driver to pick us up at the airport and drive us to San Miguel. Our plane arrived late, and after clearing customs, I searched the muddle of waiting drivers for one holding up a placard with my name on it. When I spotted a man holding a piece of cardboard with "JUDAS" scribbled across it in huge black letters, I realized he was our driver. When my kids saw the sign, they nearly tripped over each other, laughing at the man's mistake. If I hadn't still felt so guilty about Claudius losing out on his commission, I would have been laughing, too.

AND SO, ON THAT INAUSPICIOUS NOTE, my family and I began our life on Callejón de Chepito. In the coming years we would establish a routine of traveling back and forth between Seattle and San Miguel several times a year, spending most of our spring breaks, summer vacations, and winter holidays at Casa Chepitos. Each time we went, we learned more about the town, the neighborhood, and our new neighbors.

It didn't take long for us to figure out that many of the Mexicans living along the callejón were related to each other. Will seemed to possess an instinctive understanding of who was related to whom, but I had a difficult time keeping all the relationships straight. I knew that Gracia's husband was a man named Salvador and that they had three children: Lupe, Marcos, and Marthín. I also knew that they had brothers, sisters, in-laws, grandmothers, great-grandmothers, first cousins, second cousins, and cousins through marriage who lived in many of the houses in our neighborhood. Gracia's older sister Remedios and her family lived two doors down from us. Remedios and Gracia's grandfather had owned much of the land surrounding Callejón de Chepito, and their father and uncles had built a number of the twenty-two houses hidden behind the callejón's colorful stucco walls.

Only a handful of non-Mexicans lived there when we first came to Casa Chepitos. There was Betsy, a reclusive American woman who lived behind a formidable salmon-colored wall at the far end of the alley. She rented out rooms in her fortress-like enclave to support herself. A younger, blonde-haired woman named Connie owned the house with the lovely cerulean blue wall. Connie had arrived in San Miguel, fallen in love with a Mexican, and decided to buy the house. When the relationship didn't work out and an architect from San Francisco built a spec house next door with upstairs rooms that looked directly into her patio garden, she decided to sell the house and return to the States. Or so I heard.

At the head of the callejón, where it opened onto a street named the Cuesta de San José, there lived an older man from Atlanta and his German-born wife. Mr. Stafford, or J.P. as he was known, was one of a dying breed of Americans: a true Southern gentleman. It turned out it was J.P. — trying to be helpful as always — who'd given Claudius the key to the house the day we first visited Casa Chepitos.

The expatriates living on the alley didn't appear to socialize with our Mexican neighbors. Like the majority of foreigners in San Miguel, they lived outside the web of tangled relationships that make up a Mexican barrio.

My kids, however, quickly made friends with the other kids in our neighborhood.

Within days of our arrival, Will had not only befriended Marcos and his cousin José, he'd also teamed up with Rocky and Ramiro, 17-year-old twins from San Antonio, Texas, whose *abuelita* lived next door. They played pickup basketball in the Parque Juárez in the afternoons and hung out at the hamburger stand on Mesones Street late at night. Lupe and Remedios's three daughters (*las bellezas del callejón* as I referred to them, since they were all *very* pretty) invited Will to concerts and all-night discos. I had to be flexible about the one o'clock curfew he had during high school; San Miguel's nightlife doesn't start until around eleven, and the kids often didn't make it home until three or four in the morning.

It wasn't long before both Will and Hannah were being invited to local fiestas, parades, wedding celebrations, Nativity *posadas*, and extravagant *quince años* parties. Mexico is a land of infinite fiestas, cultural celebrations, and religious rituals, and San Miguel is blessed with more of them than any city in Mexico. There are Saints' Days to celebrate; Semana Santa or Holy Week (which actually spans nearly three weeks); the San Miguelada, a Pamplona-style running of the bulls in September; the Virgin of Guadalupe's day in early December; El Día de los Locos in June; and the spring celebration of Candelaria in February, to name just a few.

Our neighbors introduced my kids to Mexico's diverse gastronomy. Gracia gave them their first tastes of chicken in *mole* sauce, sweet *tamales*, and *tuna*, the fruit of the nopal cactus. They were willing and adventurous about trying most of the new foods, but drew the line when she offered them boiled chicken's feet. Gracia's sister Remedios shared *horchata* and *atole* drinks and during the Christmas *posadas* invited them in for a delicious spicy apple punch. The twins' grandma, Señora Rosa, always had a pack of grandkids at her table during the summer, but she made room for Hannah and Will, too. They came home extolling the virtues of her savory *sopas* and succulent *estofados*, and wanted to know why I couldn't create tasty soups and stews like hers.

In turn, we took carloads of neighborhood kids on picnics to the water park at Xoté and La Gruta hot springs. We brought Lupe and Marcos with us to the Mummy Museum in Guanajuato, and their younger siblings to the Mexican circus. We threw birthday parties with milky *tres leches* cake and giant piñatas that threatened to burst spontaneously from the weight of too many fruit sours and taffy chews. Will organized and played chef at our most popular events: American-style hamburger cook-offs and pizza parties for all the neighborhood kids.

I watched with a degree of envy as our kids easily integrated themselves into callejón life because it wasn't so easy for Paul and me. Though we spent most of the kids' school breaks, summer vacations, and Christmas holidays at Casa Chepitos, I made no adult friends among the Mexicans on the alley that first year. It was obvious from the limp, noncommittal handshakes and the blank faces I encountered — Mexicans were not like Midwesterners. Getting to know them was not going to be easy.

A prominent feature of callejón society is its focus on family. I noticed that most of our Mexicans neighbors spent all their spare time doing family-oriented activities. Guarding their privacy was another characteristic, and this tendency was reinforced by the giant stucco walls surrounding their houses.

The town's large expat community filled cafés and restaurants all over town, but seemed insular and poorly integrated into San Miguel's Mexican society. On the alley, our Mexican neighbors didn't seem to go out of their way to form relationships with the foreigners who lived there, and the foreigners, for the most part, ignored the Mexicans.

My husband doesn't mind living in isolation. By Jung's theory of personality types (attitudes, as he referred to them), Paul would be considered quite introverted. He can spend great stretches of time alone and be content doing so. He tends to be cerebral and lacks confidence in social situations.

I'm on the opposite end of Jung's personality scale. I'm an unabashed extrovert who enjoys mixing it up with anyone and everyone and usually find it easy to make friends. Among the weaknesses of excessively extroverted people like me, is that we need to feel we've made a good impression and that we fit in. In my case it goes beyond needing to be liked: being in healthy relationships energizes me. Having a deep sense of connection with another person makes me happier than almost anything. Feeling disconnected or isolated can throw me into despair.

One would think that the years I spent alone in Paris and other parts of France would have prepared me for the role of Insider-Outsider. Parisians are notoriously standoffish. It is common for Americans visiting France to interpret the French reserve as rudeness. But it's not just tourists that the French keep at arm's length. You can be "friends" with a Parisian for a long time and still not be certain what he or she truly feels about anything other than the current political regime or the quality of the cuisine at local restaurants. In Paris I eventually did form friendships, with the other students in my daily classes at the Sorbonne. In Mexico, I didn't even have that.

Living outside the closed social network of our barrio was challenging for me. I loved our colorful new house. I loved being back in San Miguel. I loved the fiestas and cultural events. I loved learning more Spanish and Mexican history. But I worried that Paul and I might never really fit in. That we'd end up traversing the alley, barely acknowledged by the people we lived among. Like temporary guests on some exotic island.

12 | *Amigas*

LIKE WILL, MY DAUGHTER HANNAH bonded with other kids in the alley during our first visit to Casa Chepitos. But she formed one surprising relationship that would surpass all others in importance to her and everyone in our family.

She was leaning over the railing of the upstairs terrace one day, watching the kids on the callejón kick a soccer ball around, when Lupe leaned out the second-floor window of their house — slightly more than two meters from ours — and waved at her. In that small gesture, a friendship was born. One that would grow and endure, despite an eight-year age difference and the many changes the future would bring.

From that day forward, whenever we were at home in Mexico, Lupe and Hannah spent hours at Lupe's house — braiding hair, painting nails, watching TV, playing cards, listening to music, gossiping about Britney Spears's latest antics, or babysitting for Gracia's "surprise" baby, Cholo (whose nickname is Mexican slang for "homey").

I once asked Hannah what her favorite thing to do in San Miguel was, and wasn't surprised when she responded, "Hang out at Lupe's house."

Lupe was always kind and patient with my daughter. She ushered her around town, taking her to *el centro* for corn-on-the-cob or ice cream. She taught her Spanish, and watched American videos with her even though she couldn't understand them herself, and always invited Hannah along when the girls on the callejón gathered to recite prayers on Friday evenings, or went somewhere interesting. Lupe also defended Hannah from the Mexican boys who harassed her and the curious women who asked too many questions. Hannah was adopted from Korea, and the Mexicans frequently reacted to her Asian features.

"*Chinita, chinita,*" boys hissed at my daughter as she walked around San Miguel. At first I corrected them, explaining, in my naïveté, that she was Korean, and not Chinese. But I soon learned that Mexicans might call any girl who looks Asian *Chinita*. A cousin of Lupe's is affectionately nicknamed China because she has almond-shaped eyes.

Adoptions are rare in Mexico, and interracial ones almost nonexistent. Mexicans also have a different code of behavior around what is polite, and because of this, they frequently stared unabashedly at Hannah and me as we walked through the *jardín*, or asked awkward questions when we were in the market together.

"Is she your daughter?" Mexican women often asked. When I told them yes, they looked even more puzzled. How could this happen? *Una güera*, a blonde woman, with a black-haired, almond-eyed daughter? The concept of a mixed-race adoption just didn't register in their minds.

I think Lupe could empathize with Hannah because she too was searching for her own sense of self. She understood just how difficult feeling okay about one's self could be for a young girl. Lupe, herself, had a complicated story.

BORN UNDER THE SIGN OF SCORPIO, Lupe reveled in the clandestine, and like all girls her age, she yearned to feel special. When she was fifteen — the age when Mexican families throw extravagant coming-of-age parties called *quinceañeras* for their daughters — there was no mass at the San Francisco church or fancy party honoring Lupe's transition from childhood to womanhood. For a fifteen-year-old, devoutly Catholic Mexican girl, to not have a *quinceañera* celebration is equivalent to a thirteen-year-old Orthodox Jewish boy or girl missing out on their bar or bat mitzvah celebrations. Next to her wedding day, it's the most important day in a Mexican girl's life.

It was several years before I knew Lupe well enough for her to confide in me how distressing that time in her life had been. But one day up on our terrace she told me why she hadn't had a *quinceañera* celebration.

"For years my mother saved money for my *fiesta de quince años*. She gave the money to a neighbor lady for safekeeping," Lupe said. Her face twisted into a little frown, as if she were fighting back tears. "The year I turned fifteen, my mom asked for the money back, but the woman told her her sons had lost it."

To her father's outrage, Lupe insisted on marrying her twenty-two-year-old boyfriend. When the boy left for Texas to work and never returned, Salvador had the marriage annulled.

Unfortunately, Lupe's father was a man who harbored a deep and unexamined anger. He'd never really forgiven his daughter for defying him. Their father-daughter relationship was fraught with tension and unresolved feelings.

Unlike her relationship with her father, Lupe and her mother were very close. Like many women who live in close proximity and get along, their minds seemed to work in tandem. They often finished each other's sentences and shared a quirky sense of humor.

Gracia relied heavily on her only daughter. Lupe tended the store in her absence, corralled her three younger brothers, cooked meals, helped with the laundry, and ran errands.

By the time we met the Cordova family, ten months after the annulment, Lupe seemed sobered by her experience and circumspect about finding another *novio*. Still, she gravitated toward secretiveness, craved adventure, and, like so many sixteen-year-old girls, yearned to meet someone who would love her and make her feel special.

DURING OUR FIRST YEAR in San Miguel, I often frequented Gracia's store to buy milk or yogurt for breakfast, snacks for the kids, or beer and soda when our American friends came to visit. Hannah and Will went in and out of her store and house the same as they would any friend's house in the States. But I was never invited into the inner sanctum — the kitchen or living room or any other room in their home, which was located behind the store. I had only a formal relationship with Gracia and her family; the invisible barrier of cultural difference and my minimal Spanish skills conspired to keep me at arm's length.

Then one night, our second year at Casa Chepitos, Hannah and Lupe rented the movie *Bend It Like Beckham* from the Block-buster on Ancha de San Antonio. The girls asked if I wanted to watch it with them in Lupe's room, directly behind the store. Hannah, Lupe, and I sat together on one of the lumpy twin beds under a gilded crucifix, watching the movie as Gracia roamed in and out of the room, folding laundry, selling beer and snacks out front, and scrounging for coins to make change. When I tried, in my feeble Spanish, to explain to her what the movie was about — two extraordinarily gifted girl soccer players, one of whom sneaks out to play despite her family's disapproval — she looked doubtful. Yet, not long into the movie, she sat down on the other bed and I noticed she was intently watching the action, even reading the subtitles. Not wandering in and out of the room like usual. At the point in the movie where the protagonist attempts to score a do-or-die point, Gracia began shouting encouragements at the TV. She leaned toward the screen, her eyes wide, concentrating on the play. When the ball made it into the goal she jumped up and jubilantly waved her dish towel in the air.

When the movie ended and Lupe asked what the English words "girl power" meant, I demurred. Not because I didn't have the vocabulary.

Working-class women in Mexico often shun the label "feminist." They consider feminism as a denial of their commitment to their families.

"*La fuerza de chicas*," I said to Lupe, giving her the literal translation and passing on my usual feminist rhetoric. But I did wonder, since only men played soccer in the fields surrounding San Miguel at the time, if Gracia's enthusiasm for the movie's heroine hinted at a furtive feminist inclination. Curious to know what she thought about the idea of champion girl soccer players, I asked her.

"It was okay," she said with a shrug. Then she wandered off to sell two more Coronas to a neighbor.

FEMINIST OR NOT, Gracia eventually became my closest friend and ally in the callejón, though it took a year to get her to stop addressing me as Señora, and another year for her to actually call me by my name. In spite of my derelict Spanish and her complete lack of English, we found ways to communicate and soon discovered we had a lot in common. Like me, she is a born entrepreneur with a calculating mind and good business sense. Due to family troubles, she'd been forced to quit school and begin working after the sixth grade.

"My father drank all the money away," she said. "I had to go to work at age twelve so I could buy myself shoes."

Though she's had little formal education, she can add the price of a kilo of beans, a dozen eggs, and a liter of beer in her head faster than I can on a ten-key. She runs her store efficiently, tracking each item that comes in or goes out, like a human point-of-sale system, and keeps close tabs on the bottom line.

In addition to being the neighborhood grocer, Gracia is the unofficial mayor of our callejón. People look to her for information, support, and, at times, protection.

"*Es una buena persona*" is her mantra, her way of conferring grace upon the people of our alley. She repeats it with regularity, extending the benefit of the doubt to everyone, even the Americans, like us, who were beginning to overrun her neighborhood.

At her core, Gracia is a social worker and a caretaker. In addition to attending to her own brood, she watches over the elderly, the infirm, and the homeless on our alley, and keeps them from falling between the cracks. She often takes them in and feeds them or helps them find shelter.

"The saddest thing in the world," she said one day after I'd watched her give a taco to a homeless woman, "is to have no family."

13 | *A New Language*

THE CALLEJÓN SOON turned into a living Spanish lab for the kids and me. We learned more Spanish vocabulary and idiomatic expressions hanging around our neighborhood than in all the classes I was forever signing us up for combined. I was determined not to be counted among the numerous foreigners living in San Miguel who had little or no ability to converse in Spanish.

I also knew that if I were to ever become immersed in our neighborhood, I had to be more fluent. Though the going was slow and I had a hard time retaining vocabulary — the synapses of my brain weren't as snappy as they once were — I plugged away, memorizing verb conjugations, expanding my vocabulary, and growing my repertoire of *mexicanismos*.

Gracia made a great *maestra*. She wasn't shy about correcting me, and like any good teacher, she was willing to slow down and repeat herself if I didn't understand something the first time. My friend Wendy, who is fluent in Spanish, asked if Gracia always talked to me as if I were a first grader. I told her I guessed so, and that it didn't offend me in the least. I was grateful for the help.

My Spanish slowly improved to the point where I could carry on simple conversations. But finding a genuine sense of connection with the matriarchy that ruled our callejón continued to elude me.

DRESSED IN SKIRTS AND APRONS and sensible shoes, my female neighbors stared at my feeble attempts to sweep the area in front of our house clear of accumulated debris and dog poop. Feeling the heat of their gaze, I would imagine their thoughts: *Who is this silly gringa, old enough to be a grandmother, wearing blue jeans as tight as our teenage daughters' and rubber sandals on her feet? And she's so useless with a broom!* Years later my neighbor Cristina would tell me she'd been convinced our house in the United States was full of wall-to-wall carpeting because I was so inept with a broom. "You Americans and your vacuum cleaners!" she exclaimed in mock disdain.

Another reason it was difficult to connect with my neighbors is that Mexicans are wary of outsiders. Understandably so. Their long history of being conquered and colonized by Spain and then dominated and bullied by the United States has resulted in what Octavio Paz refers to as the "Mexican Mask." In *The Labyrinth of Solitude*, he sums it up: "The Mexican, whether young or old, *criollo* or *mestizo*, general or laborer or lawyer, seems to me to be a person who shuts himself away to protect himself: his face is a mask and so is his smile."

Between the Mexican's natural reserve, the vast disparity in our economic circumstances, and our strikingly different life experiences, it was hard to imagine how I could befriend the aproned women who gathered in the callejón every day.

They nodded politely at me and the other Americans renting houses along the callejón when we walked by. But rarely were any words, other than *buenos días* or *buenas tardes*, exchanged. I wondered what I could do or say to engage and connect with these women in a meaningful way. I decided hanging out with them and doing a lot of active listening was the best way to begin. I was careful not to express my spiritual beliefs, except for my affection for the Virgin of Guadalupe. The devoutly Catholic women would likely have considered my personal version of the Holy

Trinity—the Virgin of Guadalupe, Kwan Yin, and the Buddha—a sacrilege.

———

AT CASA CHEPITOS WE ARE FLANKED by grandmothers named Rosa—one lives to the south of us and another to the north. We began referring to them as Señora Rosa to the North and Señora Rosa to the South, as a simple way of distinguishing one from the other. Señora Rosa to the North is Ángel's mother; Señora Rosa to the South is the grandmother of Will's friends Rocky and Ramiro.

Señora Rosa to the North, whose face epitomizes Paz's impenetrable mask, is one of the callejón's most formidable women. She frequently sits on the concrete bench opposite our house, tuning in on the day's gossip. Even though I found her a bit intimidating, I began sitting with her, hoping to catch bits of the daily *chisme* and to learn more about her life. Then one day, while attempting to make small talk, I accidentally offended her by making a semi-serious blunder in Spanish. And believe me, Señora Rosa is not the kind of woman who finds silly grammatical mistakes amusing.

A stout woman with silver-gray hair pulled back in a tight bun, she has skin like burnished bronze and a mouth that is drawn into a permanent grimace. The pain of arthritis and other health problems she's battled for years has weathered both her body and her spirit. She's nearly blind in one eye from glaucoma and has serious vascular issues, and lack of dental hygiene has left her with only a handful of healthy teeth. Like many Mexicans, she grew up poor and malnourished.

The result for her and large swaths of Mexico's population has been an epidemic of diabetes, high blood pressure, heart problems, dental disease, and other serious maladies.

As we sat together on the bench that day, she catalogued the long list of health issues currently plaguing her, but emphasized that it was her arthritic elbow that bothered her most.

"It's very painful; the medication they've given me doesn't work," she said. "It's hard to sleep at night."

I wondered if glucosamine or some other over-the-counter supplement might help, but lacking the vocabulary needed to offer advice, I decided to try to sympathize by dredging up a phrase I'd memorized in a junior high school Spanish class — a passage in a seventh-grade textbook where Juan was offering sympathy to Maria, who had broken her arm. It *seemed* appropriate.

"Oh my goodness, I hope it's better soon," I said, repeating the phrase in Spanish, exactly as I remembered it.

Señora Rosa turned and glared at me with her one good eye, as if I'd just cussed her out instead of offering sincere sympathy.

"What did you say?" she asked.

Wincing from the sting of her gaze, I decided not to repeat the phrase. I simply shrugged and smiled. Then I excused myself and wished her a good afternoon before ducking into the safety of Casa Chepitos, where I made a beeline for my Spanish dictionary.

I looked up the words I'd said and discovered the problem — instead of saying, "I hope it's better soon," I'd actually said, "So much the better."

I'VE MADE MORE THAN A FEW GAFFES in Spanish. Most of them were silly mistakes, like the time I called goat cheese *queso de cabrón* instead of *queso de cabra*. But on occasion, my mistakes have ended up causing larger problems.

One time I called Eleazar's home from Dallas to confirm that he would be at the León airport that night to shuttle Hannah, two of her friends, and me to San Miguel. He wasn't home, so I spoke with his wife. But I mistakenly used the verb *escoger*, instead of *recoger*, inadvertently telling her that I wanted her husband to choose me, instead of pick me up. Needless to say,

I found myself and three teenage girls stranded at the León airport at eleven o'clock that night. (A few years later I heard that Eleazar and his wife divorced.)

After my slip up with Señora Rosa, I felt more insecure than ever about speaking Spanish around my neighbors, and confused about how to explain to her what I'd intended to say.

For a while I fretted about it, but eventually decided to drop it, assuming she and the other women of our callejón would forever think of me as a ridiculous, know-nothing gringa, who couldn't even handle a broom.

But then one day something happened that gave me reason to hope, in the smallest way, that a shift was under way in my relations with the sensible matrons of our alley.

Once again, I'd packed my suitcase for the return trip to Seattle and was headed out the door of Casa Chepitos toward the Cuesta de San José, where a shuttle van was waiting to take me to the airport. Walking through our home's inner courtyard, I felt the familiar pang of remorse I experienced each time I have to leave San Miguel and my lovely, orderly Mexican home to head back to the chaos of my life and work in Seattle. As I rolled my suitcase through the heavy iron door, I was surprised to see six, maybe seven, neighborhood women standing in their doorways in the early morning shadows. Gracia was there and her sister Remedios, Señora Rosa to the South and several others. I was halfway down the alley before it dawned on me: they'd all come out to say good-bye. To *me*. Even Señora Rosa to the North was there, leaning her good hip against the doorframe of her house.

"*Vaya con Dios*," she said, nodding at me as I rolled my suitcase past her. Go with God.

14 | Lost and Found

Nothing great in the world has been
accomplished without passion.

FRIEDRICH HEGEL

FOR A WHILE THERE WAS a drag queen who stood in front of the Walgreens that had once been City People's, playing a worn-out guitar for money. Wearing a Jackie Kennedy pillbox hat, a rope of plastic pearls the size of jawbreakers, and heavy pancake makeup to cover the evidence of a persistent five o'clock shadow, she stood on the corner strumming and singing Dylan's songs, slightly off-key. I always stopped when she was there, sometimes to drop a dollar in her open case, and other times to harmonize a little. I was drawn to her for many reasons, but most of all because I could see that she had something I'd once had and hoped to have again someday: she had a *passion*. She had this thing she loved doing and would keep on doing, whether she was rewarded with coins in her case or dismissed as ridiculous, because strumming that old guitar filled a place inside her that nothing else could.

I'd had a passion once upon a time. I'd believed in what I was doing. I'd dreamt of creating a chain of the coolest, most useful retail stores in Seattle while, at the same time, providing a diverse, equitable, and supportive workplace for the employees. My goal had been to develop a new business model, one that transcended traditional managerial models and focused as much on the quality of the workplace as on the bottom line. My vision for the future had, at one time, included expanding the concept into more neighborhoods, maybe even other cities some day.

But when we were forced to close the Fremont and Capitol Hill stores, the process of liquidating and shutting them down left me exhausted and demoralized. When the two-year ordeal finally came to an end, I found the bucket of enthusiasm I'd always carried for my businesses had sprung a serious leak. The passion I felt for my work had all drained away.

Though we still had two stores to manage, and one was in desperate need of a major managerial overhaul, for the first time since I'd started the business I began to think of my work as a job. I put in my hours, and eventually managed to bring the Sand Point store around to profitability. But the excitement I'd had for the business and my work was gone. I no longer thought of City People's as my future; I began to think of it as my past.

There was another, more complicated reason I felt so deflated. My self-confidence was shaken to its core when we closed the stores. My identity had been inextricably tied to my work and the success of City People's, and losing the stores was a sucker punch to my self-esteem. Going through menopause during those difficult years didn't help either. I saw it as an omen of old age, and did not adjust to the changes with ease or grace. Hot flashes, night sweats, insomnia, and migraines plagued me during those years. Worst of all, my vanity was crushed. It seemed that only yesterday when I looked in the mirror, a fresh-faced, faintly pretty woman had stared back at me. Now all I saw were dark circles under my eyes, sagging, blotchy skin, and a network of fine facial lines that resembled a road map of Ohio. All the anti-aging serums and wrinkle creams in the world couldn't hide the fact that I was coming down to life's finish line faster than I'd ever thought possible.

None of my accomplishments seemed to matter anymore

either. I felt adrift and unhappy. I focused on everything that was wrong with my life and grew overly critical of my family, coworkers, and business partners. I'd been so caught up in the busyness of running City People's and raising my kids that I'd lost track of who I was and what made me happy.

I floundered around for a couple of years, searching for a new passion and identity as any forty-nine-year-old who's had the rug pulled out from under her would. I took classes at the University of Washington. I even completed a certificate in Fundraising Management with the idea of switching to a new career in the nonprofit sector. I envisioned working for an NGO doing business development in Mexico or Central America. But even before her words of support had tumbled from my mother's lips — "Why on earth would anyone hire *you* as a fundraiser?" — I'd already decided that full-time fundraising wasn't for me. Eventually I did discover several new passions, and as with many things, they weren't at all immediate or obvious. Instead, one small thing would eventually lead to another. But it all started with yoga.

I took up practicing yoga with the simple desire of stretching my way through middle age in hopes of increasing my flexibility in my later years. Longevity runs in the family and so do bad knees. Since virtually every middle-aged woman in central Seattle practices yoga, I knew it wouldn't be difficult to find a class. And indeed, locating a studio was the easy part. The only easy part. Everything else, from learning the Sanskrit names for the *asanas* (postures), to holding a plank pose, to sitting still for long periods in meditation, felt like a huge grind. As I struggled to get my body to cooperate in *adho mukha svanasana*, the yoga pose commonly known as downward-facing dog, I remember thinking to myself: How can anything that looks so *easy*, be so *hard*?

But I stuck with it, and after about six months of struggling with sore muscles and the humiliation of falling on my face numerous times, I loosened up. When I stopped worrying about being the best in my class, the postures became easier. My arms and legs and back grew stronger, though the first downward-facing dog of the day still felt like a challenge. My stamina for sitting quietly increased, though my mind was hardly ever truly tranquil. As someone who had never readily signed up for groups of any kind, particularly ones where sports or exercise were involved, I surprised even myself with my dedication to practicing yoga.

My yoga practice brought me more than I had expected: It provided me with the support of other women my age, calmed my persistent agitation, and helped me to stop responding to life's crises with hysteria. And when I couldn't be in sunny San Miguel, it also helped brighten my days. And, as I said, yoga eventually led me to another practice, one that would truly change my life for the better.

15 | *The Fight*

MY YOGA TEACHER MEG often ends class with a reminder that life provides us with daily opportunities to demonstrate compassion, both for ourselves and for others. The problem is, when we're at home in Mexico, I'm sometimes confused as to whether I'm being compassionate or merely imposing my values on our Mexican neighbors. Like the day a fight broke out in the alley.

I was upstairs reading on the terrace, enjoying an unusually quiet, sun-drenched afternoon.

The dogs, roosters, goats, and burro that live below us had worn themselves out braying, barking, and bleating since four in the morning. Now stretched out in the shade of a mesquite tree, they were, miraculously, silent.

No wonder siesta time is so popular in Mexico, I thought as my body relaxed into the mid-afternoon calmness. It was often the quietest time of day.

My Zen moment was shattered when shouting broke out in the alley. When it didn't subside, I got up and walked over to the railing to see what was going on. Below me, near the mouth of the callejón, I could see two boys punching and shoving each other. Other kids were quickly gathering around, including Will, who was right in the middle of the pack. Along with the others, he was shouting encouragements to his friend Hector, a runt of a kid with a cowlick, a quick temper, and a perpetual chip on his shoulder. I thought I heard Will urge Hector to punch the other kid. Within seconds I had dropped my book and was trotting down our spiral staircase.

By the time I was out the door, many people from the neighborhood had gathered and were cheering on one kid or the other. Scattered among the kids from our callejón were ones I'd never seen before and a smattering of adults, who stood on the sidelines, cheering the two adolescents as they pummeled each other. I was shocked to realize that not only were the other adults not interested in breaking up the fight, they were encouraging the prepubescent Fight Club.

I edged my way into the middle of the noisy mob and caught a glimpse of Hector's bloodied nose as he threw a punch at the other kid. I scanned the crowd for another adult I knew and saw Remedios opposite me. She shot me a concerned look. When I returned a questioning one of my own, she shrugged.

Gracia's older sister is nearly her opposite. She is reserved and naturally mindful, whereas Gracia, like me, often blurts out whatever comes into her head. Remedios is a deep thinker and slow talker who will often look to the heavens as she searches for the exact word to describe some aspect of human nature or psychology. I'm pretty certain her element would be water, whereas Gracia's is fire.

Though she clearly was troubled by it, quiet, sage Remedios seemed helpless to intervene in the fight that afternoon. Not one for being quiet or sage, I began shoving my way through the horde of screaming kids toward the brawling pair. Then, suddenly, someone grabbed hold of my arm and yanked me away from the crowd.

"Stay out of this, Mom!" Will yelled at me. His face was flushed from screaming. "You don't understand! This is not your culture!"

I equivocated for a moment. He had a point. It was *not* my culture. There was so much about life on the alley that still mystified me. Like why was I one of only two adults in the crowd who thought the fight should be stopped? Didn't anyone else care if these kids got hurt? Didn't any of the other adults watching the fight believe—like we do in politically correct Seattle—that using your words is the appropriate way to resolve your problems?

I wondered if maybe Will was right. Maybe I didn't understand. Maybe it wasn't my obligation as an adult to intervene.

As I stood debating my conscience, I heard a chilling sound. A sound that would summon a protective response in any warm-blooded mother. The sound of a child's skull smacking into concrete.

Within seconds I was in the center of the swarm, yanking the other kid off Hector, who was lying on the ground gripping his head. I grabbed him by his shirt with my left arm and lifted him to his feet, while keeping the other kid at bay with my right.

"That's enough! Stop it! Stop it, right now!" I hollered at them in English. I was no longer conscious of being in Mexico. I could have been on a playground anywhere in the world right then and I believe I would have done exactly the same thing. Maybe it was a mother's instinct, or maybe I was simply channeling my own inner bully, but the idea of a child's fractured skull was too much for me.

I told the other kids to go home, in Spanish this time, and the crowd dispersed. Will flashed me a furious look and stomped away. In his mind, I'd not only committed a cultural faux pas, I'd also embarrassed him and spoiled everyone's fun.

PEOPLE WHO CHOOSE TO LIVE in a foreign culture tread a delicate path, especially when there are pronounced cultural disparities. There's a fine line between helpfulness and hegemony, and it's sometimes hard to know the difference when you're in the thick of things. To this day I can't say with any certainty if I was motivated by compassion or merely imposing my will on a situation that really was none of my business. But I knew Hector's dad. He was the man with the leg shriveled from polio whom everyone on the callejón paid to haul their garbage down to the corner for pickup three times a week. Right or wrong, culturally insensitive or not, I imagined an expensive hospital bill was not something he needed.

16 | *Christmas in San Miguel*

Along with the easter bunny and jack-o'-lantern, the manifestations of America's overtly commercial take on Christmas have insinuated themselves into the heart of Mexico. Beginning in early December, artificial Christmas trees crop up in hotel lobbies. Plastic Santas, multicolored Christmas lights, and packages of shiny Christmas balls hit the shelves at San Miguel's Mega and the Bodega Aurrera (a chain of Walmart-owned stores in Mexico). Even St. Nick's tiny reindeer occasionally stray into the holiday décor of restaurants south of the border.

Still, most people in central Mexico do not observe *la Navidad* the way our family does in Seattle. As its name suggests, *la Navidad* centers round the nativity, with families recreating miniature manger scenes in their homes and city officials proclaiming their towns' central plazas as places where living creatures shall abide — in life-size wooden crèches.

Being in retail for so many years has caused me to develop an aversion to Christmas. At City People's, we begin buying holiday merchandise in January and then decorate and stock the store with Christmas merchandise in late October. In addition, retail gift businesses like ours are dependent on successful holiday seasons. Failing to achieve your sales goals in the fourth quarter can put a small store out of business, and the pressure to make your sales is formidable. Customers also feel pressure around the holidays: pressure to make them "extra special," to choose the "perfect" gift for everyone on their list, to spend way more than they can afford. Add long lines or the occasional failure of credit card processing equipment to that stressed out feeling, and the result is often a lot of grumpy, unhappy people on both sides of the cash register.

By the time I bought the house in San Miguel, the holiday routine at our stores exhausted and depressed me so much that by Christmas Day I often had no energy left to celebrate, or was sick with the flu.

Our first Christmas at Casa Chepitos provided a refreshing change from my normal Seattle Yuletide routine. The celebration of Christ's birth began on December 16 with the *posadas*.

The word *posada* translates as "inn" or "shelter." Groups of neighbors wander, as Mary and Joseph did, in search of the one home that would welcome them, and then feed and entertain them with music, a piñata, and lots of spiked punch. These nightly door-to-door pilgrimages culminate in Catholic masses at San Miguel's churches on *la noche buena*.

Christmas Eve that year was a quiet affair with just the four of us and my sister Rachel. She and I walked over to St. Paul's Anglican Church for a sing-along of the old familiar Anglican carols.

However, the second Christmas we spent at home in Mexico, in 2004, was more eventful. Paul's mother, Maxine, was turning eighty, and to celebrate the occasion my husband invited his entire family to come stay at Casa Chepitos. I was happy that he wanted his family to visit us in San Miguel, but I was equally glad that only four of his six siblings showed up with their families, because with all of them plus the four of us, there was literally no more room at the inn.

BEING AN ENTHUSIAST FOR THE IDEA of doing what Romans do while in Rome, I thought we should dispense with the requisite Christmas tree that year. But Hannah pitched a protest.

"Think of poor Jake!" she said, referring to her seven-year-old cousin, who would be at Casa Chepitos with us for Christmas. What she really meant was think of poor *Hannah*, who, at ten years old, loved decorating the eight-foot-tall noble firs we'd always brought home from our garden store in Seattle. So when our property manager, the woman who rented Casa Chepitos for us when we weren't there, emailed to ask if we'd like the gardener to pick out a Christmas tree for us, I figured it must have been preordained by some higher power that we would have an *árbol de Navidad* in San Miguel that year.

Our "Christmas tree," slumped against the wall near the front door, was the first thing we noticed upon arriving at Casa Chepitos that December. While I'd known better than to expect a freshly cut noble like we have in the Northwest, I'd assumed a Scotch pine or Douglas fir might be available in Mexico. But our *árbol de Navi-dead*, as Will referred to it, was a balled and burlapped, overly yellow, and rather sickly specimen of *Thuja plicata*, or western red cedar.

Hannah was not impressed.

"We can't decorate that!" she announced with unveiled dismay. "Can't we get a real one, like the kind we have in Seattle?"

"We'll see," I said, falling back on the noncommittal response my mother always used.

But Hannah kept after me about the tree, so when Cousin Jake and his sister Ariel arrived from Texas two days later, we organized an expedition to the Ignacio Ramirez market, tasked with finding an acceptable Christmas tree and a few decorations.

I inquired about a tree among the market merchants, who met my question with either a blank stare or a shrug. No one seemed to know where I could find a freshly cut fir or pine tree. One woman told me such trees didn't exist in Mexico. We finally found one *puesta*, a little makeshift Christmas stand, at the mouth of the market, where they were selling three-foot-tall fake trees and piles of tacky decorations. For less than a hundred pesos we bought a tree, a string of lights, and a surplus of shiny

Mylar ornaments dusted with glitter. Our little expedition, with arms full of cheap Christmas cheer, marched back up the hill to Casa Chepitos and set to work decorating. Even Lupe came over to help string lights and hang ornaments, something she'd never done before.

"It's *extwodinawee!*" exclaimed Jake when we were finished. At age seven he possessed the vocabulary of a high school graduate and the speech patterns of Tweety Bird.

I wasn't certain that our bargain Christmas tree measured up to extraordinary, but the kids seemed satisfied, and that was all that mattered.

That evening, when Hannah and Will and Ariel joined our neighbors going house to house for a *posada*, Paul and I opted to stay behind with Jake and his parents. A bitter wind had blown in earlier in the day, bringing with it the coldest weather our Mexican neighbors could remember. Central heating doesn't exist in most of Mexico. Houses are designed to stay cool during the hot months of April, May, and June, but architects and builders typically give little thought to how to keep them warm in winter.

When the thermometer inside Casa Chepitos dropped to forty-three degrees Fahrenheit that evening, I began wishing that our Mexican builder had thought more about how to heat the house, and that I'd remembered to bring my down jacket along. It would be a week before the temperature inside the house got much above fifty degrees. We discovered that it was usually at least ten degrees warmer outside.

Presented with the choice of sitting inside and freezing, or going outside to freeze, we opted to head downtown to the *jardín* to show our guests the grand dame of San Miguel: La Parroquia de San Miguel Arcángel.

San Miguel's original parish church, built on the site in 1683, was a modest structure. But in the late nineteenth century, a Chichimec Indian named Zerefino Gutiérrez was commissioned to design a new church on the same site. Gutiérrez, an illiterate man only informally trained in construction, studied French postcards of European churches as inspiration for his design. His only working plans are reputed to have been pictures drawn with a stick in the dirt for his stoneworkers. As the five of us stood huddled together against the cold, marveling at the beauty of his striking design, the lights illuminating the church's magnificent spires and campanile flashed on. They radiated a golden incandescence on that frozen December night that would have warmed even the coldest of souls.

On our way home, we passed by El Pegaso, one of our favorite restaurants, where our friend Fernando was closing up shop for the night.

"Come in out of the cold, and have some hot punch to warm yourselves. We're going to have a piñata for the little ones," he said, pointing to Jake.

A small crowd congregated to drink hot apple punch while the piñata was strung across Corregidora Street between the post office and the restaurant. We all took turns whacking the piñata with no effect until Jake's dad, Andy, struck it hard and the candy spilled out onto the cobbled street.

Our ungloved hands were so stiff from the cold we could hardy bend our fingers to pick it up.

17 | *Los Viejitos*

MY MOTHER-IN-LAW, MAXINE, whose birthday was the reason we'd all gathered in San Miguel, had invited her boyfriend along to Mexico for the celebration. Her new beau bore a remarkable resemblance to jolly old St. Nick. He was short and round, with a serious belly, longish wavy white hair, and a beard that appeared as soft as snowy angel hair. His gold wire-rimmed reading glasses completed the look. The irony of this was not lost on Gracia, who began referring to him as Santa Claus — only in her heavily accented English it came out *Sahn-tah Clowz.*

I didn't mind that he'd joined us. In fact, I'd happily chipped in to help pay for the small house we rented, three doors down from Casa Chepitos, where he and Maxine were staying.

But I prayed that Santa Claus, who'd undergone quadruple-bypass surgery the year before and still had not followed his doctor's orders to reduce his three-hundred-pound bowl full of jelly, would not suffer another heart attack climbing the long, steep hill up to Callejón de Chepito.

ALONG WITH THE RECORD COLD temperatures of 2004 came an epidemic of winter flu that spread itself equitably among the Mexicans and Americans on our block.

"It's the air going from warm to cold so suddenly," said Gracia, who doesn't adhere to the germ theory of disease. When her kids are sick, the cause is always something to do with a sudden change in the weather. Paul, the son of a doctor, holds fast to the germ theory. Personally, I think it's a combination of the two. But regardless of the cause, none of us were spared from the upper respiratory flu going around that year. At Casa Chepitos, it started with poor Cousin Jake, then raged through our house and neighborhood like wildfire in a Santa Ana wind. By Christmas all of us living along Callejón de Chepito were runny-eyed, sniffling, and wracked by fits of coughing. For most of us, it wasn't a serious illness, but one person didn't fare so well.

Before the sun had risen on Christmas morning, I was awakened by the high-pitched whine of an ambulance siren. My mind immediately jumped to the worst-case scenario, the one I'd been imagining all week: Santa Claus was having another coronary. And it was all my fault.

He'd gotten into the habit of getting up before dawn each day to come check his email and make entries on his blog on our computer at Casa Chepitos. But the night before, I'd asked him to refrain from arriving so early on Christmas morning and waking everyone up. People were sleeping everywhere in the house, including the living room where the computer was located.

When I heard the screaming siren of an ambulance ascend the Cuesta de San José that morning, I assumed that Santa Claus, in an early morning search for a computer to blog on, had keeled over in the street. I ran up to the terrace and spotted the Red Cross paramedics bouncing a gurney over the alley's uneven concrete and was momentarily relieved when they passed the house we'd rented for him and Maxine. But they stopped at the house next door.

The home of Señora Rosa to the North.

Señora Rosa's husband, Don José, had recently suffered several serious bouts with a mysterious stomach ailment, and I figured it was her husband who had fallen ill again. But fifteen minutes later, it was Señora Rosa, looking pale and lifeless, who they brought out on the stretcher. The paramedics attached it to the gurney, and as they rolled her away, I looked down and saw Gracia leaning out her bedroom window. She too had watched the Christmas morning drama unfold, and I knew she'd have all the details in short order.

As soon as breakfast was over and a few presents were exchanged among the kids, I hurried over to her house to find out what had happened.

"*Doña Rosa tiene neumonía*," she said. Señora Rosa had been taken to the small general hospital on Hidalgo Street, where she'd been diagnosed with pneumonia. Pneumonia in older people with compromised health like Señora Rosa's is always dangerous, but the high altitude, frigid temperatures, and prevalence of smoke from wood fires in San Miguel make it even more perilous.

For the next week, Señora Rosa convalesced in the hospital. Gracia gave me the daily updates she received from the señora's youngest son, Mario. Though her recovery was bumpy, by the end of the week, the antibiotics took effect and the pneumonia began to subside. When Gracia told me that Señora Rosa was finally coming home from the hospital the following morning, I asked if there was anything we could do to help, and she said no. But with nighttime temperatures still dipping into the forties, I went downtown, bought her a thick blanket, and asked Lupe to deliver it.

WILL PLAYED A LOT of pickup basketball in the Parque Juárez during the holiday break that year. A group of men, young and old, played there every day at siesta time, and whoever showed up was welcome to play, so Will hustled over there around two o'clock most days.

One fellow who always showed up was a man the other players called El Viejo. El Viejo was the owner of an iconic San Miguel institution: La Colmena (or the Blue Door Bakery as it's known among expats). El Viejo wasn't really old, as his nickname suggested. I suspected it was his head, which was as bald as the Buddha's, that prompted the *apodo*. With a sinewy, athletic frame, mirthful eyes, and a head so shiny it looked as if he polished it each morning, I thought El Viejo was a rather attractive middle-aged man.

The day after Christmas, I was sitting next to him on the concrete steps adjacent to the basketball court, watching Paul and his family goof around on the court after the "siesta" game was over. Paul and his brothers had played a lot of basketball in their youth, and a good-natured competitiveness still existed between them. But that day, with wives, kids, and even Santa Claus joining their game, it was more about having fun.

El Viejo sat wiping sweat from his brow with a towel and carefully studying the scene.

"*¿Es su familia?*" he asked.

"*Sí, es mi familia,*" I said, confirming that it was my family clowning around the court.

He began pointing and asking what my relationship was to each of the people running up and down the court. I plumbed the depths of my Spanish vocabulary to come up with the words for brother-in-law (*cuñado*), nephew (*sobrino*), and mother-in-law (*suegra*). He asked how I was related to Santa Claus, who was chugging his way toward the hoop.

"*Es el novio de mi suegra,*" my mother-in-law's boyfriend, I said. I pointed to Maxine who was sitting on a nearby park bench, cheering him on.

"*¿Cuantos años tiene el?*" asked El Viejo. I told him Santa Claus was sixty-five. Next he wanted to know how old Maxine was. I told him Paul's family had come to San Miguel to celebrate her eightieth birthday.

"*Ahh,*" he said, a sly grin crossing his face, "*El es su gatito.*"

I burst out laughing. Loosely translated, a woman's *gatito* is Mexican slang for what in the States we might call her "boy toy."

THE DAY AFTER our game in the park, Paul's siblings packed up and headed back to Texas. Even after suffering through the unseasonal cold weather and nasty flu, being stepped on in the middle of the night and awakened at six in the morning by our resident blogger, everyone seemed sad to be leaving Casa Chepitos so soon. I was sorry to see them go. That low-key, San Miguel Christmas with Paul's family had been one of my happiest in years.

Santa Claus and Maxine decided they liked San Miguel so much, they stayed for another month. Gracia rented them the new apartment at the back of her house at a very good rate, and they spent many mornings breakfasting on hot cinnamon buns bought from El Viejo at the Blue Door Bakery.

To this day, Gracia still inquires after *Sahn-tah Clowz* and Maxine, wanting to know if they are both still healthy and together. And I always tell her yes, they are. My mother-in-law and her *gatito* are doing just fine.

18 | *The Pepper Tree*

T HE OTHER SEÑORA ROSA, our neighbor to the south, is the mother of eight and *abuelita* to a passel of grandkids who come down from the States to stay with her during the summer months. The rest of the year she lives alone, or travels by bus to Texas to visit her children, grandchildren, and the roster of doctors who minister to her numerous maladies.

Unfortunately, life has not always treated our aging neighbor well.

Years ago, her husband abandoned her for a younger woman, and the extreme poverty of her youth has taken its toll on her health. At times she reminds me of Mexico itself — ravaged yet beautiful, riddled with disease, bullied by a man with an oversized ego. A man who continues to come around, but only when he wants something.

Despite all of this, Señora Rosa is surprisingly generous, both in spirit and with what little she has. She always seems genuinely glad when my family and I return to Casa Chepitos, and frequently invites my kids to eat at her table along with her own grandchildren.

We grew closer through the years as I learned small bits about her life. I knew the names of her children and had heard stories about each of them. I knew she'd lost two to alcohol and accident. I knew that all but one had migrated across the border to San Antonio years ago and that she had joined those who went to Texas when her husband left her in the early '80s. For fifteen years she worked in San Antonio, as a cook in a Chinese restaurant.

"If you bring the ingredients down, I will cook Chinese food for you!" she has said on more than one occasion.

In addition to cooking, she loves gardening and songbirds; her patio is flooded with cages of parakeets and pots of impatiens, hibiscus, geraniums, and ferns.

Señora Rosa is a gentle soul, soft-spoken yet talkative, and an eager hostess, who loves visitors. Each time I return to San Miguel, I make a special point of stopping by her house for a chat. I find it peaceful, sitting in her cool, darkened living room with its marble floor and mauve-colored furniture covered with hand-tatted antimacassars. The centerpiece of the room is a large black-and-white portrait of a pretty fifteen-year-old: the daughter she lost to a car accident in 1965.

However, it wasn't until one scorching afternoon when she invited Gracia and me over to share a beer and a plate of perfectly sliced papaya that I learned just how difficult her early life had been.

"My family was extremely poor, poorer than you could ever imagine," she said. She told us that she had been a sickly child yet never saw a doctor, and that her family had existed on a meager diet of beans and tortillas, when they were available. She didn't own a pair of shoes until she was twelve, and as a consequence, she hadn't been allowed to attend school.

"I didn't learn to read or write until I was forty years old!" she said with a little laugh. "For the longest time I signed my name with a thumbprint."

Poor nutrition and the untreated illnesses of her youth have ruined her health. She suffers from a number of things including diabetes, high blood pressure, and heart disease.

But unlike the other Señora Rosa, to the north of us, she never complains. Only once in ten years did I hear a complaint from my soft-spoken neighbor to the south. And even then, it was her sons who brought it to my attention on her behalf.

IT BEGAN one day when I answered a knock at the door. Ramón, Señora Rosa's youngest son and the father of Will's friends Rocky and Ramiro, stood there, his baseball cap in hand. A dark mop of fine black hair hung over his eyes as he politely requested permission to speak with me.

"¡*Sí, claro!*" I said. Of course.

"It's about your tree, Señora," he said, shoving an unruly shock of silky hair out of his eyes. "It's causing problems for my mother."

He explained that our pepper tree, which leaned over a common wall between our houses, was shedding leaves, twigs, and berries onto his mother's back patio.

"She's getting older, you know—it's too much work for her to sweep it up." As he spoke he twisted the cap in his hands into a knot.

"*Entiendo*," I said. I understood perfectly well and wanted to put Ramón at ease. "We'll trim it back, right away."

THE TREE IN QUESTION was the focal point of our courtyard garden at Casa Chepitos. It also held the dubious honor of being listed on the California Invasive Plant Inventory. But *Schinus molle*, the plant the state of California regards as a noxious weed, provided our Mexican home with dappled shade and us with the sense that we lived in an eagle's aerie. Its pinnate leaves and strands of tiny pink pearls are what the best florists use to green up their vases. I had a lifetime supply.

My husband estimated that our pepper tree was close to fifty years old. It stretched fifteen feet across and was nearly thirty feet tall, reaching above the third-floor terrace of our home. Its feathery branches, visible from every room, were natural antidepressants. Their bright green leaves gave the house a feeling of ecological well-being. Still, I didn't want the centerpiece of our home's landscape to cause problems for Señora Rosa.

So I trotted across the alley to consult with Gracia. Within minutes, Salvador arrived with a ladder, a saw, and an axe. For more than an hour he clipped, sawed, and chopped. Later that evening, he hauled away the offending branches. Problem solved.

At least until the following summer when we returned for a month in June.

This time it was Ramón's older brother, Pancho, who came knocking at my door. He was considerably bigger than Ramón, taller and broader across the chest, and he spoke more English.

"*Señora*, we must ask you to prune your tree again. It is causing problems for the renter in our *casita*." He crossed his arms over his chest and stood a little taller, making me feel even smaller than I am.

"Maybe you could come show me which branches you want removed," I said, waving him through the door. I hoped assessing the problem together might ease some of the tension I was feeling.

Out in the courtyard, I watched in dismay as Pancho pointed to all the branches he wanted removed. If I followed his plan, half the tree would be gone. Still, I didn't want to create any ill will with my neighbors, so I acquiesced.

"I'll talk to our gardener and ask him to prune the tree again."

The following Saturday I consulted with José Luís, the man who tends our garden. Together we decided on a compromise between Pancho's plan and mine, which would have been to trim only the few branches hanging over the wall. José Luís pruned back about half the number of branches Pancho wanted eliminated. At least that way, I figured, the branches were a good distance from our common wall, and yet the tree wouldn't look as if it had been split in two by lightning. I prayed Pancho wouldn't notice that I hadn't exactly followed his directions.

THE THIRD SUMMER, when we returned to Casa Chepitos, I was troubled to see how much the tree had grown. The branches José Luís had pruned the summer before had sprouted anew and doubled in size. It seemed as if the pepper tree was growing new limbs over my neighbor's wall just to spite me. I suspected I'd soon be hearing from one or the other of the brothers.

But neither of them came knocking. In fact, it was extraordinarily quiet next door. Señora Rosa had gone to San Antonio for the month to visit her family, and the cranky, chain-smoking renter who lived in the rear apartment had vacated. I was beginning to think that I might get a couple of weeks reprieve from pruning.

Then one afternoon I was napping when our doorbell's shrill note echoed through the house.

At first I ignored it. I wasn't expecting anyone. But it rang again. And again. The insistence of the bell ringer made me wonder if the kids in the callejón were messing with it again. Or if it was the propane guy, anxious to make a sale.

I grudgingly walked downstairs and opened the door. Standing there, with hands on his hips, was a sinewy, five-foot-tall Mexican man. He wore gold-rimmed aviator glasses with tinted lenses and had a pencil-thin mustache that looked as if it had been drawn on with eyeliner. I'd barely said hello when the man launched into a feverish monologue I could barely understand. The only word I recognized was *árbol*, which he repeated often and loudly. It didn't seem to matter to him that I didn't understand. He continued his rant at warp speed anyway. As he ranted, he kicked at a rock with a weathered cowboy boot and flung his arms into the air.

"*Cálmate*," I was tempted to say. That's the command Will uses when he wants me to calm down. But I was a little afraid of the guy. He seemed really upset, and a bit crazy, too. I worried he might be dangerous. So I calmly asked in Spanish who he was and if he would mind speaking more slowly.

"I'm the man of the house next door, that's who I am!" he said, jabbing a finger in the direction of Señora Rosa's house. "And that tree has got to go! My sons have been too nice to you. We're tired of asking and we're tired of being nice. Either you cut the tree down or there will be problems for you!"

I suddenly realized who he was. And what he wanted. He was Señora Rosa's ex-husband, Don Pancho, who came around only when he needed something or got a hankering for some of his ex-wife's home cooking. According to Gracia, the younger woman he'd shacked up with wasn't much of a cook.

"You Americans think you can come down to Mexico and do any old thing you want!" he said, stomping his foot. "Well, I won't stand for it!"

I didn't interject or argue. I just let him vent.

Eventually, he ran out of steam.

"Señor, I don't want to offend you or cause problems for my friend, Señora Rosa," I said. Which was somewhat disingenuous of me because the truth was, I would have loved to have lectured him on what I thought of his running off with a woman half his age, leaving the sweetest woman on our alley to fend for herself.

But in lieu of a scolding, I pulled myself together and said: "I only want to be a good neighbor. I promise I'll take care of the tree."

"You better mean that. This is serious!"

"*Entiendo, Señor*," and really, I did understand. The scrappy little *macho* meant business.

SOMETHING I'VE LEARNED during my years in Mexico is that the word *macho* has several different meanings in Spanish. Definitions range from "overbearing male" or "tough guy" to simply "male" or "masculine." Like many Americans, I'd always thought of a macho man as one who bullied females in order to prove his masculinity. But for Mexicans, *macho* doesn't always carry the same negative connotation. *Macho* is often seen as a positive characteristic, meaning strong or virile.

Of the many Mexican men I'd met in San Miguel, particularly the ones living along our callejón, there was not one I would label *macho* in the negative sense of the word. I had been treated with friendliness, respect, or sometimes polite indifference by my male neighbors. But not one had ever been disrespectful. Until I met Don Pancho.

Gracia didn't care for Don Pancho either. Like me, she found him rude and was mad that he'd walked out on Señora Rosa.

"It was Don Pancho who sold the land to the architect who built your house," she said when I told her how I'd met him. "If it troubled him so much, he should have chopped that tree down before he sold it!"

SINCE I WAS ONLY IN SAN MIGUEL for one more week, I called my property manager and asked her to arrange for a specialist to prune the tree — again. After returning to Seattle, I got an email saying she'd retained an arborist who would prune the tree for $500 (dollars, not pesos), a small fortune by Mexican standards. But I figured the man was an expert at pruning while José Luís was not, and compared to the $10,000 my business partners and I had just laid out for another arborist to remove three cottonwood trees from our Seattle garden store property, the man's bid seemed like a bargain. Plus he could complete the work while we were gone.

I returned to Casa Chepitos the following October. It was nearly midnight by the time I arrived home, and I went straight to bed. But when I awoke the next morning, I noticed the bedroom was unusually bright. I walked to the window, drew the curtain aside and gasped.

The branches of our pepper tree, once verdant and majestic, were totally gone. The "arborist" my property manager had hired had cut off every single limb. Not a twig, not a leaf, not a berry cluster remained. All that was left of our beautiful tree was a brutalized trunk. A stump that resembled an angry fist raised in protest. I was devastated.

I called Paul in Seattle. When he answered the phone, I broke into tears.

"Our beautiful pepper tree! It's been pollarded!"

I knew he too would be upset. We both think of pollarding — a radical pruning practice developed during the French Revolution — as a crime against nature. But for once my husband was the optimistic one. He said there was a good chance the branches would grow back.

The following spring the tree had some shoots and leaves, and even a few berries on it. But the new growth turned out to be our tree's last hurrah — its final attempt at survival. By the next autumn, the new leaves had withered and died. When José Luís arrived to tend the garden one Saturday morning, I asked him what he thought.

"*Se murió*," he replied.

Our tree was dead. I wanted to cry, all over again.

I paid José Luís and a friend to remove the stump. In its place, he planted a lime tree Paul and I had bought a few years before that had outgrown its pot. At least that gave us hope for the future.

THOUGH IT HAS BEEN GONE for several years, and our lime tree is now laden with tiny green fruit, I still regret the loss of the Peruvian pepper tree. But the incident did provide me with one priceless moment.

Not long after my encounter with Don Pancho, Señora Rosa returned from her visit to San Antonio. While chatting with her in the alley one day, I explained how I'd finally met her cantankerous ex-husband. I even did a little impersonation of him, strutting around, like the Mexican comic Cantinflas, puffing out my chest, and ranting and raving a bit in Spanish. Just like Don Pancho had in front of my door. A fit of giggles suddenly bubbled up in the señora that soon spilled over into deep, full-bellied laughter. Seeing my sweet neighbor so completely amused made losing the pepper tree somehow seem worth it.

19 | *Finding Nacho*

ONE OF THE MANY THINGS I appreciate about San Miguel's expatriate community is its unspoken agreement that says, *If you take up residency here, you will give something back to the community.* Practically every foreigner living in the city volunteers for one charitable cause or another. They raise money for scholarships, literacy programs, clean water projects; they build houses for the poor, volunteer to teach ESL, run medical programs, work with orphans and in battered women's shelters (and this is only a partial list of what expats volunteer for in San Miguel). I've visited and lived abroad in many wonderful and interesting places, and I've never found a community of people so committed to doing good.

One night at a dinner party at Casa Chepitos, the topic of volunteering came up. A mix of friends from San Miguel and Seattle were there, including my friend Patrice.

To describe Patrice as a colorful character would be a serious understatement. She is the quintessence of color. Her store Abrazos, her home, her clothing, her lifestyle, her opinions are all bold, bright, and full of color.

So when the topic of volunteerism in San Miguel came up that night, I wasn't a bit surprised when Patrice, who was also the former owner of a feminist bookstore in Berkeley, told us that there was another, more class-conscious component to the volunteer frenzy sweeping the city.

"What you volunteer for says a lot about where you fit into San

Miguel's social hierarchy," she said. According to her, there were prestigious volunteer opportunities and lower-status ones.

I was certain my family and I were low on San Miguel's social totem pole. Our house was not one of the exquisitely ancient, meticulously renovated houses of *el centro*, nor was it a chic, new home in one of San Miguel's exclusive gated communities. Though we love it, our narrow, littered callejón was hardly a high-class address.

LATER THAT YEAR, during a six-week sojourn at Casa Chepitos, I decided it was high time our family volunteered for something in San Miguel. When I read one day in *Atención*, the town's bilingual newspaper, that the Sociedad Protectora de Animales (S.P.A.), was looking for volunteers, I figured it was perfect. We are all animal lovers in our family, and I thought our lack of pedigree shouldn't matter to the folks running an animal shelter. I imagined their need for volunteers was likely to be enormous, and few skills would be required. An abundance of enthusiasm, and strong backs and arms, should be enough. I figured we could provide those.

Paul couldn't be convinced to join us, but the next day Will, Hannah, and I took a taxi across town to 7 Los Pinos, where we found a single-story, grass-green building with windows secured by iron bars, and a torn screen door hanging loosely from its hinges.

Inside the shelter's tiny office, sitting behind a makeshift desk, was a grim-faced, chain-smoking woman who was talking on the phone. She ignored us, while her cigarette burned down amid the pile of butts spilling over the ashtray.

We moved outside, where the smell of urine mixed with disinfectant filled the air, and rows of four-by-eight-foot cells with chain-link gates lined the interior of a dusty lot. There was little grass or other vegetation, and the handful of trees looked distressed. Yet, as void of greenery as it was, I noticed the floors of the kennels had been freshly hosed; and although the din of attention-hungry dogs was deafening, they appeared well-fed. Their coats were shiny and free of mange, which is rampant in Mexican street dogs. It was clear that the poor, abandoned creatures were well cared for.

A few minutes later, a tall, enthusiastic woman with a Canadian accent hustled up and asked if we needed help.

"We're here to volunteer," I told her.

"Great!" she said, quickly sizing up my strapping, eighteen-year-old son. "We could use a strong fellow like you to exercise the big dogs."

Hence Will was roped into a job he adored. It didn't take him long to bond with a number of the shelter's lop-eared mutts and choose favorites: a Bluetick hound mix named Hank and a sweet-tempered bitch named Lola. Lola and Hank took turns dragging Will uphill every day to a junk-littered lot above the shelter. After Lola was adopted by a gay couple from Connecticut, Will lobbied hard for me to let him adopt Hank. I reminded him that Katy, our golden retriever, was enough big dog for our small backyard in Seattle. But the thought crossed my mind that a smaller companion for our aging retriever might be something to consider.

Over the course of the next two weeks, Will exercised the dogs while Hannah and I volunteered for a few of the shelter's easier jobs: playing with kittens or walking the smaller dogs up to the *jardín* on Thursdays, where we chatted up people who showed interest in adopting them.

One sunny afternoon at the shelter, Hannah and I were laboring hard at "socializing" the puppies — one of our favorite jobs at the S.P.A. But after a while we grew tired of the mass of wriggling furballs shredding our shoelaces and nipping at our fingers with their needlelike teeth. So we wandered around to a group of kennels housing the smaller adult dogs.

A goofy-looking miniature gray poodle, sequestered in one

of the kennels along with a long-haired, brown and white mutt straight out of the annals of Dr. Seuss, charged up to the fence when we arrived. Hannah and I amused ourselves watching the little poodle perform tricks behind the chain-link enclosure. All twelve pounds of the wriggling mass of gray fur seemed to be showing off for us. Like a dog auditioning for a circus, he walked on his hindquarters, turned elaborate circles, paddled his paws in the air as if swimming. The only thing he lacked was a little sign that read, Will Dance for Food.

For some reason the dog was tagged with the unfortunate name Major Mosby. John Singleton Mosby, an officer in the Confederate army, was nicknamed the Gray Ghost for his rapacious, surreptitious activities. How a Mexican street dog came to be named for a Confederate rogue was a mystery. But there were many mysterious things about the little gray dog. Like how he ever survived San Miguel's traffic-choked streets in the first place.

I found out from Karen, the Canadian volunteer, that Major Mosby had been living off garbage and dodging cars in San Miguel's cobblestone streets when he was brought to the shelter. Even harder to believe was what she told me next: this dog, with his Tickle Me Elmo personality, had viciously attacked a shelter worker when he was first brought in. As is my habit, I ignored this alarming bit of information and relied instead on my intuition and the evidence now curled up in my lap. Compared to the other small dogs, including one frantic male poodle that refused to pack up his privates, and another that yapped relentlessly, Major Mosby looked like a winner to me. Hannah agreed.

As soon as Will returned from walking Hank, we eagerly introduced him to Major Mosby.

He, of course, thought it was a great idea. Having spent his first eight years — before we got Katy — lusting for a dog, Will would have been up for bringing home the shelter's entire canine population.

We tracked Karen down again, and in the smoke-filled office she gave us the paperwork we needed to fill out to adopt Major Mosby. She told us that adoptive families were required to make a donation to the S.P.A., which I was happy to do. Then Will, Hannah, and I left the Gray Ghost to sacrifice his manhood for the comfort of a new home and family. We were told to come back two days later, and we could then bring him home to Casa Chepitos.

"NO WAY! WE'RE NOT GETTING ANOTHER DOG," Paul declared, when the three of us arrived home with the news that we'd just adopted the cutest miniature poodle. For a guy who'd been a pretty good sport about me liquidating my retirement account to purchase a house in Mexico he'd never seen, I thought he was being a little recalcitrant. But I decided to let the kids battle it out with their dad. Normally he caves in to their requests with enough persistent begging.

"Come on, Dad, you'll like him when you see him. He's really cute," Hannah said. "His name was Major Mosby, but we're going to call him Nacho."

Will was more contentious. Like a pair of alpha males, he and Paul often went head-to-head during Will's teenage years.

"How can you make up your mind just like that?" Will shouted. "You haven't even seen him!" They went back and forth, arguing for a long time.

"Katy is the only dog we need," Paul said with finality. I was beginning to think he wasn't going to back down. Then Will piped up again.

"Okay, let's put it to a vote," he said. I immediately saw through my son's ruse.

He was relying on our family's tradition of running things democratically. Majority rules in our house.

"All those in favor, raise your hand," he said. Three hands flew into the air, none belonging to my husband.

"I guess you're outvoted, Hon," I said, giving him a little hug. He stomped off to the living room to sulk and read the *International Herald* I'd brought him. And Nacho, the little circus dog, had a new home.

FRIENDS AND DOG LOVERS who hear Nacho's story always ask if it was difficult to bring a dog into the United States from Mexico. What we discovered was that it is infinitely easier for a Mexican dog to immigrate to the United States than a Mexican human. All we needed was a certificate from the veterinarian verifying that he was current on his rabies and distemper vaccines, and a letter stating he was in good health. Finding a crate in which to ship him home on the airplane was by far the hardest part. We finally found one at a Costco outside of Puerto Vallarta while on a weeklong search for warmer temperatures that winter.

The day Hannah and I were to travel with Nacho back to Seattle, I picked up some tranquilizers from the vet. Paul had already left, since he was traveling back through Texas to visit more family. My daughter and I plastered the dog crate with signs that read "*Por favor, no ponga nada encima de la caja,*" in hopes that the Mexicans would not place anything heavy on top of our cheap, collapsible Costco crate and crush our new dog.

At the airport in León, I gave Nacho half a tablet of Calmivet, a Valium-like drug for dogs. In two hours we'd be in Dallas where —we were told by an agent at American Airlines—we would pick him up as we passed through customs. I planned on giving him another tablet of tranquilizer before transferring him to the five-hour flight to Seattle.

When we cleared customs in the Dallas airport, we found our luggage but Nacho was not with it. An agent directed us to a special area of the airport where animals were processed.

"He's already been transferred to the Seattle flight," a perfunctory uniformed customs officer informed me. I panicked. I was afraid traveling untranquilized on a thunderous jetliner for five hours would be more than our luckless Mexican street dog could endure.

When we arrived in Seattle, Hannah and I were relieved to find the crate waiting for us at the baggage claim. We rushed over and opened the door, but when I reached in and pulled him out, poor Nacho was catatonic. His body was stiff and unyielding. He had a wild, distant look in his eyes.

Not knowing what else to do, I piled our luggage on a cart and whisked him outside, where I searched in vain for a patch of grass where he might relax and pee. I finally put him down on a corner of the concrete sidewalk, but he didn't move. He just stood there, frozen with fear.

I tucked his rigid body under one arm and with the other helped Hannah push the luggage cart onto an elevator.

In the elevator, Nacho finally came back to life, and along with his decision to live came a sudden need to urinate. Pee began spraying out of him like water from a pressurized hose. I screamed and held him away from me, pointing him first in one direction and then in the other, trying to avoid getting Hannah and our luggage soaked. By the time the elevator's doors finally glided open, the walls were thoroughly rinsed in the urine of a Mexican street dog with a new lease on life.

20 | *Crossing the Border*

OUR HOUSE IN SEATTLE was in an old neighborhood of single-family homes built in the early 1900s. The majority were four-bedroom boxes with small porches and front lawns, arranged in close proximity to one another. Yet months, sometimes years, went by when we didn't see or speak to our neighbors. We lived in a state of disconnectedness, rushing from house to car to work and back, each of us barely aware of the people living right next door. It's not that we had nothing in common; we had everything in common.

An ocean of disparity separates me and my Mexican neighbors on Callejón de Chepito. Unlike in our Seattle neighborhood, the social, economic and educational differences between us and our neighbors are marked. Yet the languid pace of life in the alley allows time for daily interaction and, *poco a poco,* I established relationships with a number of women who live there. Central to our relationships are humor, empathy, and the role we all have in common — motherhood.

Margaret Mead once said that no matter how fundamentally different cultures may seem on the outside, there are certain roles that transcend political and cultural boundaries. Motherhood is one of them. Mothers everywhere — from Mexico to Myanmar, Seattle to Timbuktu — share a fundamental bond: the struggle to ensure the survival of our children.

A BREEZE WAS KICKING UP DUST one day in the summer of 2005 as Gracia and I huddled around the stone bench where Remedios and the two Señoras Rosas sat discussing the immigration debacle in the United States (H.R. 4437 — the proposed Border Protection, Antiterrorism, and Illegal Immigration Control Act was being debated in Congress) and Ángel's recent border crossing.

With arms folded over her aproned chest, Señora Rosa to the North kneaded her arthritic elbow as she recounted her son's harrowing journey across the Rio Grande.

"Ángel nearly drowned crossing the river," she said, her gravelly voice echoing off the alley's stucco walls. The others nodded, knowingly.

"He left in October. My oldest son got him a job working construction in Austin. The baby, Ángelito, is anemic, you know. He was born premature and needs a lot of expensive medicine," she shook her head slowly. "Ángel needed the money or he would never have gone *al otro lado*."

El otro lado is what my Mexican neighbors call the United States. They also refer to it as *el norte*, but they rarely call it the United States and never America, since they consider themselves also to be North Americans. To them "the other side" means the other side of the U.S. border, but historically it was a reference to the other side of the Río Bravo del Norte, the river we call the Rio Grande.

Since the late 1840s, when U.S. troops invaded Mexico and forced their own resolution to the border dispute (the Mexican government believed the Nueces River to the north to be the official boundary), the Río Bravo has been the legal boundary between the two countries. Today, crossing to the other side of the river means the possibility of a better life for my Mexican neighbors.

Ángel had managed to survive the raging waters of the Rio

Grande, but the anguish of losing him and three of his brothers to *el norte* was etched into the creases of Señora Rosa's leathery face. "I don't know when I'll see him again," she replied when I asked if he would be returning soon. "It's very dangerous and expensive for him to cross." Tilting her head to the side, she unfolded her arms and let out a shallow, ragged breath. Her lungs were still weak from the pneumonia she'd contracted during the last winter's record-breaking cold spell.

SINCE ARRIVING on Callejón de Chepito in early 2002, I had witnessed an unrelenting exodus of my young Mexican neighbors. With wages south of the border 25 percent (or less) of those in the United States (construction workers earn an average of twenty dollars a day in Mexico for the same work that they earn ten to fifteen dollars an hour for in the States), it was no surprise that my neighbors continued to stream across the border. The lure of America's job market and our material lifestyle — now being broadcast 24/7 to Mexico via satellite TV — was a powerful magnet. By 2005, it was estimated that ten percent of Mexico's population was working in the United States.

Writer Wendy Call, whose years living in Tehuantepec were the basis for her book *No Word for Welcome*, once told me that she believed crossing the U.S. border was a rite of passage for young Mexicans.

"The challenge of going *al norte* has a near mythological appeal for them," she said. "Success in crossing brings not only more lucrative employment, but a kind of prestige among their peers."

The vast majority of men and women who migrate across the border do not *want* to leave their families, friends and lovers behind. The challenges many of them face on the other side are, at best, difficult, and often horrific. They leave Mexico because they need to put food on the table for their families, and because they want to pull themselves and their families out of abject poverty.

But as a result of this exodus of workers, a new subculture has emerged in Mexico: the hundreds of thousands of wives, mothers, and children who are left behind. They live in a state of limbo, not knowing when, or if, a husband, son, father or mother might return. If the wage earner across the border forsakes them or creates a new life in the United States, those left behind fall into even more desperate poverty. In Mexico there are few resources to help those who have been abandoned — there is no unemployment insurance, no welfare, no food stamps or government aid to women and children.

AFTER THE DEFEAT OF H.R. 4437 in the Senate, vigilante patrols began waging their own war against undocumented workers and it became even more dangerous and expensive for Mexicans to cross back and forth. Coyotes who used to charge $1,200 to guide someone across were now charging as much as $3,000. As a consequence, Mexican families were forced to live with yet more uncertainty about when, or if, they might see their loved ones again.

It's a conundrum, because the health of Mexico's economy and the welfare of these families are inextricably tied to these workers (who may never come back) going north. Remissions — the money sent home by Mexican workers — are the country's third largest revenue stream, after oil and tourism. Without the tide of remissions it receives from workers in the States, Mexico's economy would collapse.

Ironically, Americans are equally dependent on the labor of undocumented workers. Migrant workers roof and side our homes; they build the roads we drive on; they wash our windows, clean our houses, mow our lawns, and plant our gardens; they cook the meals we eat in restaurants, bus and wash our dishes.

They pick fruit, vegetables, and flowers for our tables. According to the U.S. Department of Agriculture, nearly half of all crop farm workers are in the United States illegally. Seven in ten of them are Mexicans.

LIKE SO MANY MOTHERS south of the border, those gathered around the bench that day were concerned about the persistent exodus of their children. Nearly every woman living on our alley had at least one child, and many had several, who had left San Miguel to work in the United States.

Both Señoras Rosas had multiple children who had gone *al norte*, and Remedios's oldest daughter, Alejandra, was a U.S. citizen who lived with her American husband and child in Texas. Remedios had never met her two-year-old granddaughter because she needed a visa to visit the States. In order to obtain one, she would have to make the long bus trip to Mexico City or Guadalajara and spend hours, maybe days, waiting at the consulate to request an appointment. Then, at some future date, she'd have to return for the appointment. Even if she were to do all of this, there would be no assurance she'd get a visa. Obtaining a tourist visa to the United States is a crapshoot for a Mexican, even for a person like Remedios, who is an upstanding citizen and has children living there.

Gracia's family was the exception; she and Salvador and their four kids all still lived under the same ever-expanding roof. Their house was frequently under construction as they added new rooms to accommodate their growing family or to house more renters.

It was evident that their standard of living had improved since our first visit to Casa Chepitos. San Miguel was experiencing a real estate bubble that mirrored the one in the United States, and Salvador had regular employment building new homes for both Mexicans and Americans. He had not had to work in the

States since the mid-1980s, when Lupe was a baby.

The income from Gracia's store and her apartment rentals provided the extra cash for their remodeling projects, a new color TV, and a computer — with Internet service, thanks to her upstairs tenant. Gracia had even made a few capital improvements at the store, including a bright red awning with *Abarrotes Gracia* written in white block letters over the entrance.

Lupe and Marcos were both old enough to work, and that made things easier for the family. Lupe worked part-time in an art gallery owned by our neighbor Frieda Stafford, and Marcos, now in high school and driving, helped run the store and made excursions to Celaya for supplies. Gracia, ever the entrepreneur, was scheming to buy a used Ford Explorer.

"Marcos can earn money driving tourists around," she said. "That way maybe he won't be tempted to go *al norte*, like his cousins."

Gracia was a woman who was clearly happiest when her kids were hovering nearby. Family is the most important thing in a Mexican woman's life, and for my friend it was no different. Keeping her brood intact was clearly her priority.

ON A SUBSEQUENT TRIP to San Miguel that year, I walked over to the Galería Colibrí, where Lupe worked the afternoon shift. She looked up from her paperwork as I walked in and her eyes brightened with excitement.

"I've got a secret to share with you," she said. "But you have to promise not to tell anyone."

I promised, but the idea of keeping secrets from Gracia made me uneasy.

"I don't want Frieda or my mother to know," she said, "but Paola and I are thinking of going *al norte*."

The news alarmed me.

What about Gracia's feelings? How would she react if Lupe and Paola left for the United States? Lupe was her oldest child and only daughter, her closest confidant whom she depended on for many things. What if Lupe left and never returned?

I also had an allegiance to Frieda, who was my friend in addition to being Lupe's employer. I knew she would need time to find and train another salesgirl.

But mainly, I was worried about Lupe and Paola. The idea of them making the arduous trek across northern Mexico with some *cabrón* for a coyote unnerved me. I'd recently read *The Devil's Highway*, Luis Alberto Urrea's story of the Yuma 14 — the fourteen Mexicans who died in 2001 when their coyote abandoned them in the desert south of Tucson. Nearly all of them, including young boys, died of sunstroke and dehydration. Remembering Urrea's description of desiccated corpses — bodies stripped naked, skin broiled black and dried like leather — made me want to warn Lupe of the foolishness of her fantasy. I wanted to tell her that life in the United States might not be what she expected, nor was it going to be easy for someone who spoke so little English.

But I saw a craving in her eyes, a craving to see the world outside San Miguel. A hunger I understood all too well. I knew it was useless to try to dissuade her. At the same time, I wondered if I might be partially responsible for her desire to expand her horizons. Had her hunger to experience the outside world been brought on by a seaside vacation we'd taken her on the previous winter?

January 2005. I'm about to pitch her overboard into the Pacific Ocean when I catch myself wondering if Lupe really possesses the audacity I've attributed to her. Shivering and covered in goose bumps, a neon-orange life jacket fastened tightly around her soft, bare midriff, she leans over the boat's bobbing bow and shrieks as a wave crashes against it. She closes her eyes.

"*¿Lista?*" I ask. She nods her readiness.

So I toss the nineteen-year-old, who has never learned to swim, way in over her head. She sinks momentarily but corks back up, gasping and choking on the salt water. She grins at me tentatively. Then she begins paddling around, proving that I have not mistaken her for someone else. She really does possess the courage I credit her with.

During that weeklong sojourn to the seaside village of Sayulita, Lupe experiences a litany of firsts. In addition to seeing the Pacific Ocean, she swims and snorkels, tries surfing on a boogie board, rides a horse, comes within a boat's length of a pod of breaching whales, eats at fine restaurants, and saves an iguana from drowning in a swimming pool. Watching her, I wondered if in future years she would summon these memories. Would she grow restless with her life in San Miguel, like I had with mine in Kansas?

Our weeklong vacation to Sayulita marked both a beginning and an end for Lupe. Part of having new experiences is learning what we are capable of. All children, no matter what conditions circumscribe their upbringing, undergo certain rites of passage. Like seedlings destined to bloom, they push forth from the earth's dark womb toward the promise of the future's brilliant light.

OVER A CUP OF COFFEE with Frieda Stafford a few months later, I was got an earful about Lupe's recent adventure crossing the border.

"That silly girl just left for the States! She disappeared with her cousin Paola and didn't even tell me she was going," said Frieda. A German beauty with bluntly cut blonde hair and piercing blue eyes, her German accent became more pronounced when she was riled. "I should never have taken her back!"

Frieda and Lupe were like oil and water. Frieda understood little Spanish and spoke even less. Lupe spoke a modicum of English, yet understood a great deal more. But their communication problems had less to do with language barriers, and more with the disparity between Mexican and German cultural norms and generational differences. Lupe's tendency toward secrecy and inclination toward rashness were not traits Frieda appreciated in her employees.

"Lupe is still young and a little impulsive," I said. "But she has a good heart."

IN GRACIA'S LIVING ROOM, a few days later, I got Lupe and Paola's version of the story. I was mesmerized, listening to them talk about their journey crossing the border into Texas.

Their adventure began when their uncle received a phone call from an ex-employer in Alabama, who asked him to return to a welding job. With the promise of a wage that was four times what he could earn in San Miguel, he couldn't afford to turn down the offer. This turned out to be the opportunity the girls had been waiting for since it would be safer crossing with their uncle.

They took a bus north to the state of Tamaulipas where they joined a group of eight other Mexicans, with whom they would travel across the desert by night. It was impossible to hike during daylight hours. Immigration officials and vigilante groups were ready to descend on *mojados* like bloodhounds on the trail of a scent.

"Weren't you scared?" I asked the girls. They glanced at each other, half smiling.

"Only sometimes," Lupe said. "Mostly what I remember is how beautiful the desert was at night. There were so many stars."

"What I remember is that Lupe couldn't stop laughing," Paola said, laughing at the memory of it.

The thought of Lupe giggling her way through what was likely one of the most harrowing experiences of her young life surprised me as much as it amused her cousin. Paola continued recounting the story, as I sat there imagining it.

IN MY MIND'S EYE, I see a small band of Mexicans scrambling through a desolate landscape.

A cluster of seven men and three women under the control of a *coyote*. Their safety is in the hands of this man, a man none of them trusts. They silently pray that he is honest and knows the trail. They pray he can lead them to a place where the river is low and moves slowly along the long, lonely Texas-Mexico border.

At night they walk northward through darkness, free from the blistering sun. At the first light of day, they take cover in the shade of a rocky ridge or under the Mexican scrub. They sleep, tense and restless, for a few hours each day. As soon as night descends again, they resume their northward trek.

Three nights of walking. Three days of hiding. Stumbling over boulders. Slicing themselves on barbed wire. Tearing their clothing. Puncturing their flesh on cactus needles. Stemming the flow of blood with red and blue bandanas. Eating cold tortillas and beans, which are bad for the digestion. Paying some *pendejo* to row them across the Rio Brava, who then points a pistol at them and runs away with their money.

No one can swim, but they wade into the churning river. Water rises to their waists, to their armpits, to their necks. Paola's foot slips off a rock. Panic spreads as she is swiftly carried downstream. She is sinking under the weight of her backpack when someone grabs her arm and yanks her back to shore. She shivers uncontrollably through the night.

The fourth night. Texas. The silence of the desert is pierced by a faint hum. The hum becomes a steady rumble that turns into a roar. Giant rotating blades kick up a whirlwind of dust. The dust blinds the migrants. It fills their mouths and noses. A blinding light pours down from the helicopter, highlighting dark faces covered with bandanas. An omnipotent voice from above barks commands at them, first in English, then in Spanish: "Uncover your faces! Put your hands up!" Two black SUVs slam to a stop in front of the group and four heavily armed uniformed men jump out. They point high-beam flashlights and automatic rifles at the Mexicans, who are huddled together. The uniformed men demand to know who is in charge but the coyote is long gone.

IMMIGRATION AND NATURALIZATION SERVICES transported Lupe, Paola, and the others to a detention center in Brownsville, Texas, where the women were separated from the men and placed in a cell block with a group of Honduran women. Many of them had been robbed, beaten, and/or sexually assaulted on their journey across Mexico. By the time immigration officials found them lost and wandering along the river near Brownsville, they were half-starved and dehydrated. Though they'd been at the detention center for a week and had no idea when they would be released, they told Lupe and Paola it wasn't so bad.

"At least we have food and water and a safe place to sleep," one Honduran told them.

The girls sat up all night waiting to be processed and escorted back across the bridge to Matamoros. Twenty-four hours later they arrived at San Miguel's Terminal Central and walked seven miles from the bus station back to the callejón. After hiking across northern Mexico for three nights, the walk across town was nothing. But for them, walking through town that morning was far worse: the humiliation of having friends see them unbathed and wearing torn and dirty clothes, with wild, uncoiffed hair, muddy shoes, and no makeup, was torture for the two teenage girls.

"Our friends all wanted to know where we'd been," Paola said. "We told them we went to Texas so we could say that we'd walked on U.S. soil."

Part Three | *La Ciudad*

*Many a trip continues long after movement
in time and space have ceased.*

JOHN STEINBECK

21 | *Changes*

NOT LONG AFTER I PURCHASED Casa Chepitos, friends and family began barraging me with magazine and newspaper articles about San Miguel. Its abundant colonial charm and affordable real estate had not escaped the attention of the media, which seemed as smitten as I was with the colorful Mexican hill town. At least once a month, I'd find some new review placed on my desk at work or in my email inbox. *Condé Naste*, the *New York Times*, the *Washington Post*, the *Wall Street Journal*, *U.S. News and World Report*, *Travel + Leisure*, *Town and Country*, *Architectural Digest*, and *Elle* — to name only a few — all published articles extolling some aspect of San Miguel's *buena vida*. When my mother sent one she'd clipped from *Money Magazine* decreeing it one of the "Top Ten Places to Retire," I knew my investment acumen had shot up in her esteem. But I was also aware of the consequences of an article like that: more Americans would soon be arriving in San Miguel.

The thought depressed me and gave my husband, who finally seemed to be warming to the idea of retiring at least part-time to San Miguel, one more reason to reject the proposition.

It isn't that we were anti-American; we had a number of American friends in San Miguel. We were also not blind to the fact that, being Americans ourselves, we were part of the problem.

But our plan had been to retire to a Mexican community with a *small* expatriate enclave, not to a town that lifestyle magazines were now referring to as the "New Santa Fe." Still, change was coming to San Miguel and to our tiny callejón, whether we liked it or not, and more rapidly than we could have ever anticipated.

ONE MORNING DURING our fifth year on Callejón de Chepito, I was jolted awake by a pounding so loud I wondered if an *albañil* was downstairs mistakenly tearing out a wall of our kitchen.

I grabbed my clothes, took a quick look down the spiral staircase to make sure the kitchen was still intact, then ran upstairs to the roof to see if I could figure out where the pounding was coming from. By the time I reached the terrace, the booming had subsided into the relentless *tap, tap, tap* of an iron chisel chipping at concrete. A noise that meant yet another new construction project was under way. The sound of tapping chisels and the pre-dawn reveilles of the crowing roosters, barking dogs, and bleating goats that lived beneath our bedroom window provided the sound track for my Mexican life.

I found out from Gracia that the pounding and tapping were coming from a new construction site behind her house. She said a young couple from San Francisco had purchased the large vacant lot directly behind the store. According to her, they were building three houses and eight apartments (the "apartments" actually turned out to be rooms at the couple's bed-and-breakfast inn). All of this was being constructed around a crumbling eighteenth-century chapel that had previously provided shelter for the homeless of our neighborhood.

A quick glance down the callejón might have surprised even lesser cynics than Paul and I with the speed of its conversion. The latest project behind Gracia's house was just one of many. Now paved and level and clear of debris and dog-doo, our alleyway had been gentrified in little more than five years. Many homes and properties that were Mexican-owned when we first came to Callejón de Chepito now belonged to Americans. The existing houses on those properties had all been torn down and rebuilt, or extensively remodeled. Large, imposing houses designed by architects from San Francisco, Boulder, and Dallas had replaced simple, single-story, two- and three-room homes of exposed brick or concrete blocks. Courtyards of cement and rubble had been supplanted by showcase swimming pools, hot tub spas, and terraced landscapes straight from the pages of *Garden Design*.

Our alley was not alone. As Paul and I had feared, the media's endorsements and an enthusiastic word-of-mouth campaign brought a new slew of real estate speculators and yet another construction boom to San Miguel. Developers were driving Mexicans from their homes with offers of cash too good to refuse, which in turn divided families, further corrupted officials, and distorted the importance of cash in an economy that had long been without. The boom also served to push more Mexicans out of *el centro* to the outskirts of town, where whole new barrios were springing up every six months.

By 2006, San Miguel's boomer boom, as we referred to it, was shaping up to be as frenzied as any in the last fifty years. American and Canadian retirees were flocking to town like swallows to San Juan Capistrano in mid-March. When my mother asked a cab driver how he felt about having so many Americans living in his hometown, he answered her question straight-faced: "You know, Señora, we Mexicans need a green card to work in San Miguel now."

The upside to all of this? The boom was providing jobs for the San Miguelenses. Hotels, restaurants, shops, and Spanish schools were bustling. Rentals were hot. Casa Chepitos was booked for more than half the year. Gracia seemed nearly giddy about it; more Americans in the neighborhood meant more beer and soda sales for her. Her husband, Salvador, and our other neighbors were easily finding employment. Their increased prosperity meant more discretionary income, so it wasn't only the foreigners who were upgrading the callejón with their construction projects. Our Mexican friends were remodeling, too. Gracia, Remedios, even Señora Rosa to the North, were all in the throes of various home renovation projects. One day, in a sudden fit of affability, Señora Rosa invited me over for a tour of her newly renovated house.

Inside, I felt as if I'd walked into the home of some lucky winner on *Extreme Makeover: Home Edition*. I was dumbstruck by the sumptuous remodel of her once rustic property, with its lovely rose-colored walls, Italianate tiled floor, and attractive iron windows. I cooed in appreciation.

"It was Martín's idea," Señora Rosa said. Her oldest son, Martín, who worked in Austin, Texas, had provided not only the idea, but also the cash to remodel her home from top to bottom.

"*Está muy bonita*," I said, glancing around. She shrugged unenthusiastically. As she listlessly shuffled from room to room, showing off bathrooms with shiny porcelain fixtures, large, open bedrooms with stunning views of the town, and a kitchen appointed with appliances and cabinets so new that they still had the price stickers plastered on them, she focused only on what had gone wrong.

She mourned her prized lily, which had been lost under the crush of construction debris, and complained she was having a hard time adjusting to the modern appliances. She claimed the noise and dust of the remodel had set off another round of health problems and blamed the stress of construction for her worsening cataracts. By the end of our tour, I realized what she was really saying was that she missed her old, familiar house. Like Paul and me, the señora was having a difficult time adapting to change.

MY FRIEND, writer Barbara Sjoholm, said that people tend to yearn for places exactly the way they were when they first encountered them — meaning each of us has a different perspective on what makes a place special, based on the characteristics that first drew us to it.

Among those of us who knew and loved San Miguel in the

early 1970s, a few might remember that many of the town's multicolored walls were once painted white above and dark red below; that the town ended just past the Quinta Loreto hotel on one side and the Instituto Allende on the other; that the Ignacio Ramirez market encompassed half the Plaza Cívica; and that traffic, a fraction of what it is today, flowed freely in the streets, even at midday.

By contrast, a newcomer to San Miguel might be thrilled to find new restaurants opening weekly, top-notch opera and chamber music at the Teatro Angela Peralta, an ATM on every corner, and, more recently, the familiar logo of Starbucks, kitty-corner from the *jardín*. ("Even in San Miguel!" the tourists exclaim.)

I once jokingly told Paul that if Starbucks ever arrived in San Miguel, we would have to leave. It's not that I believe Starbucks itself is a party spoiler, but its presence is a good indication that a party is officially out of control. It means that soon every kid from here to Siberia will be crashing it and messing everything up. But when I got over my initial irritation at seeing the Starbucks logo every time I approached the *jardín*, I noticed that the Mexicans loved lounging in the cozy, living-room-like café sipping their double tall mochas. Plus, I loved my life in San Miguel. It was going to take something more than the gentrification of our alley, an explosion of expats, and the arrival of Starbucks to make me consider leaving town.

22 | *El Diablo y la Virgen*

Dios te salve, María,
llena eres de gracia, el Señor es contigo.

FROM THE AVE MARIA PRAYER

O F THE AMERICANS POURING into San Miguel de Allende in the mid-2000s, a disproportionate number were female and over fifty. Women my age are drawn to San Miguel like June bugs to a porch light on a hot summer's night in Kansas. The allure of the irresistible colonial town seems to fan the flames of postmenopausal passion, making middle-aged women fall hard in love.

When the sirens of San Miguel call, some of these women tumble into a state of love-induced insanity that lasts long enough for them to imagine a whole new life here. Many even purchase a whole new house to go with their whole new life — just like me.

But if they truly are like me, these women are drawn to more than just the brilliant walls, picturesque churches, cheaper housing prices, and bargains in the markets. They're drawn to San Miguel because they want to be part of the lively Mexican and American artists' community and to live in this unique part of Mexico, where expatriate women are free to be themselves and speak their minds (except on the subject of Mexican politics, which by law, noncitizens are not allowed to get involved in). It is a place where they will be accepted for who they are and can contribute something to the greater good of all who live here.

Unlike many Mexican towns, especially those along the border, San Miguel is not overwhelmed by gang and drug violence. In the mid-2000s, its expat community, for the most part, felt safe living there.

Since my family and I had begun making our multiple annual sojourns to San Miguel, I'd never had reason to worry about our security. The stabbings Eleazar had mentioned turned out to be a feud between two cousins who were now working in Monterrey, and the altercation had actually occurred on the callejón below us. Our neighborhood was a peaceful place where my family and I felt safe coming and going any time of day or night. With Gracia and her family watching out for us and for the house, we had little reason to fear being victimized.

But in the early spring of 2006, our peaceful artists' colony — the darling of travel and lifestyle magazines — began making international news for something other than chic remodels of ancient haciendas.

ON A CHILLY MORNING in March, I was slowed to a near standstill trying to cross one of Seattle's many bridges on my way to work, when the *Father Knows Best* voice of NPR's Steve Inskeep poured from my car radio with ominous news:

"Some Americans who thought they'd found a haven abroad now have to worry about an attacker. A serial rapist has been targeting foreign women in the town of San Miguel de Allende."

The next thing I heard were the familiar voices of my friend Patrice and other women I knew in San Miguel issuing forth from the radio. In the five months I'd been away, an attacker had raped four women. All were expatriates, all spoke English, and all, except one, were over fifty.

Just like me.

By the time I returned the following June with Hannah and two of her friends, fear and uncertainty had taken up residency in San Miguel. Like a pair of overbearing relatives who've long overstayed their welcome, they were sucking the energy right out of our fair city.

The heat that year didn't help. The summer rains, which normally begin mid-June, did not arrive on schedule to break the oppressive late-spring temperatures. Landscapes languished in arid profusion; the jacaranda trees looked tired and thirsty; the brilliant magenta blossoms of the bougainvillea quickly faded to tepid mauve. Everyone was testy, worn out by the relentless heat, the lack of a much-needed rainy season, and a preoccupation with the belief that the rapist was still living among us.

TWO DAYS AFTER OUR ARRIVAL, I met with friends from the S.P.A. over *huevos rancheros* in the shady courtyard of the Café de la Parroquia. We were working on a new fundraising plan for the animal shelter. Over the clatter of plates and a gurgling fountain, I caught snippets of conversation from the table next to ours.

"Isn't it awful?"

"I knew it was going to happen again."

"The ineptitude of the police is so infuriating!"

"I've heard they know who he is; they just don't *want* to catch him."

"I'm scared sick. I don't sleep at all when my husband is away."

When I asked my S.P.A. friends if they knew what the women at the next table were talking about, they told me that the rapist had struck again, the night before last. His latest victim was a well-known author and high-profile member of the expat community who, like the man's other victims, was middle-aged and American. The attack had occurred just blocks from my friend Joyce's house, where the girls and I were staying since Casa Chepitos had been rented for two weeks.

"When the first rape happened last October, it was unsettling," said Karen, the Canadian shelter volunteer who'd helped us to adopt Nacho. "But since then there've been four more attacks. Everybody's really getting wiggy." She said the rapist's predilection for middle-aged, English-speaking women had her, and every other Anglo woman in San Miguel, living under a veil of anxiety, wondering who among them might be the man's next victim.

Over dinner with my friend Miriam the following night, she told me the rapist's first victim was a close friend of hers, a yoga teacher I'd practiced with several times.

"He got in by climbing a ladder at a construction site behind the house Charlie and I were renting at the time," Miriam said, looking visibly distressed. "She was house-sitting for us while we were in the States last fall."

I felt sick as she recounted the details of the first four attacks: women held at knifepoint and raped repeatedly over several hours by a deranged man who climbed over walls and picked locks to get in. Between violating them, he made his victims drink wine and speak English with him.

"With all the building going on in this town, no one is really safe," Miriam said.

AT DAWN THE NEXT MORNING, I peeked into the small, stuffy bedroom at Joyce's house where Hannah and her friends were sleeping. Clad in tank tops and boxer shorts, their nubile bodies were splayed across damp, rumpled sheets. The listless whirl of the ceiling fan's blades barely moved the room's thick, humid air.

I climbed the steep concrete steps to the rooftop terrace in search of a fresh breeze and to sit for morning meditation. A rosy haze blanketed the city below. A hot air balloon floated on a sultry breeze beyond the apricot spires of the Parroquia and the blue and white tiled dome of the San Francisco church. I sat down on a cushion and folded my legs Indian-style. I closed my eyes and began concentrating on my breath.

Minutes into my meditation, I heard a faint scrabbling on the other side of the stone wall I was leaning against. The noise became louder. Bits of scree peppered my scalp. I opened my eyes in time to see a scrawny young man in a ragged T-shirt tumble over the wall. Like a feral cat, I sprang to my feet and eyed him suspiciously as he dusted himself off.

"*Con permiso*," he said, excusing himself. He explained that he was working on the construction site next door. He only wanted to attach a hose to the spigot on our roof.

His calc-covered blue jeans and worn leather work boots supported his story.

"*Está bien*," I answered tentatively. But as I watched him grab the rope and rappel back down the twenty-foot wall, anxiety began spreading through me like an aggressive cancer.

AFTER THE MORNING's rooftop incident and the lurid reports I'd heard detailing the rape that had happened three days ago, and only two blocks away, I began hyperventilating at the thought of being alone with three adolescent girls in a house with no locking inside doors and walls that opened to the sky — walls that strangers were climbing over.

I was relieved that the girls seemed unaware of the recent attack and decided not to mention the guy on the roof to Hannah. That night I waited until they were asleep before rolling a giant potted ficus plant in front of their door to block access.

As I shoved the pot into place, Hannah rolled over, propped her sleepy head up on her hand, and asked "Is that to keep out the rapist?"

"He isn't interested in us, Sweet Pea," I said, giving her a little pat on the leg before I left the room. "You know me, I'm just being paranoid."

Then I booby-trapped the door of my own room with precariously placed chairs and lamps, tucked a spear-like rod under my mattress, and lay awake until three in the morning ruminating on the only other time I'd felt so frightened in Mexico. My first trip to the beaches of Oaxaca.

April 1974. My boyfriend and I have gotten separated from our friends, who have rented a *cabaña* we plan to share. But we think nothing of it. Instead of looking for them, we decide to roll our sleeping bags out on the lovely white sand beach and lie under a navy blue sky watching shooting stars zigzag across the night canopy. We've heard it's dangerous to sleep on the beach, so we bury our money and other valuables in the sand.

Sometime around midnight, the gentle slapping of the luminescent surf lulls us to sleep.

But not for long. We are kicked awake by two Mexican men wearing steel-toed boots and smelling of cheap Oaxacan mescal. They shine flashlights in our faces and aim a Luger pistol and a semi-automatic rifle at our heads.

"Get up," we're commanded in Spanish.

We do as we're told and are herded like animals, barefoot and wild with fear, through patches of creeping cactus. Our feet are shredded by the time we reach a coconut grove where a late-model Chevy pickup with a cedar-shingled camper is parked. A man with a stringy blond ponytail, wearing a Mexican peasant shirt, sits on the tailgate of the truck. A single kerosene lantern illuminates the night.

The men with the guns tell us to stay put, and they disappear again. We assume the guy with the ponytail is in cahoots with the armed men, since he seems unperturbed by their actions, but he explains: "These guys are *federales*, Mexican federal police, who get their kicks rounding up hippies who sleep on the beach and shaking them down." Evidently this wasn't the first time he'd been shaken down.

Minutes later the men reemerge from the darkness with two more boys and a pretty strawberry blonde from Chicago. They insist that the girl's visa is no longer valid and give her the choice of paying them 200 pesos or going directly to the "police station" with them. The man with the ponytail interprets their demand for the Chicagoans, who speak no Spanish. The boys shake their heads and insist they don't have the money. They try bargaining with the men, as if in a market.

"This isn't a business transaction," says one of the *federales*, "it's the law." They grab the girl by the arms and lead her toward the beach. She shoots me a beseeching look, as if being female, I'm the only one who can help her.

"They'll probably just rape her and let her go," says the guy with the ponytail when the three of them are out of hearing range.

I feel as if I'm going to be sick. I know that girl will never make it to the police station. The two drunk men have the cover of night and the silence of Mexico to conceal their crimes. A silent scream wells up in me as I watch them disappear into the darkness.

"Maybe we should have just given them the money," one of the boys from Chicago says.

I want to punch each of them for their stupidity. Instead I run to catch up with the *federales* and the girl. With the pistol trained unsteadily on me, I beg the men in my child-like Spanish to let her go. I tell them the boys have the money and that they will give it to them.

THE FOLLOWING DAY IN SAN MIGUEL, I wandered over to the benches in the *jardín* where Americans gather every day. The square was abuzz with more details of the rape. Beneath the shadow of the Parroquia, I heard anger and distrust spilling into nearly every conversation. The police's inability to capture the rapist was subverting the confidence and goodwill that normally exists between San Miguel's foreign community and its local bureaucrats. Like the ancient stucco walls of the town's many colonial mansions, it was beginning to crumble. Even the carefully polished image of our handsome young mayor, Luis Villarreal, had been tarnished.

American women were outraged by the lack of concern and

sensitivity demonstrated by San Miguel's police force. Victims had suffered double humiliation when, after being raped, they were interviewed about the intimate details of their attacks in rooms open to the public. One woman was furious when she discovered she'd been the butt of jokes made by the police after reporting her rape.

Mexican women were angry too. They were angered by the attention the American victims were receiving from the police, while their pleas for justice for Mexican rape victims had for years been ignored. They claimed, and it was well-documented by human rights groups, that Mexican police frequently blamed the victims. Archaic laws regarding rape only served to inflame the outrage: the age of consent was twelve years old. Historically, incest was considered a consensual act under Mexican law, and the victims of incest were frequently punished as severely as the perpetrators.

On top of all that, a number of foreign residents were in a standoff with the chief investigator over his refusal to release a composite sketch of the rapist. But many San Miguelenses supported his decision to withhold the rendering. The chief claimed it was an unreliable sketch, but I suspected there was more to it. There's ample evidence that crime victims who are white frequently have difficulty accurately identifying non-white criminals. A false accusation would be a public relations disaster for the police chief and for our dashing young mayor, whose sights were set on a higher office.

The most exciting news percolating among the Americans gathered in the *jardín* that morning were the rumors of FBI involvement. I was amused at the the idea of the FBI rehabilitating its image among the skeptical group of ex-protesters. The bastion of oppression from our youth were now the good guys.

Worn out by the incessant negative chatter and too little sleep the night before, I decided to leave the *jardín*. I wandered past the town's newspaper hawker and bought a copy of *Atención*, San

Miguel's bilingual paper. Tucking it under my arm, I traversed the shady square and ambled down Calle Reloj, past the Blue Door Bakery where the perfume of fresh-baked *bolillos* filled the air. I turned up Calle Mesones, en route to gather the girls from an art class, and arrived at the Plaza Cívica. There our town hero, Captain Allende, was guarding the newly planted landscape from his bronzed mount. Daylight had washed away the previous night's feeling of menace. I studied the faces of the people around me: limbless and sightless beggars with outstretched hands; bow-legged ranchers in neatly pressed Levis; bespectacled, stern-looking nuns; weathered *vendedoras* peddling overripe avocados. The faces of people preoccupied with the effort of eking out a living, making ends meet, keeping their families together, and serving their God.

No diabolical men bent on violating middle-aged, English-speaking women lurked among them.

LATER, WHILE LYING IN BED perusing the *Atención*, I was surprised to find an article by the writer who'd been raped only a few days before. She described the events leading up to the attack. How she neglected to lock an inside door and woke up a few hours later with a knife at her throat. But something else she reported really intrigued me.

After she was raped, the woman somehow summoned the courage to ask her violator to leave, knowing he had raped his previous victims multiple times, over many hours. When that failed, she began to pray. First in English, then in Spanish. As she invoked the Virgin, reciting several Hail Mary prayers in Spanish, her attacker became agitated and asked why she was praying. When she replied, "I am praying for you," he abruptly left.

"The prayers, or more likely the Virgin herself, drove him from my house," she said in the article. The *Atención* printed the full text of the prayer in both Spanish and English, and the victim implored the women of San Miguel to recite it.

I memorized the prayer and began reciting it with regularity, not so much for the girls' and my protection but for a greater purpose. I drew comfort from the idea that maybe, through focused intention, we could accomplish what the police hadn't been able to in the last nine months. It turned out I wasn't alone. By early July, I knew many expatriate women who were regularly reciting the Ave Maria prayer.

Within days, San Miguel de Allende was, again, crawling with police. More than fifty federal, state, and local agents occupied the city. Truckloads of uniformed men patrolled the streets. A restive hum filled the hot, humid air. The *click* of steel-toed boots on cobblestone made it feel as if our city were under siege.

AS WITH MORE NOTORIOUS and violent predators — Ted Bundy, the Boston Strangler, the Green River Killer — the odds finally caught up with the rapist of San Miguel. His ruse came to an end on July 5, 2006, when federal police arrested him a few blocks west of Casa Chepitos. Ironically, it was the same day Felipe Calderón, vowing to fight crime and take down the drug lords, was elected president of Mexico.

The FBI had indeed intervened, identifying José Luis Álvarez Gonzáles through a DNA match and providing police with a photo that was confirmed by his victims. The paunchy, balding, fifty-eight-year-old Álvarez more closely resembled an aging computer programmer than the stereotype of a crazed rapist I'd imagined. He'd done time in California and Texas for thefts and break-ins and, not surprisingly, was an experienced locksmith. He confessed to all five rapes and numerous burglaries too.

As word of his arrest spread, a communal sigh echoed through San Miguel's streets.

That evening, as if to contribute to the celebratory mood, the rains arrived and brought relief to the parched landscape. I breathed deeply for the first time in weeks, removed the iron spear from under my mattress, and recited one more Ave Maria.

23 | *A New Path*

AN ASTROLOGER, READING MY NATAL CHART, once commented that the north node of the moon was in my third house. When I asked what it meant, she told me it suggested that writing was an activity that would allow me to work through my karma and grow spiritually. A palm reader later confirmed it: the lines crisscrossing my right hand also indicated a writer's life.

Since childhood, I've been an avid reader. In elementary school, I volunteered in the school library, where, instead of shelving stacks of books according to the Dewey decimal system, I crouched in corners, reading what I was supposed to be filing. At age ten, I wrote my first book, a mystery set at the farm behind our house in Kansas, and, like many young girls, I kept journals and penned lengthy, uninspired prose poems. In an essay on the subject of career aspirations for Albert Hunsley's ninth-grade English class, I wrote that my one aspiration in life was to write the next great American novel. I felt certain I was among the chosen because I shared a birthday with an author named Harper Lee who had written the greatest American novel I'd ever read. Mr. Hunsley, apparently unimpressed with either my essay-writing skills or my career ambitions, gave me a C– on the essay, but I didn't let that deter me.

Throughout my twenties, I filled still more journals during my travels abroad, authored dozens of articles, and edited newsletters for various progressive groups and liberal causes.

Then I began opening stores, and all of my energy went into growing a retail business. There was little time left for writing. When my son was born I was so exhausted from balancing the needs of a high-energy baby boy and my work life that my ambition to pen anything got permanently consigned to the back burner.

Even the pages of Will's baby book were left blank.

I've never spent much time ruing what "might have been." I don't dwell on the what-ifs, and I feel as if life, thus far, has been more than fair to me. But the urge to write again nagged me through the years and as I closed in on the half century mark, that urge became more like an obsession marching through my consciousness, like the "long rows of devoted ants" Billy Collins speaks of in his poem, "Advice to Writers."

But it had been years since I'd written anything other than advertising copy. I'd also matured and grown more reticent about expressing my innermost thoughts on paper. (One of the beauties of youth is that life is so immediate and uncensored.) I really had no idea how to get started again.

Then one day I ran into Nick Gallo, a man I'd warmed benches with for years at our sons' high school and city league baseball games. I'd spent many soggy spring evenings huddled together with Nick and his wife, Laurie, on cold aluminum bleachers. While making small talk, I learned Nick was a travel writer, and his passion was writing about Mexico. He'd published numerous articles in travel magazines and in newspapers. Twice he'd been awarded the Pluma de Plata, Mexico's award for the best travel article of the year.

Both he and Laurie loved Mexico. They were familiar with San Miguel, having spent a year there when their kids were young. Nick was actually of Italian descent, but he said that because of his thick, black hair, olive complexion, and deep-set brown eyes, Mexicans frequently mistook him for a *compadre*.

The day we ran into each other I told him about the house in

San Miguel and took the opportunity to ask if I could pick his brain about the business of travel writing. We set a date to have coffee.

"It's a hard business to make a living at," Nick said the day we met. "I suggest you don't quit your day job." He went on to say that he still struggled to make a decent living, even though he'd been at it for over twenty years and was widely published.

We talked about ideas we each had, including one I had for a guidebook on Mexican handicrafts that I hoped to put together someday. I asked a few more questions about the writer's life, including just how poor was poor in a writer's world. I was astonished to find out how little professional writers are paid.

"Most guidebook authors are paid less than thirty thousand per book," Nick said. "Books that take them a year to research and write. And that includes travel expenses."

As we were leaving the coffee shop, he turned to me. "I hope I haven't discouraged you. Writing can be a lot of fun … if you don't have to make a living at it."

Our conversation shed some light on some of the mysteries of publishing, including how long the odds were that I'd ever get anything published, or be decently paid, if I did. But I didn't let that conversation with him dissuade me.

I have a foolhardy fascination for challenging odds, something I inherited from a pro. Whenever my mother hears the words "No way," she thinks it's time to put on the gloves. Like the time she took on the Mafia as a young beat reporter for a Chicago weekly. When word got out she was writing an article implicating the Mafia in the torching of a local Italian restaurant that had refused to pay "protection" money, she received a phone call.

"You're gonna be sorry if you run that article, lady," the stranger on the phone warned.

"You can go to hell," my mother responded, "and take your mob buddies with you!"

THE SUMMER AFTER my coffee date with Nick, I was back at Casa Chepitos. One sultry afternoon, at the last minute, I decided to attend a reading sponsored by the San Miguel Author's Sala. Tony Cohan would be reading from his new book, *Mexican Days*.

I rushed downhill to the small theater at the Bellas Artes, where a throng of gray-haired Americans dressed in brightly colored silks, flowing skirts, and strands of silver and semi-precious stones were filing in. Stagnant air blanketed the crowded room as we waited for the reading to start. After a series of announcements, and a reading by another writer, Tony finally took the stage. He came across as mildly self-effacing, with a gentle manner and a soft voice. The humor and poignancy of his words resonated with me, and I could tell from the extended applause that they had captivated all who'd sat through the stifling heat to listen.

Afterward I purchased his new book and felt a bit like a groupie in thrall of a rock star, as I stood in line waiting for him to sign it. When I finally made my way to the front, I surprised myself by blurting out a question.

"Do you ever teach writing classes?"

In lieu of the annoyed expression I'd half expected, he regarded me kindly. Though I was holding up the line of eager, overheated book buyers, he took time to answer.

"In August I'm teaching a workshop at a travel writing conference in California," he said, as he signed my book. Later I noticed that at the bottom of the page he'd written "Book Passage."

Within twenty-four hours of the reading, I'd googled Book Passage, a Bay Area bookstore, and enrolled in their Annual Travel Writers Conference.

THE WRITERS' CONFERENCE I'D SO EAGERLY signed up for was little more than a month away, and I had nothing to bring or show or even talk about. I wasn't eligible to attend Tony's workshop; it was on advanced narrative writing for experienced travel writers, and all I'd written about in the last twenty years were the merits of patio furniture and organic fertilizers. I studied the conference website in search of a workshop that a true beginner could sign up for and chose "Travel Writing for Beginners." Though the workshop focused on writing travel articles for a rapidly evaporating newspaper market and magazines that rarely published anything by anyone other than established authors, I didn't care. Getting published was the least of my concerns.

Among the various conference offerings I found something intriguing:

"A Chance for Great Prizes!" it read. I'm a sucker for contests even though I'd never won anything except a giant chocolate Easter bunny at an egg hunt when I was five, and I've always suspected that was rigged.

The conference organizers were sponsoring three contests: a photography contest, a 1,500-word essay contest on the topic of Cultures in Transition, and a postcard contest. The postcard contest's requirements were to write 200 words (or fewer) on the most exotic spot you'd ever visited. I figured I'd try that. It would be fun. As a woman who'd managed four multimillion-dollar-a-year businesses while volunteering on numerous boards and raising two kids all at the same time, I figured I should be able to write a measly 200-word postcard before the deadline, which was two days away.

I sat down at the computer and spent about an hour trying to think of something to write. Nothing came to mind. The most exotic place I'd ever been? I'd made numerous journeys to Europe, Canada, and Mexico, and even lived abroad for months or years at a time, but never in places I'd exactly call "exotic."

Unlike many of my friends, I'd never traveled to the jungles of Borneo or South America, the temples of Cambodia and ashrams of India, or the island paradises of Bali or Tahiti. I hadn't kayaked the waters of Patagonia, scuba dived off Belize's coast, toured the Galápagos Islands, trekked in Nepal, or retraced Captain Cook's journey through New Zealand.

I finally settled on the one travel experience that was the closest thing to exotic I could remember: My first trip to Mexico, to the pyramids of Chichén-Itzá, with my family in 1967, and specifically, about the night I woke up at midnight to find myself alone in a motel room with a giant, furry tarantula.

I spent the morning racking my aging brain for details of that disastrous family vacation thirty-nine years ago and tapping away at my keyboard. Four hours later, I had something I kind of liked. It was a goofy story, told in the voice of a thirteen-year-old me, but the nouns and verbs and the few adjectives worked. However, there was one small — or, should I say, *big* problem: My 200-word postcard was over 700 words. I was forced back to my computer to take a stab at self-editing, that merciless act of slashing your untamed writing so it can be brought forth into polite company. Sort of like teaching social skills to children. Only harder.

Four hours later, I checked my word count and was more than a little dismayed to discover that it was still eighty-three words over the limit. I thought, *How the heck could anyone tell a good story in fewer words than that?* I pruned it some more, eliminating every possible superfluous word. After twelve hours at the computer, my lower back ached and my toes were numb from sitting in one position. But I finally printed out the postcard and limped to the post box with it.

THE FIRST DAY OF THE CONFERENCE, I was sitting at a patio table, shivering in the cool marine air of Marin County in August, with my official-looking Book Passage Travel Writers and Photographers Conference portfolio on my lap. A sweet, perky young woman in a miniskirt bounced up and asked if she could join me.

"Sure," I said, anxious not to look like the lonely outsider I was.

"Did you enter any of the writing contests?" she asked after the usual intros.

"Oh, yeah," I said casually, "I sent in a postcard." My breezy act was intended to hide the fact that I probably could have hiked the Pacific Crest Trail in less time than it took me to write that postcard. I mean, seriously, most people complete the STP, the Seattle to Portland bicycle race, in less time.

"I entered that one, too!" she said and launched into a description of her postcard. It was about eating strange body parts of an even stranger animal while on a trip to China. I had to admit, hands down, it sounded way more exotic than the story I'd knocked out in just under thirteen hours.

The conference went well. The workshop I signed up for was excellent. I took copious notes and asked too many questions, as usual. I met all kinds of people: travel editors from the *Dallas Morning News*, the *San Francisco Chronicle*, the *Los Angeles Times*; publishers from *Lonely Planet* and *Frommer's* guides; editors from *Island* and *National Geographic Traveler* magazines; agents and writers and photographers. Among the people I befriended was a photographer named Lori who was originally from Tennessee but now divided her time between California and Mexico. She had edited *Best Places, Baja* for Sasquatch Books. She was funny and cool, and I figured if I ever did try my hand at writing a guidebook on Mexican handicrafts, she'd be a great resource. We traded contact information before I left to fly home on Saturday night. The conference wasn't over until Sunday afternoon, but I had to be back at work on Sunday morning.

ON SUNDAY NIGHT, we were just sitting down to dinner when the phone rang. Hannah answered and handed it to me.

"Hey, Judith! You left too soon!" A woman's southern drawl ricocheted over a crackly cell phone connection. It took me a minute to realize it was Lori. "'Cause guess what?" she said. "You won the postcard contest! And I got second place for my photograph!"

She told me that Don George, the former editor of the *Lonely Planet* travel guides and natural-born jester, had read the postcard aloud at the conference, mimicking my thirteen-year-old voice.

"They loved it!" Lori said, "Don had everyone in stitches!"

Thus began my second practice.

24 | *Los Novios*

I HAVE SOMETHING TO ADMIT that's more than a little embarrassing: I am a closet romantic. A complete sucker for quixotic love. I well up over the sappiest things. Teenage pop-songs of love gone awry, romantic movies with tragic endings, stories of obsessive, impossible, star-crossed love — think *Brokeback Mountain, Cold Mountain, The English Patient, Shakespeare in Love.*

When I was a teenager and Franco Zeffirelli's *Romeo and Juliet* finally made it to theaters in Kansas, I was first in line to see it. Afterward my date, Bobby Hughes, had to punch me in the arm to make me stop bawling.

So when Lupe, in the fall of 2006, only weeks before her twenty-first birthday, pulled me aside in Frieda's gallery one day and surprised me with the news that she was engaged to a boy named Juan who lived and worked two thousand miles away, I gave her an enthusiastic two thumbs up. When she asked if I would be her *madrina* for the wedding, I was even more delighted.

"*Sería un honor.*" I said. It would be an honor. Though I had no idea what being the godmother for a Mexican girl's wedding entailed, my romantic alter ego was happy to step up.

Lupe told me her *novio*, Juan, was a few years older than her and from Santa Rosa, a small town thirty minutes outside San Miguel on the road to Querétaro. He'd been working in Virginia as a roofer for the past year, but had returned home recently to visit his mother and Lupe. She radiated contentment as she described him for me.

"*Juan es un buen hombre*," she said. A good man. "He's poor, but very hardworking and sincere."

The words she chose to describe him were a reflection of how much she had grown up since we'd first met.

I proposed throwing a party to celebrate both her upcoming birthday and her engagement.

We decided on dinner at Méchica, the hip new bar on Canal Street where her cousin Teresa's husband, Esteban, was the manager. It was only two blocks from the bar where I'd celebrated my own twenty-first birthday, thirty years before. Teresa and Esteban helped plan the menu for the get-together that included a dozen of Lupe's relatives and friends, and, of course, her future husband.

There was no standing on chairs, no White Russians, and no unrealistic promises for the future, only an abundance of good food and drink and a genuine feeling of *amistad* that night.

But as friends and family toasted the happy couple, I noticed Gracia was quieter than normal. More reserved than I would have expected her to be on the night celebrating her daughter's engagement. It made me wonder how she felt about Lupe's new beau and the idea of her daughter marrying again.

JUAN, A SLENDER, QUIET YOUNG MAN, has earnest light-brown eyes and the square, calloused hands of a manual worker. In Virginia he was part of the shadow workforce that does America's most backbreaking work — shingling roofs and siding homes — work many Americans regard as boring, difficult, or dangerous. There are no benefits — no health or dental insurance, no Medicare or Social Security — for the men who work these jobs. If one of them falls from a roof and injures himself, L&I will not come to his aid. He must return to Mexico and pray that his family can take care of him until he is able to work again.

Juan made nine dollars an hour roofing houses for a Pakistani developer in Manassas, Virginia. There was plenty of work; he often put in fifty or sixty hours a week, though he was never paid overtime wages. Still, he was making four times what he could make in Mexico, and despite the lack of benefits and overtime pay and the dangers of working on roofs each day, he was intent on returning to Virginia as soon as possible. He and Lupe were convinced that the United States was a place where, if they worked hard enough, their dream of making enough money for a traditional Catholic wedding and to build a small house on Juan's family's humble farm would come true.

IN THE WEEKS FOLLOWING our dinner celebrating the engagement, I noticed Gracia's mood did not improve. In fact, it seemed to be getting worse. Her chatty, happy personality had been displaced by a moroseness I'd never seen in her before. She wandered the alley glum and preoccupied, and seemed distant and distracted as she went about her business. When I went over to buy eggs one day and noticed her struggling to make change — something she never has trouble with — I asked if something was bothering her.

"Lupe is moving out. She's going to live with Juan up at *el rancho*," she said, meaning the small acreage where his family lived. "Salvador is not happy about it. He doesn't think Lupe should marry a poor boy from the ranches."

We talked for a while longer, and I began to see how she was struggling with Lupe's choice on two accounts. First, she was coping with the fact that her first child, her only daughter and closest confidant, was now grown up and preparing to move out. I could empathize, remembering how I'd felt when Will went off to college in Iowa. Second, and more distressing, she was being forced to play intermediary between her volatile, unhappy husband and their strong-willed daughter. Something she'd often had to do through the years. Salvador and Lupe, both bright, emotionally complex people, had always struggled to understand each other.

From the beginning, their father-daughter relationship was difficult. Not long after Gracia became pregnant with Lupe, Salvador left Mexico to work in Texas. Like Juan and millions of other Mexicans, he went to the States in order to earn enough money to support Gracia and their future family. But he stayed in Texas for three and a half years. By the time he came back, Lupe was nearly three. Instead of returning to the adoring child he'd imagined, he arrived home to a little girl who refused to have anything to do with a man she'd never seen before. As a little girl, Lupe was intimidated by her fiery, energetic father and frightened by his boisterous laughter and mercurial temper. Their bond developed slowly, but Lupe remained her mother's daughter while Salvador related more easily to his three sons.

Still, his feelings for his only daughter ran deep.

"*Extraño a Lupe*," he told me after Lupe moved up to the ranch to live with Juan.

I went home and looked the verb *extrañar* in my dictionary. Though it sounds like the English verb *estrange*, it means the opposite in Spanish. Salvador missed his daughter.

24 | *The Soul of Mexico*

THE SAME YEAR I BOUGHT CASA CHEPITOS, I befriended a couple from Seattle who were moving to San Miguel. Charlie had opted for early retirement from a marketing job with a large commercial developer, and his wife, Miriam, subsequently left her job in human resources for an international aid organization so they could move to Mexico.

Miriam and I are near opposites in stature and appearance — she's tall, willowy and of Italian descent, while I'm small, blonde, and fair-skinned like my Scotch-Irish ancestors — but it turned out we have a great deal in common. We both have traveled and lived in many of the same places, enjoy learning languages, are nonstop talkers, and most important of all, share a passion for Mexican folk art, culture, and cuisine. It wasn't long before we were traveling around Mexico together, attending festivals and art shows; searching for the best *artesanía* (folk art) at markets, artists' cooperatives, and galleries; and visiting artisans in their homes and villages. Given our many shared interests, Miriam and Charlie became two of my closest friends in San Miguel.

IN THE FALL OF 2006, along with the news of Lupe's engagement, came my own big news. I got my first writing assignment.

Well, I *sort of* got my first writing assignment. I'd pitched an idea for an article on Michoacán handicrafts to the travel editor at the *Dallas Morning News*, an amiable fellow I'd met at the travel writers conference, who had emailed back to say that he *might* be interested. If I actually got around to writing an article, he promised to take a look at it. Being a complete ingénue in the travel writing business, I assumed this was as good as having an actual assignment. So I called Miriam, who was an avid note-taker and always up for the next adventure in Mexican *artesanía*, to help organize a trip to Michoacán for the Day of the Dead. One of the largest, most important folk art markets in Mexico takes place there during *el Dia de los Muertos*, and I knew we could gather all the info we'd need for the article. I also emailed Lori in California and invited her along as our official photographer. A month later the three of us, plus Charlie who graciously agreed to be our chauffeur, set off from San Miguel on a five-day junket to the city of Pátzcuaro.

Pátzcuaro: The Door to Paradise

Charlie's Chevy Tahoe barreled across Mexico's vast *altiplano* beneath an azure October sky. The *altiplano* is a six-thousand-foot-high plateau that spans the breadth of central Mexico, from the Sierra Madre Occidental in the west to the Sierra Madre Oriental in the east, and north from the trans-Mexican volcanic belt to the mountains of Zacatecas. Behind us: our home state of Guanajuato. Ahead: Michoacán, a state the size of West Virginia that boasts both conifer-covered mountains and lush tropical forests, acres of avocados, millions of monarch butterflies, and more artisans per capita than any state in Mexico, outside of Oaxaca.

We'd been driving for nearly four hours when we finally spotted a sign over the highway welcoming us to Michoacán. After circumnavigating the capital city of Morelia, we turned onto the highway leading to Pátzcuaro.

"Only a half hour more!" Miriam called back to Lori and me.

I shifted in my seat, eager to arrive in the lovely lakeside town I'd visited only briefly once before. Ten minutes later, however, the car suddenly slowed.

"Oh, hell!" Charlie exclaimed. I looked up from the brochures I was poring over in the back to see what was up. It was a Mexican-style roadblock: two pickup trucks angled across the road. A dozen camouflage-clad federal police hovered as Charlie grudgingly eased the car off to the side of the road. Within seconds four or five of them, each carrying an AK-47, encircled the car. Being surrounded by a group of gun-toting Mexican police, with their closely shaved heads and blank faces, unnerved me. My distrust of the Mexican federal police runs deep, as a result of that frightening first night on the beach in Oaxaca:

April 1974. Satisfied with the money coughed up by the boys from Chicago, the *federales* release the girl and go in search of other hapless hippies sleeping along the beach at Zipolite that night. My boyfriend and I, still trembling uncontrollably, leave the man with the ponytail perched on the back of his truck, and spend a long night huddled under dense brush on the far side of the coconut grove. Dawn finally arrives and breaks the spell of the prior evening's nightmare.

In the light of day, we relocate our belongings on the beach and easily find our friends in the tiny seaside village. We spend the afternoon close to the rented *cabaña*, where we feel safe. I lounge in a hammock, reading and recovering from the sleepless night, and talking with my boyfriend, trying to make sense, in our immature and unworldly way, of the injustice we'd experienced.

That evening our friends decide to hike down a narrow dirt path through the jungle to a taco stand they've heard is cheap and popular with travelers. I break a sweat at the thought of wandering through the jungle at night; I can still feel the cold barrel of the Luger pistol pressed against my thin cotton T-shirt. I go along merely because I'm more afraid to stay behind, alone. But under the dense, shadowy canopy, away from the safety of the *cabaña*, I feel anxious and exposed. "Maybe we're on the wrong road," I repeat over and over, like an obsessive child.

It seems forever before the trees open up. In the clearing, we find the restaurant — a simple, open-air place with a rusty corrugated tin roof and a handful of long communal tables covered in brightly flowered oilcloth. The six of us gather around one of the tables and sit on metal folding chairs bearing the logos of Mexican breweries — Dos Equis, Corona, La Blanca.

Night descends. A generator kicks on and a scattering of bare bulbs hung from wires above our heads light up. While we wait for someone to take our order, I notice a guy dressed in khaki pants and a khaki shirt, standing in front of a jukebox in the corner. He stuffs pesos into the slots and punches the buttons, and the energetic voice of the forever seventeen-year-old Ritchie Valens booms from the chrome and glass box: "*Yo no soy marinero, soy capitán, soy capitán.*"

We've ordered beer and tacos when the man in khaki comes over and sits down at our table.

I recognize the indolent gaze of his nearly black eyes and the large red mole on his left cheek. He strikes up a conversation with sixteen-year-old Nancy, a naïf who has escaped the rigors of East Coast prep school to learn Spanish in Mexico. Unfortunately, Nancy is a good student, conversant in Spanish, and when the man informs her that he is a federal police officer, she seizes the opportunity to report the events of the previous night. I frantically kick at her shins under the table, to no avail.

"You should hear what happened to my friends last night!" she says with innocent conviction. As she details our night from hell for the man, his dark, sleepy stare remains riveted to my face. My heart bounces around in my chest as Nancy chatters away. Finally, he tires of the silly American and her story and returns to the jukebox, where he punches more buttons.

The theme song from *Hawaii-Five-0* pours out of it and into the humid Oaxacan night.

HAVING THE FEDERAL POLICE surround his car outside Pátzcuaro unnerved Charlie a bit too.

A sandy-haired, neatly-tucked man, he possessed a temperament that vacillated between a relaxed jollity and a slow boil.
Under stress, the heat could come up quickly, and I could tell,
from the color in his face, that he was already up to a steady sim-
mer. I was relieved when he waved the men over to Miriam's side
of the car. She spoke more fluent Spanish and was calmer under
pressure.

A man with the beaked nose of an Aztec warrior sidled up to
Miriam's side and began questioning her. When she showed him
their FM-3 cards and calmly explained that we were headed to
Pátzcuaro for the Day of the Dead, he tilted his head toward the
road. A stern-looking younger officer with black fuzz for a mous-
tache backed one of the trucks out of the way. No passports con-
fiscated, no trumped-up charges, no nips at our pocketbooks. It
was our lucky day.

"Welcome to Michoacán!" Charlie bellowed when we were
safely out of range.

WITH THE ROADBLOCK BEHIND US, I turned back to my travel
brochures. "Come fall in love with Michoacán, the soul of Mexico," they implored. I knew it was only an imaginative piece of
advertising copy conjured up by some agency in Morelia or
Mexico City, but the line appealed to the copywriter-poet in
me. I found a map in one brochure and discovered that the "soul
of Mexico" was filled with places possessing strange-sounding
names: Tócuaro, Erongarícuaro, Ihuatzio, Zacapu, Tzintzuntzan. I traced my finger over the names and stumbled trying to
pronounce them. The names were Purépechan, from the indigenous people and language of the area. The same language and
people the Spanish conquistadores referred to as Tarascan.

These places with the odd names, I learned, were the artisan villages ringing Lake Pátzcuaro. Thanks to the efforts of a

sixteenth-century Spanish bishop, each one had its own spe-cialty handicraft. Today the work of Bishop Vasco de Quiroga, a lawyer by training, would be called community development. He taught the fundamentals of self-government and craft skills to the indigenous people of Michoacán. In the 1800s, his work would have been considered an act of sedition against the church and sovereign. Exports were a main source of income for Spain and allowing colonists and Indians to be self-sufficient became intolerable to the Spanish crown as their hold on New Spain grew more tentative.

Tata Vasco, as he was affectionately known by the Purépecha, persevered in teaching various trades and handicraft production, and the people living beside Lake Pátzcuaro became self-suf-ficient. Nearly five centuries later, village artisans still produce the Spanish guitars, leather saddles, ceramic crockery, *huarache* sandals, copper pots and vases and jewelry, hand-hewn toys, hand-loomed textiles, carved wooden furniture, and palm-fiber baskets once fabricated by their ancestors.

IT WAS LATE AFTERNOON before our small entourage finally caught sight of Lake Pátzcuaro in the distance. The long, lan-guorous, island-dotted lake shimmered silvery gray in the after-noon sun. Lining the road between the lake and the city were rows of towering trees with trunks painted white below. I rolled down my window and inhaled deeply. The air outside was filled with the pungent, therapeutic perfume of eucalyptus.

Our first night in town, we met a man from California who invited us to an art opening at a new gallery down the street from El Refugio, the bed-and-breakfast inn where we were staying. The vibe among the silk- and linen-clad group gathered at the gallery that night was decidedly more Beverly Hills than Pátzc-uaro. Boldly colored oil paintings hung on freshly painted stucco walls, but they were mostly ignored by the cabernet-sipping crowd. The artists, also primarily American, seemed more interested in cruising the hors d'oeuvres table than mingling with potential patrons.

I struck up a conversation with a man who told me he'd immigrated to Mexico from Los Angeles to escape the smog, traffic, and increasing gang violence. During our chat, he explained the reason for the roadblock we'd encountered.

"Five severed heads were rolled onto a dance floor at a nightclub in Uruapan last month. Since then this place has been crawling with cops."

The state of Michoacán, home to Mexico's newly elected president, Felipe Calderón, has one of the country's worst drug-trafficking problems. Several of its largest drug cartels are ensconced in the mountains there, and turf battles between them and government officials erupted regularly. In addition to the gruesome news from Uruapan, the mayor and chief of police of Pátzcuaro had been murdered in the local square, in broad daylight. The irony of the Los Angeleno's situation seemed lost on him: he'd traded sunny Southern California's pollution and gang wars for the wet, cool weather and horrific violence of Michoacán.

Minutes later, Lori, a wiry sprite of a woman with closely cropped blonde hair and ten pounds of camera gear hanging from her neck, clattered up to me. She was fidgety and bored. "Wanna go check out the plaza?" she asked.

I was as eager as she was to escape the Californians-in-Mexico scene. We waved at Charlie and Miriam across the room and slipped out the door.

AFTER A SHORT DOWNHILL HIKE, we arrived at Pátzcuaro's Plaza Grande. Arched porticos, stately ash trees, and bustling sidewalk cafés lined the large colonial square on four sides. At the plaza's center, a verdigris-stained statue of the benevolent bishop stood watch over the tide of burnished clay pottery, wheat-straw ornaments, leather chairs, Spanish guitars, and lacquered boxes that had washed up at his feet earlier in the day. Lori, seduced by the brilliant colors and interesting textures of the handicrafts, began snapping away.

A pair of costumed urchins carrying squashes carved into jack-o'-lanterns approached me asking for handouts. Seeing them reminded me: it was Halloween night. I thought of Hannah, who was likely roaming our neighborhood with her two best friends and garnering another year's supply of mini candy bars.

Clusters of children wandered about the plaza, some in costume, some not, looking for handouts of pesos or candy. A knot of little girls, dressed as witches in tattered rags and pointy hats, swarmed me like the pesky bees that hovered around the decorated sugar skulls sold under the square's arches.

"*Pesos, Señora, pesos?*" they cried. "Trick or treat!" one girl shouted. I gave them the few pesos I had, but more kids arrived, also wanting coins, while the first ones still hovered. They shadowed me and pulled at my shawl, and pouted when I told them I didn't have any more.

Unable to shake them off, I grabbed a *viejitos* mask — an old man's grinning, toothless face — from an adjacent handicraft stand. I covered my own with it and turned on the little girls, letting loose a blood-curdling imitation of the Wicked Witch of the West. They screamed with delight as I chased them around the plaza. Finally, worn out, I brought the mask back to the vendor I'd borrowed it from and was relieved when she smiled at me.

Tzintzuntzan: The Sound of Hummingbird Wings
After breakfast the next morning, we stepped out of El Refugio and were stunned by Benigno Serrato Street. Overnight, the cobbled, one-way street had been transformed into a giant outdoor flower market.

A river of marigolds, cockscomb, stock, and tuberose flowed

down the street as far as we could see. Keen to capture its colorful abundance on film, Lori sprang into action. Miriam, Charlie, and I stood by, listening to the dissonant clang of the basilica's bells and breathing in the sweet scent of tuberose in full bloom.

Though *el Día de los Muertos* is observed throughout Mexico, the villages and islands of Lake Pátzcuaro are the epicenter for Day of the Dead observances. Benigno Serrato was only one of many streets where makeshift markets had sprung up overnight. Sidewalk stalls peddling sugar skulls and candy skeletons, Tarascan bean soup and fried chicken tacos, crisp sweet flatbreads, donut-shaped *rosquetes*, and giant coconut macaroons had cropped up everywhere. Artisans from places as far away as Chiapas, Oaxaca, and Guerrero had staked their claims in a city where hotels and inns were booked to capacity. The main event, however, and the reason so many tourists come to Lake Pátzcuaro on that day, is to wander through *los panteónes* on the night of November 1. Full of candlelight and festooned with thousands of flowers, the cemeteries are where Mexican families gather to commune with the souls of recently departed loved ones through the long, chilly night.

EARLY IN the afternoon of November 1, we piled into the Tahoe and drove seventeen kilometers through a pastoral countryside dotted with chalet-style wooden houses that brought Switzerland to mind. Our destination was the village of Tzintzuntzan.

The word *tzintzuntzan*, when spoken rapidly and correctly (*tsin-tsoon-tsahn*), is onomatopoeic for the sound of hummingbird wings in flight. In the pre-Hispanic era, the village of Tzintzuntzan was known as the place of the hummingbirds and was the capital of the Purépechan empire. Today it's known for the Yácatas pyramids, a large handicraft market, and the two cemeteries skirting the main road through town. Thousands of tourists from all over the world visit the cemeteries at Tzintzuntzan on the night of November 1 to wander among the graves.

We'd come early in the day to watch families prepare the grave sites before the crowds arrived.

The two cemeteries were buzzing with activity. Mexican families — from young children to ancient grandmothers — were busy sweeping or raking debris, cleaning the closely set marble headstones or mausoleums, and decorating them with candles and flowers. Giant wooden frames had been erected and people were covering them with marigolds. The careful planning, designing, and preparing of the colorful displays seemed to be an act of homage in itself. Mexicans spare no expense in honoring their dead.

Great mounds of *cempasúchitl* were piled along narrow paths between graves, and the air was filled with its piquant scent. Native to Mexico, the large, ruffled, orange marigold is used to decorate the graves because it is believed that the bright flowers lure the dead back to earth. Among the profusion of marigolds and votive candles adorning the graves were also things the departed one had been partial to: foods like guavas, mangoes, papayas; drinks like tequila and beer; maybe even cigarettes if the deceased had been a smoker. Stuffed animals and other favorite toys appeared on the graves of children. A few graves had photos of the deceased on them, and every tomb was lined with a multitude of candles. Later that night, the golden glow of thousands of candles could be seen from miles away.

At the top of the cemetery, Lori and I found an unusual grave decoration — a racing bike covered in marigolds. There was a pineapple on the rider's seat, and apples, oranges, and bananas were strung between the spokes. Lori gestured to the long-faced woman placing candles atop the grave below it, to ask if she could photograph the bicycle. The woman nodded her consent. Afterward we spoke with the woman's niece, who told us her cousin had been killed in a cycling accident the previous July. I thought of Will, now twenty-one and savoring the fullness of life, and a lump formed in my throat. There but for the grace of God.

BACK IN PÁTZCUARO, we returned to the market to interview and photograph more artisans.

We talked with the women from the Santa Cruz artists' co-op, who stitch brightly colored embroidery designs on pillows, shirts and blouses, tea towels, tablecloths, and runners. There is an appealing naïveté in their hand-stitched woven goods, which depict colorful scenes of typical Mexican life — farm life, weddings, Day of the Dead.

Lori befriended the backstrap weavers of Cuanajo, who weave woolen belts and shoulder bags using the ancient "dog leg" pattern. I interviewed an award-winning clay artist from the village of Patamban, where the giant green-glazed ceramic pineapples are made. Afterward, I pored over blue tarps spread with my favorite *artesanía* — the whimsical clay art of Ocumicho, a remote village in the mountains north of Uruapan.

The people of Ocumicho still speak Purépecha primarily and produce colorful clay sculptures so ironic that they verge on outrageous. At times I've wondered if the artists of Ocumicho aren't all slightly mad — in a really *sweet* way — because their art so obviously mocks the Catholic view of good and evil. While there are a few sculptures with themes like the Garden of Eden or the Tree of Life, the majority of Ocumicho ceramic sculptures (and the best sellers) are clearly blasphemous. Evil run amok is the most popular theme. There are devils playing trombones, trumpets, and guitars; devils riding motorcycles; devils driving buses full of frantic passengers; devils seducing large-bosomed beauties; devils rejoicing in the midst of burning hotels. Amid all of the diabolically themed sculptures, I found a gem: a breadbox-sized piece with thirteen fluorescent-colored mermaids covered in silver glitter sitting around a table.

"*Es la ultima cena sirena*," the artist told me in all seriousness when I asked what it was.

The Mermaids' Last Supper. I loved the way the sound of it

rolled off my tongue in Spanish and its impertinent take on the Last Supper. Imagining it on our bookshelf at Casa Chepitos, I asked how much she wanted for it. It was a bargain at twenty dollars.

As I carried my new prize back to El Refugio, a number of Mexican tourists approached me to ask what it was. When I replied, "*Es la ultima cena sirena*," they giggled and guffawed loudly. Mexicans, even devoutly Catholic ones, adore irony.

WE MET UP WITH Miriam and Charlie, and the four of us dined on bowls of creamy *sopa Tarasca* and sausage-stuffed empanadas at an outdoor café on the Plaza Chica. Afterward, we wandered up La Paz, a small side street that opened onto the park-like grounds of the basilica, where we found a huge crowd gathered along the sidewalks. Everyone was looking at something up the street, but the crowd was so dense we couldn't see what. We threaded our way to the front and were surprised to see hundreds of mounted cowboys, trotting four and five abreast down Buena Vista Street toward *la Basílica de Nuestra Señora de la Salud*. A number of the riders were young boys, maybe ten or twelve years old.

A silver-haired cowboy led the procession carrying a yellow banner with the initials INRI sewn on it. The rhythmic *clop, clop, clop* of hooves echoed off the cobbled streets as the handsome *vaqueros*, dressed in their best leather gauchos, silver spurs, and ivory- or ebony-colored Stetsons, guided their horses toward the iron gates of the church plaza.

Lori jogged back to the hotel for a lens she lacked. I dodged sweaty haunches and swishing tails to squeeze past and through the plaza's narrow gates. Cowboys whistled and shouted, or used their spurs to get their horses up the plaza's steps and into the courtyard. As more horses crowded in, the churchyard began to take on the look and smell of a rodeo holding pen.

A beautiful, twenty-hand palomino dropped a load directly in front of the sanctuary's open doors.

I found refuge from the chaos of clattering hooves in a corner of the basilica's façade next to a Mexican woman with wavy, hennaed hair and heavy makeup. She appeared to be sizing up the cowboys.

"What are all these cowboys doing here?" I asked.

"Every year there's a special mass at the basilica for the cowboys. Many of these guys have been riding all night to bring their horses here to be blessed," she replied. She ran a set of perfectly French-manicured fingernails through her hair as she spoke.

"They're very handsome," I said, referring to the horses.

"Yes, they are. You can pretty much have your pick."

I was still wondering if I'd understood her Spanish correctly when a stocky cowboy in spurs and an oversized Stetson passed close by. Without turning his head, he made a discreet hand gesture in her direction. She winked at me and followed him around the corner.

Janitzio: Abandon all hope, ye who enter here.
As Dante described in his *Inferno*, there are many versions of hell. Even if you don't fit into any of the nine categories of sinners he described, and your life is relatively sin-free, you probably still harbor your own private version of hell. For some people, hell is wading through a computerized phone message for fifteen minutes, for others it's dealing with the eternal technological glitches that plague our laptops and smartphones or the big one: dealing with customer service at Comcast. For my husband, hell is having to wait in line. For me it's being stuck in a crowd.

It was well past midnight, but hundreds of Mexican, American, European, and South American tourists were still queuing up at the maze-like entrance to the *Muelles de Janitzio* to board the launches that crossed Lake Pátzcuaro to the island of Janitzio. A steady stream of the long, narrow plywood watercraft jockeyed for a place to dock. The roar of outboard motors was deafening. More boats ply the lake's *café-con-leche*-colored waters on November 1 than on any other day of the year.

Though numb with cold and exhausted from traipsing through the cemeteries at Tzintzuntzan, Lori, Miriam, and I shrugged off thoughts of our cozy beds at El Refugio to venture across the lake at midnight. Lori's heart was set on photographing Janitzio's celebrated candlelight procession. Charlie thought we were all crazy; he headed back to Pátzcuaro and went to bed.

By the time we disembarked on the island, it was after one in the morning. We soon discovered that the famous candlelit procession had ended hours ago and since then, the island's solemn tribute to the dead had digressed into a writhing mosh pit for the living.

Like Mont Saint-Michel in France, the island of Janitzio has only one steep, narrow walkway through it. Pearl Jam blared from scratchy speakers above us as we were shoved along past tacky tourist shops and fishy-smelling restaurants by a crowd of exuberant underage drinkers pressing their way toward the party on top of the island. Being averse to crowds (I'm an enochlophobe at heart), the crush of exuberant youth was more than I could handle. At one point I found myself pressed bosom to bosom with a harem of teenage girls. The sickeningly sweet scent of Clinique's Happy perfume clung to my nostrils. It was all I could do not to scream.

LORI, MIRIAM, AND I all agreed that the drunken scene on the touristy island was more than any of us could bear, so we pressed our way back through the youthful throng to the docks. Forty-five minutes later, we squeezed onto an overloaded launch with a mob of unruly teenage boys who were intent on keeping the party going. In stark contrast to the somber vigils we'd observed at the cemeteries at Tzintzuntzan, the boys were hanging over the open stern splashing, shouting, shoving, and punching one another. Our captain, the only apparent authority aboard the ten-meter-long tub, looked slightly older than my twelve-year-old daughter.

A thick fog had settled on the lake while we'd been island-side, cutting visibility to a few meters. We were halfway across the lake when I noticed that the persistent, plaintive horns of the other launches sounded disturbingly close. Out of the mist, a green and red bow light suddenly appeared, alarmingly close to our leeward side.

A collective "Aye!" filled the air as the other boat plowed into ours. We played bumper boats for a few minutes as our young captain struggled to back away from the other one. With each rev of the engine, the rowdy teens in the rear cheered louder. Chaos broke out when one of the boys fell overboard into the murky brown water.

The launch veered wildly off course as our captain struggled to rescue his passenger. By the time he'd cut the engine and yanked the boy to safety, we'd drifted into the shallow part of the lake. The propeller was now stuck in the weeds. Our warm beds at El Refugio seemed like a fleeting apparition on Mexico's Night of the Dead.

THE STORY ENDED HAPPILY. No one else fell overboard that night, and eventually our young helmsman managed to paddle us out of the weeds and restart the engine. Miriam, Lori, and I were also lucky. Our story on Michoacán handicrafts was published in the *Dallas Morning News*, and the editor bought several of Lori's photographs, too.

But the best thing about the trip to Pátzcuaro was learning that it's the simple, specific, observable details that make travel writing, or any kind of writing, come alive. The real soul of Mexico resides in the wink of a hooker's eye and the confident stride of twelve-year-old cowboy. It's in the stony face of a young *federale* and the toothless smile of an ancient weaver. It sits at the graveside vigil of a mother whose son died too soon, and inspires a migrant worker to make a three-thousand-mile journey home each year to place flowers on the graves of his loved ones. Extravagantly wealthy and oppressively poor, stubbornly corrupt yet surprisingly generous, the soul of Mexico is full of ritual, attached to tradition, fixated on death, and overflowing with life.

26 | *El Otro Lado*

THE PHONE RANG at our house in Seattle just before six o'clock one Saturday morning, startling Paul and me awake. I rolled over and pulled the pillow over my head, irritated that anyone would have the nerve to call so early. But my husband jumped up and answered it. He came back to bed holding the phone in his hand.

"It sounds like Gracia," he said.

Though still groggy, I felt my pulse begin to race. Gracia was not someone who would waste money calling from Mexico unless she had news to share of some calamity on the callejón. I sat up too quickly and the room spun as I grabbed the phone from Paul's hand.

"*¿Bueno?*" I said.

Gracia responded in rapid-fire Spanish. I couldn't understand a word, but her anxiety was clear. It sounded as if she was right next door, sounding the bell on an eight-alarm fire.

"*Por favor, Gracia, mas lento,*" I said, imploring her to slow down. She began again. Slower this time. Articulating the special way she does, so I'll understand.

"It's Lupe," she said. "She left for *el otro lado* with Juan. They made it to Houston. But she doesn't have the money to pay the coyotes. I thought maybe you could help. Juan will soon be returning to his job in Virginia. He can repay you when work begins." She repeated the last sentence twice.

I assured her that I would help, but I couldn't help wondering why Lupe and Juan would cross the border with two coyotes they didn't have the money to pay. Like the animals they're named for, the men who guide people across the border are skittish and unpredictable. They're often part of the Mexican mafia and infamous for the abject violence they're willing to perpetrate on their own people if things don't go as planned. Crossing without having the money to pay your coyote is crazy. It's not like you can arrange credit with Mexico's underworld.

Before she hung up, Gracia told me that Lupe was at her cousin's house in Houston. She gave me the phone number, and I promised to call.

"You understand that what she's asking is illegal, don't you?" Paul said after I'd hung up.

I did, in fact, know that aiding an undocumented alien was a federal offense. I also knew that if one is convicted of helping an undocumented person, the result could be fines, forfeiture of property, or time in jail. I thought about it for about a minute or two, then I shrugged off Mr. Voice of Reason.

My friendship with Gracia and relationship with Lupe trumped any personal concern I had about the INS coming after me. In our years on Callejón de Chepito, she and Lupe and Salvador had often helped us.

"They've always helped us when we've asked them to. Now it's our turn to help them," I said as I dialed the phone number Gracia had given me.

"She's sleeping," her cousin Alejandra said when I asked to speak with Lupe. Exhausted from her four-night trek across Mexico's northern state of Tamaulipas, she'd been crashed out for hours, so I ended up talking at length with Alejandra instead. With Lupe fast asleep, she felt free to vent about her cousin's behavior.

"I don't know what she was thinking, crossing the border when she didn't have the money!" she said. "I don't have that kind of cash."

I spent the next five minutes trying to calm Alejandra, who was understandably panicked at the thought of two unhappy coyotes knowing where she lived. She finally settled down when I told her that I was willing to help pay them off.

It took several hours and four more phone calls, but together Alejandra and I worked out a plan for my friend Jim, who was living in Houston at the time, to meet her husband at ten o'clock that night and give him the required cash. Jim — a dyed-in-the-wool liberal who is also extremely anxiety prone — later told me they met on a desolate, out-of-the-way street corner in a neighborhood in southwest Houston. After briefly acknowledging one another, they ducked into a dark alley, where, like a pair of Sinaloan drug dealers, they completed the transaction.

During one of the phone calls to Houston, I spoke briefly with Lupe.

She told me she wasn't feeling well, but said nothing that explained her behavior. Though she can be impulsive at times, she's not reckless or crazy, which is what you have to be to mess with coyotes. As it turned out, there was more to it than I knew at the time.

TEN MONTHS LATER, in early December, I received a letter postmarked Manassas, Virginia. Inside was a brief note in Spanish and a photo of Lupe holding a chubby-cheeked infant on her lap. The photo suddenly made everything clear.

Her note explained how she went into labor on the night of September 18, and with Juan by her side at a Virginia hospital, delivered a healthy baby girl early the next morning. Though Lupe knew nothing about the Fourteenth Amendment, she did know that because her baby was born in Virginia, she was automatically a U.S. citizen.

"Maybe someday she will attend college or work legally in the U.S.," she wrote in tidy, schoolgirl script that she embellished with little happy faces. But in closing, her tone became serious and she equivocated about staying in the United States. "Things are not so good for the Mexicans here in Manassas. I think we'll return to San Miguel in February, or maybe next summer."

It would be the following summer before I understood exactly what she meant.

"At first things went well for us," Lupe would tell me months later. "We paid off the coyotes, then took the bus to Manassas. Juan's sister owns a small house there, and we had our own room."

Work was abundant, she said, in the town of thirty-six thousand that is best known as the site of the Second Battle of Bull Run, one of the bloodiest battles of the Civil War. Juan soon got his roofing job back and had a regular paycheck coming in. He earned enough money to pay rent to his sister and dispense with his debts from their trip across the border.

"We even had a small amount in savings," Lupe said.

She admitted to missing her family and San Miguel, but she and Juan had been hopeful about their future and their plan for improving their lives.

Then, in early July, when she was seven months pregnant, things began to fall apart.

27 | *Seeds of Animosity*

ANGER TOWARD UNDOCUMENTED WORKERS had been building in and around Manassas for years, but when Juan and Lupe arrived in early 2007, the anti-immigrant vitriol in Prince William County had reached a new pitch. The seed for this animosity took root between the late 1990s and early 2000s, when the county was growing faster than any other in Virginia. Its proximity to Washington, D.C., and its affordability compared with D.C.'s costly housing market, made it attractive to prospective home-buyers who worked in the Beltway area. Money for construction loans was cheap and flowing freely. Developers jumped on it, and projects began sprouting up.

With construction booming and employers eager to hire cheap, non-union laborers, thousands of Latinos flocked to the area. By 2007, they made up 9.7 percent of Prince William County's total population — roughly the same percentage of expatriates living in San Miguel de Allende today.

Latino laborers dominated local construction sites. Men from Mexico, El Salvador, Guatemala, Nicaragua, and Honduras worked as laborers, painters, roofers, bricklayers, and landscapers. New migrant workers arrived almost daily in Manassas and the surrounding towns. They rented apartments, houses, and storefronts; opened grocery stores and restaurants; parked their taco trucks at job sites and other places around town. Latino-owned businesses grew as the population grew, and they prospered as the Latino community prospered.

But Help Save Manassas, an alliance of neo-nativists, was growing too. (I call them neo-nativists because, unlike true nativists, they weren't really interested in reclaiming Virginia for the descendants of Pocahontas.)

The group was led by an avid blogger named Greg Letiecq. Letiecq and his followers watched in irritation as Latino businesses continued to sprout up and thrive. They were enraged by the day laborers who gathered at local 7-Eleven and Home Depot stores in hopes of finding work.

Ironically, Letiecq's parents were immigrants themselves: they had immigrated to the United States from Quebec, Canada. But Letiecq, who seemed to have forgotten his own family's immigrant roots, blogged daily about the "problems" posed by Manassas's latest immigrants. He referred to day-labor centers as "open air toilets." He photographed Latino workers without their permission and urged police to go after them for minor infractions, like loitering or spitting. He associated Latino activists with what he called the "Zapatista conspiracy." According to him, this imagined international conspiracy included the French youth who set cars on fire in the Paris suburbs. In an essay titled "Our Culture Under Assault," Letiecq wrote: "We are obliged to defend our embattled culture before we inexorably veer off onto that destructive path. But we fight on many fronts. Whether our battle is combating the 'press one for English' insanity, or preventing the pollution of our longstanding cultural traditions with pagan harvest rituals from Mexico in our Christmas celebrations, we must engage in the struggle."

The final straw for Letiecq and his Help Save Manassas adherents was when the new immigrants began wanting in on the Great American Dream — the dream of homeownership. As more Latinos began buying homes in Manassas and surrounding towns, Prince William County's anti-immigrant fervor ramped up.

Then, in early 2007, Corey Stewart and John T. Stirrup Jr.,

new members of the Prince William County board of supervisors, introduced a resolution to implement the most draconian anti-immigration policies in the United States. If passed, the proposed resolution would deny immigrants access to all social services in the county: there would be no in-home care for the elderly and disabled; no rental or mortgage assistance to immigrant families in crisis; no drug and alcohol counseling; no health care services at local doctors' offices, clinics, and hospitals. There would be no aid for homeless migrant workers; no food stamps or other food assistance for women and children; and no access to programs focused on reducing gang violence.

In addition, the resolution required local law enforcement officials to check the residency status of anyone they *suspected* of being in the country illegally and report people to the INS if they could not provide the necessary documentation. Even if they had not broken a law.

Stirrup and Stewart turned out to be the new messiahs the anti-immigration crowd had been praying for.

Like Letiecq, Stirrup articulated their deepest fears by generalizing the issue and making unsubstantiated claims such as "illegal immigration is causing economic hardship and lawlessness." He was quoted in the *Washington Post* saying his proposed measure was only "the first step toward taking back our community."

Despite the objections and concerns voiced by hundreds of Latinos and their supporters during hearings that spring and summer, the board went ahead with the vote. On July 10, 2007, with more than two thousand people spilling out of their chambers and into the lobby of the county offices, the Board of County Supervisors of Prince William County, Virginia, made history: they passed the country's first comprehensive anti-immigrant legislation — unanimously.

Overnight, construction jobs for Latinos began drying up. Spanish-speaking workers were turned away from job sites where they'd always found work. Even those who had worked for the same employers for years suddenly found they were no longer needed. Manassas's Latino population soon began migrating north to Baltimore and Pennsylvania, or south to New Orleans and Mississippi, where recovery work from Hurricane Katrina was still under way.

With the workers gone, Mexican grocery stores shuttered their doors. Restaurants went under. Taco truck owners pulled up anchor and joined the caravan of displaced workers as they headed for states with laws more accommodating to migrants.

The new legislation affected Lupe's impending delivery too, though she only discovered it the day before she went into labor, when her doctor announced that he was no longer able to deliver her baby at the Prince William County Hospital.

"A nurse told us to go to a hospital in Warrenton, in the next county over," Lupe later told me. "But it was an hour away, and we didn't have a car."

She said that her water broke the following afternoon, but it was after midnight before Juan finally found a friend with a car who was willing to drive them to Warrenton.

NEARLY A YEAR TO THE DAY after Gracia had called to ask for help in paying off the coyotes, I called Lupe in Manassas to find out how things were going with her and Juan.

"Not so good," she said. Juan had lost his roofing job and in the six months since then he'd been unable to find steady work. Their savings were depleted. The bank was after her sister-in-law, who was behind in her mortgage payments. And on his way home from work one night in late July, Juan had been jumped by a gang of young men who robbed and beat him badly. Because of this and the county's new anti-immigrant laws, he and Lupe were nervous about being seen on the street. They spent most of their time holed up in the house with the baby, Gisela.

I'm usually ambivalent about telling my Mexican neighbors what I think they should do, but I knew Gracia would endorse what I said next.

"Maybe it would be best if you returned to San Miguel."

"I want to go back, but there's no money. Juan is thinking of going to New Orleans. A friend told him there's work down there. But I don't know what Gisela and I will do if he goes."

"I think your mom would feel better if you went home. I can help you get back to San Miguel."

I asked her how much money she needed to get home. She wasn't sure, but said she would ask around the Mexican community in Manassas to see if she could find a ride back home.

"I'll call you back if something turns up," she said.

Two days later she called to say she'd found a man with a truck who was leaving for central Mexico the next day. If I could get the required sum to her within twenty-four hours, she and Gisela would make the trip with him. She said Walmart did money transfers, and that if I went there that night and made the transfer, she could pick it up at the Walmart in Manassas the following morning. A good plan, I told her.

There were, however, a few minor obstacles. First of all, we live in central Seattle, fourteen miles north of the closest Walmart. Second, by the time Lupe and I hung up it was after six in the evening. Paul was out of town, and Hannah had a gymnastics meet that wasn't over until nine thirty.

By the time I dropped Hannah off at home and got back in the car, it was after ten. Fortunately, I'd called earlier that day and found out that Walmart was open until midnight.

It took forty-five minutes to find the Walmart in Renton, Washington, a place I'd rarely visited in the thirty years I'd lived in Seattle. The surrounding area turned out to be a slice of little Mexico. On the way I passed numerous Mexican restaurants, two taco trucks, and the La Familia used car lot. Walmart's parking lot was hopping for a Friday night at eleven; it was full of Mexican families with small children in tow, rolling giant carts full of disposable diapers, baby formula, and cases of Budweiser to their cars. It felt familiar, like the parking lot of the Mega store in San Miguel.

Inside, hearing the sound of Spanish with its melodic cadence and seeing the open, friendly faces of Mexicans helped soothe the tension I'd accumulated driving through poorly lit and unfamiliar neighborhoods along Lake Washington at the late hour. Making the transfer turned out to be easy. An efficient girl, who looked no older than fourteen, completed the transaction in about three minutes and assured me Lupe would have the money by eight o'clock the next morning.

A WEEK LATER, I RECEIVED my first non-emergency call from Gracia. She wanted to thank me for helping Lupe and Gisela get home. It was the first time she'd seen her first and only grandchild, and she sounded ecstatic.

"*Muchísimas gracias*, Judith!"

"I'm glad she's home," I said. "I think it's better this way." Knowing that Gracia would be her perky old self again made me happy. Lupe and Gisela were home safe, and life in the callejón would be fun again. It was always more interesting when Lupe was around. Plus now there would an added benefit: Hannah and I would have a cute, cuddly nine-month-old baby girl to play with.

After Lupe returned to San Miguel, Juan left Virginia too. He went to New Orleans, where he met up with his friend who had told him there was work there. However, he found The Big Easy flooded with day workers, and most were just scraping by; the work was spread too thin already.

So in the late spring of 2008, after months of looking for work and finding little, Juan abandoned his dream of working toward a better life in the United States and returned to Mexico.

Juan was the first to lose his job, but eventually all of his family in Virginia was out of work. His brother-in-law, who had lived and worked in Manassas for twelve years, was let go, and his sister lost her office cleaning job. Her employer said he was sorry, but with the new laws, he couldn't afford to take the risk of keeping her on. With little or no income coming in each month, Juan's sister got further behind on her mortgage payments, and within a year, she lost her home to foreclosure. Her life savings were gone, too — she'd used them for the down payment.

The real estate market in Prince William County soon hit the skids, and Manassas became second only to the city of Woodbridge for the highest rate of home foreclosures in Virginia. Thousands of lives were ruined or turned upside down.

IN JUNE THAT YEAR Hannah and I flew through León on our way to San Miguel. Unlike Lupe and Juan, we waited in the queue at customs for fifteen minutes, confirmed with the immigration officer how long we intended to be in Mexico, and automatically received a six-month visa.

As I stood there reflecting on their journey, I felt acutely aware of the freedom that possessing an American passport brings me. But for the first time in my life, the small navy booklet also felt like a burden.

Our reunion with Gracia and Lupe was a joyful one. Gisela took an immediate liking to Hannah, who in turn discovered her affinity for babies. Having a baby had slowed Lupe down, but we all enjoyed the more relaxed pace.

One balmy afternoon we were sitting on the store's steps together. Gisela was in Lupe's lap, gurgling happily as Gracia passed around cups of *horchata*. As we sat, sipping on the cinnamon-infused rice milk, the subject of Juan and Lupe's adventure across the border came up. Gracia frowned and shook her head, but Lupe ignored her mother and turned to me.

"Someday I will tell my grandchildren the story of how I went *al otro lado,*" she said. A look of defiance crossed her face, and she hugged her daughter a little closer. "So they will know how I tried to give them a better life."

BORDERS ARE ARBITRARY. Livelihoods are not. For nine generations, Mexicans have crossed the Río Bravo in hopes of improving their own lives or the lives of their children and grandchildren.

The story Lupe will tell her grandchildren is a tale as old as human migration itself. One that for centuries has been told by mothers and grandmothers and great-grandmothers to their children and grandchildren.

It is an enduring narrative, interwoven with risk and hardship, loss and denial, perseverance and self-sacrifice, spun from the slender threads of faith and hope.

28 | *El Tianguis*

ONE TUESDAY MORNING later that summer, Lupe came knocking at our door to ask if Hannah and I wanted to go up to the *tianguis* with her family. The Tuesday Market, as American and Canadian expats call San Miguel's *tianguis*, is the highlight of Gracia's week. She invariably closes the store for a few hours every Tuesday to make the trip up there. Not only does she find great buys, but she frequently runs into friends and relatives and picks up choice bits of news or gossip.

Since the market is on the outskirts of town, and we don't have a car in San Miguel, we rarely go. But I needed a couple of mattress pads for the twin beds in Hannah's room, and I thought I might find some there. I also knew I could rely on Gracia to bargain for me since she and Lupe consider me a wimp when it comes to fighting for a good deal.

THE WORD *TIANGUIS* is derived from the Nahuatl word *tianquiztli*, which means "marketplace" in the language of the ancient Aztecs (1.5 million Mexicans still speak Nahuatl). The *tianguis* has a long history in Mexico. In pre-Hispanic times, the largest *tianguis* was at Tlatelolco (the same plaza north of Mexico City where student demonstrators were massacred by a paramilitary police force in 1968). In *The Conquest of New Spain*, Bernal Díaz writes that he was "astounded at the great number of people and the quantities of merchandise" he and Cortez encountered at the Tlatelolco market in 1519. Never had they seen such an amazing array of products or so many people (estimated at twenty to twenty-five thousand a day) in European markets. His description of what he encountered reads like a rave review: gold, silver, and precious stones; chocolate; skins of lions and tigers, otters, jackals, badgers, deer, and mountain cats. But he seemed most impressed with the canoe loads of human excrement being sold. Apparently the Aztecs used it to tan animal hides.

One popular guidebook claims that *tianguis* markets are the "most authentic in Mexico," and points them out as places where you can find "native textiles and Indian pottery." This may be true of other *tianguis*, but San Miguel's is a giant open-air flea market, where you're more likely to find pirated DVDs, car batteries, Osterizer blenders, and cheap plastic toys made in China than authentic Mexican handicrafts. On that first reunion to San Miguel in 2002, my mother and sister went up to the *tianguis* expecting to find some rare gems of folk art. "It's just a bunch of junk!" my mother reported with dismay.

HANNAH AND I trotted across the alley the Tuesday morning Lupe came calling and found her, Gracia, and the kids, including her soon-to-be-thirteen-year-old son Marthín, sitting on the steps waiting for us. I looked around for Marcos or Salvador, who generally did the driving, but they weren't there.

Since neither Lupe nor Gracia drove, I wondered how we were getting up there.

"Are we taking the bus?" I asked.

"Oh no, Marthín is going to drive us," Lupe said, nonchalantly.

"Marthín?" I asked, incredulous at the idea of Gracia's chubby, baby-faced preteen son behind the wheel of a car. The halcyon, car-free days Claudius and Octavio had spoken of in 2002 were long gone. There were plenty of cars to hit in San Miguel now.

"Oh, yes, Marthín drives now," Lupe said confidently. "I taught him how." As if that was somehow supposed to reassure me. I wondered aloud how you could teach someone to drive, when you aren't a driver yourself.

"I tell him when to hit the brakes, when to accelerate, when he's turning the wheel too far," Lupe said. "It's easy. I taught Marcos how to drive, too. My dad gets mad too easily; no one wants to learn from him."

Fortunately, just as I was about to snag the wheel from our preteen chauffeur, Marcos came walking up the Cuesta de San José. Having completed his course at Lupe's driving school three years ago, the eighteen-year-old was an excellent driver. I was happy to ride with him.

DRIVING IN SAN MIGUEL, even if you're experienced, is somewhat like taking a trip through Mr. Toad's Wild Ride at Disneyland. The steep, narrow streets are crowded with cars and often deeply rutted from missing cobblestones. Mexicans on motorbikes and Americans on ATVs weave in and out between cars navigating one-way streets that often change direction in midstream. Drivers also have to dodge pedestrians who cross at random, burros bearing loads of firewood or garden soil, and those Mexican dinosaurs of mass transit, the rattletrap local buses known as *urbanos*.

In addition, about 25 percent of the cars in San Miguel are taxis, and many are driven by young men who think of driving as a sport and themselves as Mario Andretti. One time, an overeager young taxi driver, with my mother and me in back, pulled in front of a bus careening down the Salida á Querétaro. When the bus only narrowly missed plowing into the side where she sat, my mother invoked Jesus so loudly that the young driver sobered right up. I noticed his speedometer didn't top twenty miles per hour the rest of the way home.

Few people, other than foreigners, use seat belts regularly in Mexico. Taxis rarely have functioning ones, and friends visiting from the States frequently make frantic searches for them after climbing in. Once, a very cautious friend of mine who was unable to find her seat belt asked, "Do you think we should get out and find another taxi with seat belts that work?"

"Good luck," I said.

EIGHT OF US crammed into the Explorer for the trip up to the Tuesday market that day. Naturally, there were no seat belts or car seats for the babies. Marcos, Hannah, and Lupe were snugged in up front. Marthín and Gracia, with Gisela on her lap, and I were in the back seat. Behind us, Cholo, Gracia's youngest, who was now three-and-a-half, rolled around in the cargo hold. As we bumped along up streets with ridiculously steep grades, Gisela grew fussy. Like many nine-month-olds, all she ever wanted was her mother. Gracia soon grew tired of her whining and wiggling to get loose. So she took aim and tossed Gisela, like a football, over the front seat to Lupe. As Gisela landed, she bumped her head against the dashboard. She came up screaming and gave Gracia the infant evil eye, making all of us burst into laughter. "*¡Mala abuelita!*" she seemed to say with her angry glare. If only babies could talk.

San Miguel's *tianguis* takes place on an enormous fair-ground-like lot that is void of vegetation except on Tuesdays, when it bursts into bloom. Covering an acre or more, the market is a visual landscape of its own. Mountains of used clothing and hills of fabric samples; rivers of wrenches and hammers, off-brand batteries and car parts; vast plains of plastic buckets and laundry baskets, brooms and mops. A cloud of dust fills the air, which smells of tacos frying in pools of oil mixed with the perfume of overripe papayas, mangos, and guavas being blended into smoothies at *licuado* stands.

After parking the car, we all scattered. The boys went in search of the *puesto* selling pizza. Lupe and Hannah left to scan tables full of cheap hair ornaments, makeup, and nail polish. Gracia and I marched off to find the vendor selling *colchas* and other bedding. We found him and Gracia mentioned what we were looking for. He insisted that somewhere among the piles of bedspreads, pillows, and curtains, he was sure he had mattress pads. We watched patiently as he tore the stand apart searching for them. After spending fifteen minutes disassembling the place, he finally dragged two pads out from underneath a stack of polyester coverlets. They were of mediocre quality and bigger than I wanted, but the man had gone to so much trouble to find them that I felt obliged to buy them. I nodded yes when Gracia looked at me for the signal to begin bargaining.

There are certain rules of engagement that polite Mexicans, even the hardest bargainers, adhere to when negotiating for goods. Number one: never demean or disparage a vendor or his merchandise, or insult him with an outlandishly low offer. Second: don't raise your voice or get angry. I will never forget the time I watched a well-dressed woman from Mexico City browbeat a timid Tarahumaran vendor in the Copper Canyon who refused to speak to her.

"*¡Francisco!*" the *chilanga* yelled at her guide. "Make her talk to me!"

The last rule of bargaining is this: know what your best offer is and when to walk away. Gracia obeys all of these rules and is so calm and respectful in how she deals with salespeople that they're barely aware she's driven the price down to a paltry sum before the negotiation is over. Needless to say, I got my mattress pads for a very good price.

WE CAUGHT UP WITH Marcos and with Marthín, who was holding three slices of pizza in his hands.

"He's an eating machine! Look at how fat he's getting!" Gracia exclaimed.

"Will looked just like Marthín when he was twelve," I said. At twenty-two, my son was now six foot one, lean and lanky. "I'll bet he's going to be tall, just like Will." Marthín smiled at me as he shoveled the second piece of pizza into his mouth.

Before we left, Gracia wanted to make one more stop. She and I trotted off in the direction of a secondhand clothing dealer, while the kids went to visit the "petting zoo," as I call the puppies, kittens, rabbits, and, sometimes, baby goats being sold at the market. Gracia spent a few minutes digging through racks crammed with sweaters and blouses while I waited, and finally pulled out a kelly-green cardigan, embroidered with holly, ivy, and bright red poinsettias. The kind that women in the States wear to Christmas-sweater theme parties at holiday time. When I tried explaining this to her, she looked at me as if I must be making it up. She wanted to know who on earth would throw a party just to wear a sweater? Or buy a sweater only to wear it to a party? Though it was June, she bought the festive holiday sweater.

Among the many things for sale at the petting zoo that day was a menagerie of puppies, kittens, parakeets, and poultry. The rest of us had gathered by the car when Lupe approached, carrying a small box. Inside the box were three baby chicks, all dyed in eye-popping fluorescent colors. Acid green, shocking pink, safety-cone orange.

"I really wanted a puppy but decided chickens would be better," she said. Her logic escaped me. How does one want a dog but end up with three chickens dipped in food coloring like hard-boiled eggs at Easter? I figured maybe chicken feed was cheaper than dog food. Or perhaps they could eventually eat the chickens or their eggs.

We all piled back into the car for the ride home. Marthín and Cholo were both in the cargo hold this time, with the chicks. As we headed home, bumping along at ten miles per hour over San Miguel's numerous *topes* (speed bumps), Gracia reached in her *bolsa* for the new cardigan.

She smiled proudly as she held it up for everyone to see.

"Ma! That's a Christmas sweater!" Lupe groaned. We all cracked up, including Gracia.

I began humming "Feliz Navidad" and soon we were all singing the popular Christmas song as three brightly colored feather puffs staggered about, loose in the cargo hold.

"Look!" shouted Cholo over our holiday chorus, "They're dancing!"

WHEN I TOLD THIS STORY to a Seattle friend, instead of being amused, she was horrified that there were no car seats for the babies. She seemed appalled that I'd joined in the laughter when Gisela was tossed over the seat in a moving vehicle and wondered if it bothered me that Gracia made fun of her son for being overweight or that Lupe had purchased baby chickens that had been "tortured." What she really wanted to know was how I — a person she'd always thought of as being politically correct — could reconcile myself to these things that were so obviously *not* PC.

The answer is not simple. Safety is something I care deeply about. As babies, my children always rode in car seats, and buckling up is second nature to them now. Hannah is the one who frequently has to remind me to buckle my seat belt. Demonstrating care and respect for animals and children is also important to me. But living in a country among people with different habits and lifestyles and cultural norms offers me the opportunity to step out of my judging mind and see the world through a different lens. Spending time with my neighbors, doing things their way instead of mine, has helped me become less rigid and circumscribed in my thinking. That has been their gift to me.

29 | *Sangha*

Forgiveness means giving up all hope for a better past.

LILY TOMLIN

THERE ARE WORDS WHOSE MEANINGS go far beyond the surface. Like *hope* and *grace* and *faith*. Such small words, yet they encompass such big ideals. *Hope*, a wonderful word, conjures up all sorts of possibilities. *Grace*, the name of my closest friend on the callejón, is defined as the unmerited favor of God. Something all of us could use more of. *Faith* is a complicated five-letter word, tainted by overuse and loaded with negative connotations for an unapologetic liberal like me.

Still, the older I got, the more I found myself wanting to revisit the question of faith. Or at least to explore the idea of faith as I prefer to define it: the belief in a power greater than ourselves for which there is no proof. I wasn't looking to make peace with God or for reassurance that I would get into heaven someday. My spiritual quest has always been about enriching life as it is, right here and now. But it was the quest to rediscover a sense of faith that eventually led to my third practice, the one that has made the biggest difference in my life. My meditation and mindfulness practice.

I learned to meditate on a mountaintop in France at the age of twenty-two, but had practiced only sporadically since. Then, at the age of fifty-three, I read a series of articles about the medical benefits of meditating regularly — lower blood pressure and heart rate, increased serotonin uptake, enhanced immune system function, improved concentration and energy level.

Neuroscience, it seemed, was finally catching up to what yogis and monks have known for centuries: That the practice of yoga, meditation, and mindfulness can profoundly change the way we think and act.

When I heard others in my yoga class talking about how their meditation practices had benefited their lives, I decided to join the *sangha* — a meditation and Buddhist study group — that my yoga teacher Meg was organizing. The Buddhist part was completely new to me.

Though we were baptized and confirmed in the Episcopal church, when my sisters and I grew into unruly teenagers my mother gave up her battle to get us out of bed and off to church on Sunday mornings. As an adult, I tried returning to the church but found the liturgy no longer resonated with me.

I still love sitting under the lofty arches of Grace Cathedral in San Francisco or St. Mark's in Seattle with sunlight pouring through the immense stained glass windows, and feelings of goodwill well up in me on Christmas Eve when the church choir breaks into the familiar strains of "Lo, How a Rose E're Blooming." But the Episcopalian's Sunday sermons, prayers, and hymns were too traditional and staid relative to who I had become.

THE APPEALING THING about Buddhism is that you can walk the dharma path at your own pace. There's no requirement to become an adherent or develop a monastic lifestyle to garner the benefits. I've studied Buddhism for several years, and yet I don't identify as a Buddhist any more than I consider myself an Episcopalian. I think of myself as a spiritual eclectic and of the world's religions as a theosophical smorgasbord from which I can pick and choose the tenets and philosophies that fit my moral principles. I object to the idea that any single religion has all the answers, and have developed an interest in reading about many different spiritual and religious traditions, including Islam, Judaism, Taoism, Hinduism, Christianity, and some native traditions. Each of them has a unique set of laws and guiding principles and their own particular approach to the divine.

BEFORE JOINING THE *SANGHA*, I'd never studied Buddhism in depth, nor had I consciously tried to follow its tenets. In the beginning I found sorting out the Four Noble Truths, the Eightfold Path, the Five Moral Precepts, and the Twelve Insights (what was it with the Buddha and lists?) a challenge, not unlike learning another new language. But I came to understand the Four Noble Truths, the basic precepts of the Buddha's teachings, which are:

1. Life is full of suffering.
2. There is a cause for suffering.
3. There exists a state of mind free from suffering.
4. There is a way to end suffering.

These four statements may seem simplistic, but are in reality, profound. If there is anything I've learned in my fifty-plus years, it's that suffering is unavoidable and change is the *only* constant. Through reading a number of Buddhist texts and discussing them in our *sangha*, I've also learned how we compound our own suffering by clinging to the illusion that we can control what happens in our lives. One day, over lunch at El Pegaso in San Miguel, a stranger from Austin, Texas, said something that threw a spotlight on how I contribute to my own suffering.

I was sitting alone at a corner table when a white-haired gentleman with a twinkle in his eye and a distinctive Southern drawl sat down at the table next to mine. Being we were in San Miguel and the only people in the restaurant, I knew it was only a matter of time before we'd strike up a conversation.

"Have we met somewhere before?" he asked. Though it

sounded like a standard pick-up line, I too had the feeling we'd met. But neither of us could remember where or when. A conversation ensued, I eventually moved over to his table, and we ended up talking for close to two hours, confiding all kinds of personal things to each other over *sopes de pollo* and tuna sandwiches. My new friend, Richard, told me about his addictions to drugs and alcohol and how he'd ruined several marriages and a career; he told me about his current search for happiness and a new partner, and about the troubles he was having with his daughter and finding someone to take care of his cats. I told him about my obsession with achievement and proving myself, my challenging relationship with my mother, and my current effort to repurpose myself in midlife. As our conversation drew to an end, it turned into a discussion on the human need to feel in control.

"I have to admit, I'm a bit of a control freak," I confessed. "I want to micromanage everything: my business, my staff, my kid's lives, every little thing in my personal environment. I do it, I think, because it makes me feel as if I've got my *own* life under control."

Richard smiled. "Honey, I'm gonna let you in on a secret. Not only are you *not* the CEO of your own life," he said, chuckling, "you're not even on the committee!"

I'VE NEVER SEEN RICHARD AGAIN, but I think of his quip whenever life does not go according to my plan. It helps me accept things as they are, rather than how I'd like them to be, and is especially helpful in accepting the things I'm powerless to change. As dharma teacher Phillip Moffitt once said at a retreat I was on, "If we cease thinking that things should be as we wish they were, we open to all kinds of possibility."

Mindfulness — being aware and completely present in the moment — is one of the most important tenets of Buddhist psychology. Again the idea may seem simple, but in practice it's really quite difficult. Given the prevalence of TVs, computers and iPads, smartphones and iPods, attention-sucking Facebook, Twitter, and YouTube, text messaging and viral video games, I am relatively certain that the number of people living fully in the present moment is at an all-time low. But the benefits of learning the seventh element of the Eightfold Path are numerous.

When I am persistent about my mindfulness practice and following the dharma (the Buddha's teachings) as it is taught in our *sangha*, I reap many benefits, both at home and at work. It's helped me embrace Will for who he is, rather than who I think he should be, and to greet Hannah's teenage angst with less of my own maternal anxiety. The practice of mindfulness and right speech can turn difficult interactions with customers at the store into positive ones. The challenge of running a retail store provides me with daily opportunities to practice mindfulness.

My success is often hit-and-miss, but when I fail (and I often do), I try to keep a sense of humor about it and not beat myself up.

The Buddha's teachings have also helped improve the way Paul and I communicate, though my husband sometimes pokes fun at my attempts to incorporate Buddhist precepts and Nonviolent Communication into our relationship.

Like the time Meg recommended that we in the *sangha*, and our spouses, try asking each other daily, "What can I do to make your day more wonderful?" I went home and explained the idea to my husband, who seemed to be only half-listening. Then at breakfast the following morning, he surprised me. Without looking up from his newspaper, he asked, "So what are you going to do to make my day more wonderful?"

OF THE MANY BENEFITS being in *sangha* has brought to my life, none has been more important than the change I experienced in my complicated relationship with my mother.

Of her six children, I am the one most like her. In many ways we're too much alike. We're both curious, creative, passionate, and droll. We also can be pig-headed, competitive, impatient, judgmental, and unforgiving.

Since adolescence I've also been the child most likely to cross her. Our relationship has been strained over the years by my obstinate independence and her reluctance to accept it. We've often spent precious vacation time, the only time we have together, antagonizing each other with recriminations. Arguments or accusations that served only to rile each other and cause our summertime reunions to dissolve into teary feuds (the tears belonging exclusively to me). Like the row we had one August while we were vacationing at her summer cottage on an island in Ontario.

WE'D SPENT A PLEASANT EVENING at a friend's cocktail party and lost track of time. By the time we said our good-byes and got into the boat, the dusky evening sky had turned inky black.

I was in charge of getting my mother and my kids safely across the open bay, which is full of shoals. Shoals I can locate during the day, but which turn into hidden hazards the minute the sun goes down. I was frightened as I picked my way across the lake in the dark, even though as teenagers my sisters and I had frequently been out half the night on the bay, partying with friends. Stories of drownings and near-drownings abound in island country. Maybe it was because we were young and considered ourselves invincible that it never crossed our minds that we could drown. Or maybe we were just too drunk or stoned to care.

But, as the old cliché goes, time changes all things, including our youthful misassumption that we're never going to die. Now that I was a mother myself, and a panicky one to boot, it scared the hell out of me to be ferrying my children through shoal-infested waters at night.

With Will navigating, and my mother, who still possessed twenty-twenty vision at age eighty-seven, pointing us in the right direction, we reached the dock without incident. But my hands were still shaking as I tied up the boat.

The next morning, I commented to my mother how frightening it had been being out on the lake at night and asked her how it had felt, long ago, to have three of her daughters out there until the early hours of morning.

"Didn't it worry you when Margaret and Rachel and I were out there in boats at night?" I asked.

"Sure it did. But you all never listened to me anyway. You always did exactly what you wanted to." The acid tone of her voice took me by surprise. I, of course, immediately became defensive.

"What do you mean by *that*?"

"Like that time you went off with Billy Breithaupt on his motorcycle," she said, referring to a weekend road trip I took with a friend when I was eighteen. I'd lied to her about where I was going and who I was going with, and she had never forgiven me. My mother does not tolerate being lied to.

"That was thirty years ago! Don't you think it's about time you let go of it?"

"You demonstrated then that you couldn't be trusted," she said, glaring at me. "I've never trusted you since."

With that declaration she turned and marched off to the dock, where a friend was waiting to take her to church. I knew that if she felt the least bit of remorse, she would absolve herself of it before it was time for the coffee and cookies. Meanwhile I was left alone with my tears, stung and angered by the idea that my mother was determined to go to her grave resenting me for that lie and every other misstep I'd ever made. And there was nothing I could do or say that was going to change it.

THE FOLLOWING WINTER I was talking with Cathy, a friend from our *sangha*.

I told her my mother and I had not spoken since that conversation six months before. I had stubbornly refused to call my mother all fall and since she never calls me, except in emergencies, we hadn't talked. I knew Cathy would understand because she, too, had had a troubled relationship with her mom.

"My mother and I are very different people," she said. "When it finally dawned on me how hard it must have been for her to raise a daughter who is nearly the exact opposite of her in every way, I felt a lot more compassion for her." Cathy explained that once she was able to feel empathy for her mother, it broke the cycle of blame that had plagued their relationship, and feelings between them improved significantly.

It had taken fifty-four years for me to be able to hear it, but I couldn't ignore the truth in what Cathy said. I knew my mother couldn't have found it easy to raise a child like me, either.

I wouldn't have wanted to raise me. As a teenager I was reckless, unfocused, unreliable, impulsive, hysterical, and flirtatious. I was attracted to boys who were alcoholics or addicted to drugs. Growing up in the pre-AIDS, free-love era, I slept with more guys (and a few women) than I can count on all my fingers and toes combined.

I was a mediocre student, despite scoring high on aptitude tests. Year after year my teachers, frustrated by my lack of initiative, sent notes home complaining of how I wasn't performing up to my abilities. That drove my mother crazy.

At eighteen I moved as far away as possible, first to Virginia, then to Mexico, then to Paris, and last to the West Coast. As a young adult I became a liberal Democrat who perpetually protested against every right-wing cause.

The very core of who I became was a slap in the face to my mother, whose conservative, Midwestern values have been the hallmark of her life.

My conversation with Cathy helped me realize how none of this could have been easy for my mother. But the Buddha said that before we can have compassion for others, we must first have it for ourselves. Learning self-compassion meant I needed to stop seeing myself through my mother's eyes.

I was no longer the flaky, irresponsible teenager I'd once been. I was an industrious, responsible, and trustworthy adult. Knowing this about myself, on a very deep level, allowed me to consider my mother's side of things, and to stop reacting to her every criticism.

But the real epiphany in our relationship, the one that would fundamentally change the way we communicated with one another, took place nine months later in a remote canyon in northern Mexico.

30 | *The Hand of Fate*

WELL INTO HER EIGHTIES, my mother was a miracle of octogenarian vigor. She walked steadily without a cane, could still climb stairs without holding on to a railing, and jumped in and out of motorboats without assistance. But the closer she got to ninety, the more aware I was that her traveling days were numbered. So the year she turned eighty-eight, I booked a trip for the two of us to Mexico's Copper Canyon as a birthday present.

Described by the Society of American Travel Writers as the world's most exciting train ride, the trip seemed like the perfect present for a woman who loves train travel and thrives on experiencing new places and different cultures. Though she's traveled all over the world, my mother still feels somewhat shortchanged that she never got to do "a few things." Such as dig in the Olduvai Gorge alongside Louis and Mary Leakey, take the Orient Express from Paris to Istanbul, or go river rafting through the Grand Canyon. But at her advancing age — or maybe it was mine I was really concerned about — the Copper Canyon would have to suffice. And though it may sound as if my motivation for the trip was purely altruistic, it wasn't. I had an agenda.

I wanted that trip into the canyons of Mexico — possibly the last time my mother and I would vacation alone together — to bring closure to the years of pain we'd inflicted on each other. I didn't know how it was going to happen, or if it would, but I hoped that if we managed to have a good time, a time free from anger and drama — and if I could adhere to the Buddhist practices of empathy, mindfulness, and right speech — the emotional space to talk about our differences might open up and a healing process could begin.

IN LATE SEPTEMBER, only days before I was to leave for Mexico, I ran into my travel-writer friend Nick. He was huddled at a table in a corner of Louisa's Café one morning, nursing a latte. Though I was already running late for work, I plunked myself down in front of him.

"Hi," he said in a quiet voice. He seemed tired that morning, and the deep circles under his eyes darker than normal, but I said nothing as I peppered him with questions about the Copper Canyon.

"I'm afraid I can't be much help. I don't have good memories of my Copper Canyon trip. I was sick the entire time." It turned out his three-day train trip into the canyons had been an intestinal nightmare.

We commiserated about the gastric perils of Mexican travel, then moved on to other subjects. But a few minutes later, as I stepped out into the unseasonably chilly Seattle morning, I felt a kernel of doubt take root in my own gut.

AFTER SPENDING TWO DAYS AIRPORT HOPPING, Mother and I arrived in the colonial city of El Fuerte, where we planned to catch the train into the Copper Canyon the next morning. A day to rest up at the pleasant hotel, a meticulously renovated hacienda, was just what we needed. I signed up for a massage and swam in the pool while she chatted up people poolside and napped in the room. While she slept, I took my notebook into the bar and had just begun writing in it when a Mexican man sipping on a Corona at the next table asked what I was writing.

"Just making some notes," I said.

"Notes for what?"

I told him I was an aspiring travel writer and that I was jotting down things that I might someday use for an article on the Copper Canyon. He reached in his wallet and fished out a business card.

"Javier Bustamante. Director of Public Relations for the city of Mazatlán," he said, handing me his card.

He inquired where I was from. When I told him Seattle, he asked if I knew Nick Gallo.

"Yes! Nick is a friend of mine. A mentor of sorts. I ran into him right before I left on this trip."

He told me he'd known Nick for years, and that they had collaborated on articles about Mazatlán. We talked for a while longer, and then I decided it was time to check on Mother.

As I stood up to leave, he shook my hand and said, "Please tell Nick hello from me when you see him again. He's a great guy."

AFTER BREAKFAST THE NEXT MORNING, Mother and I took a taxi to the station to catch a nine-thirty train. The Chihuahua al Pacífico, or El Chepe, as the railway is called, is one of the last remaining passenger trains in Mexico. El Chepe's only route is a stunningly scenic four-hundred-mile course through a series of canyons that cover more square miles and are deeper than the Grand Canyon.

The station was empty when we arrived, but within minutes a small group clustered on a simple, uncovered concrete platform. The train arrived only a half hour behind schedule, an astonishing accomplishment when compared to Amtrak's past record.

It turned out that "the world's most exciting train ride" ambled along at fifteen to twenty miles per hour. But what the ride lacked in speed, it made up for in visual drama. After snaking slowly through velvety green lowlands outside of El Fuerte, we ascended to higher elevations. The terrain turned steep and mountainous, full of jagged peaks and sheer canyon walls. Deciduous forests soon gave way to subalpine landscapes where stands of juniper, pine, and madrone grew between giant boulders formed from the flow of ancient volcanoes. Native cosmos dotted the railroad's rock-strewn embankment with brilliant bursts of tangerine.

After winding around Huites Lake, the enormous drainage basin for the canyon's six rivers, the train began crossing a series of thirty-seven bridges that span the canyon's deep ravines.

I was standing in the open space between two cars talking with a German man, when the train stopped for no apparent reason. He pointed to a man wearing a khaki vest and jeans scrambling up a rocky hillside.

"He's a photographer on assignment for the Balderrama hotels," the German guy said. The fellow snapping away on the opposite hillside had been commissioned to photograph the train. We started up again, but a short while later, after clearing a narrow bridge that spanned a three-hundred-foot-deep gorge, the train stopped again. Then, slowly, it backed up to the middle of the bridge, where there were no sides and no guard rails. As the train swayed gently from side to side in the wind, my fellow traveler and I held our collective breaths as we stood in the open doorway. Being terribly afraid of heights, I backed away from the door and prayed that the photographer would hurry.

He reboarded the train and we were under way again. Mother and I were getting hungry, so we decided, for old times' sake, to have lunch in the dining car. We were surprised to find it nearly empty. My childhood memories of dining cars on the Santa Fe Railway were that they were always bustling; last-minute tables were rarely available. After preparing our meals, the rotund chef, a Mexican Paul Prudhomme in a badly stained apron, resumed his poker game with the porters at the table across from ours.

Not long after lunch, the train pulled up to our destination: Posada Barrancas. The scent of sun-baked pine needles tinged the air as we disembarked to a narrow wooden platform. Within minutes a young man in a white shirt and black trousers hustled up and herded our small group into a van for the short uphill ride to the Hotel Posada Barrancas Mirador.

Mirador means "scenic viewpoint" in Spanish, and the Mirador certainly measured up to its name. Our room's rustic log balcony hung over a cliff and embraced an expansive view of the Sierra Tarahumara. Surrounding us on three sides was a testimonial to the Río Urique's handiwork: sheer canyon walls and craggy cliffs covered in cactus and desert scrub plunged six thousand feet to a verdant subtropical floor where thin fingers of jade-green water flowed.

A riot of stars crowded the sky that night. Their proximity shocked me awake when I poked my restless head out the sliding glass door around midnight. At four in the morning my mother woke up and began running back and forth to the bathroom. I plied her with an ample supply of Imodium, but lay awake fretting, knowing I'd never hear the end of it from my siblings if anything serious came of it.

By breakfast she was rallying. We dined on toast and tea and at nine o'clock she was outside wandering around in search of our tour guide.

WE TOOK AN UNINSPIRING TOUR of the logging town of Creel and some bizarre rock formations, and afterward our guide shuttled us back to the hotel. On the way I noticed my hands felt clammy. I began to sweat. Each new curve in the road provoked a profound queasiness in my stomach.

After a lunch of yogurt and more toast, I returned to our room and crawled into bed. I spent a listless afternoon tracking my rising temperature. By early evening, I was burning with fever and sprinting to the bathroom every five minutes.

My mother hurried out to the front desk to inquire about finding a doctor for me. The hotel manager, a man named Irving, assured her he would call one. Three more hours passed with the pestilence racking my body as Mother hustled back and forth to the front desk, reminding poor Irving about the doctor.

Night had fallen when we finally heard a soft knock at the door. Mother rushed to answer it. Irving, another young man who announced that he was a psychologist, and an aging doctor with rimless glasses, graying sideburns, and a thick mustache crowded into our room. Though curious, I was too lethargic to inquire about the presence of the psychologist.

Dr. Aragón set to work immediately. He gently prodded my belly while asking questions in Spanish about my symptoms. He took my pulse and then my temperature.

Dismay spread over his face as he mumbled: "*Más que 40 grados.*"

His speculative diagnosis was salmonella. A consensus was quickly reached among the huddle of men in our room when I told them we had eaten lunch on the train. According to Irving, there was no refrigeration in the train's kitchen, and people frequently got sick with food-borne illnesses. My heart sank, remembering the chicken sandwich I'd eaten for lunch.

With the closest hospital being back in El Fuerte, the doctor began setting up a makeshift clinic in our room. He bent coat hangers from which to hang an IV drip, as my mother drilled him with questions, in English, which he didn't understand. Her anxiety spread around the room, like overcharged electrons. It bounced off the walls and clustered in corners.

For nearly two hours I was pumped full of electrolyte solution and antibiotics while the three men sat there, discussing cars. Irving seemed to know the make, model, and current sticker price of every vehicle sold in Mexico. I drifted off to sleep. When I awoke a half hour later, they'd moved on to motorcycles.

The doctor finally drained the last liter of IV fluid into my arm. Being satisfied with the color of my tongue and turgidity of my limbs, he began to make out a bill for his services and the medications. Two hours of his time, two liters of IV solution, a week's supply of Bactrim, a lifetime supply of Imodium, a bottle of Tylenol, and a box of herbal tea came to a total of ninety-seven dollars.

After thanking them repeatedly in her feeble Spanish, my mother escorted the men out. I sat up for the first time since noon and laughed when Mother crowed: "It's a *milagro!*"

THE MIRACLE WAS SHORT-LIVED. We went to bed, but within an hour I was on the floor of the bathroom, spewing all that remained in my stomach, and losing an abundance of fluids.

For once in my life I was thankful that my mother is nearly deaf without her hearing aids, so I didn't disturb her as I rushed back and forth to the bathroom every fifteen minutes. After my tenth trip, I contemplated lying down in the shower rather than returning to bed but decided against it. It would only have increased her alarm if she were to discover me lying there.

In the morning she rushed out to the front desk once again, to find Irving and ask him to re-enlist the doctor's help. But Irving was off duty that day, and Mother had to pantomime her request to the woman staffing the front desk, who spoke minimal English. She eventually understood and called the doctor, who promised to send over two injections of anti-nausea medication. A nurse on the hotel's staff would come and administer them. At least that was what my mother *thought* the woman said.

Several hours passed. The injections arrived, but no nurse to administer them. An hour later, just as I was seriously considering injecting myself, a spirited young woman with a long black pigtail and wearing a white chef's jacket showed up at our door. She exuded an air of self-confidence and the odor of the fried fish served for lunch that day.

I greeted her meekly and asked, "*Usted es una enferma?*"

She looked puzzled for a moment. Then her face lit up.

"Ah!" she said, finally comprehending my error. "*En-fer-me-ra,*" she said, enthusiastically pronouncing each syllable of the correct word for nurse, rather than "sick female" as I'd said.

"No!" she told me. She was not a nurse.

"¿*Una medica?*" I asked.

"No! Really, I have no medical education," she said sincerely.

"Ah!" I said, as she stuck me with the needle. She may not have been one, but she administered the injection as well as any medical professional ever had.

THE NEXT MORNING I was finally on the mend, but still very weak, and there was one more problem. The Bactrim was wreaking havoc on the lining of my stomach. At breakfast Mother befriended a urologist from Mexico City and consulted him about my case. He recommended a different antibiotic. Back in our room, my mother trembled with excitement as she relayed his advice. She was certain that Cipro was the drug that would cure me. If we could only find some.

I rallied a little and, for the first time in two days, left the room and shuffled out to the front desk with her to inquire how we might obtain Cipro. The clerk told us that all the hotel vans were being used for morning excursions, and were not available to take us to the only pharmacy in the area which was 15 kilometers away. Try back around lunchtime, she said.

Mother quickly scanned the hotel's dusty parking lot and spied two women packing boxes of souvenirs into a battered blue Ford pickup. Seeing my mother make a beeline for them, one of the women began waving a red T-shirt in the air, thinking she was about to make another sale. I caught up to them in time to hear Mother say (in English):

"I need to find a *farmacia*. Can you drive me to a *farmacia*?"

When the woman looked baffled, my mother repeated her request, only louder. She offered to pay the woman ten dollars for the ride, and when the woman only looked more confused, I translated my mother's request. The woman's friend, who'd been silently watching the scene unfold with a bemused expression on her face, spoke up:

"*¿Porque, no?* Help the lady out!"

The friend and I stood side-by-side, watching my mother's platinum-blonde head pitch wildly about inside the cab as the truck jostled down the washed-out, boulder-strewn road.

"Watch out for the bumps!" the friend yelled after them.

"Buckle your seat belt!" I shouted feebly at my mother.

They traveled ten miles down the road to the neighboring town of San Raphael only to find the pharmacy closed. The T-shirt vendor pulled out her cell phone and dialed the number on the sign above the door. To my mother's delight, Dr. Aragón opened the door a few minutes later.

The T-shirt vendor stared in amazement as the good doctor greeted my mother like a long-lost friend. It turned out Dr. Aragón was not only the town's doctor, he was also its pharmacist and grocer. He concurred with the urologist. Cipro was the drug I needed, and he measured out a week's supply. Though he didn't want to charge her for it, Mother insisted on paying, and left a ten-dollar bill on the counter. She gave the T-shirt vendor twenty dollars when they arrived back at the hotel, and waved off the question of change. I took the prescribed dose of Cipro. Things began to look up.

THE FOLLOWING DAY we had to board a train for the nine-hour return trip to Los Mochis or risk missing our flight back to Guadalajara. Though still shaky, I felt stronger as the day went on. But by late afternoon, when the train was held up for hours by a boulder that had fallen onto the tracks, exhaustion began breathing down my neck. When the photographer and his wife offered us a ride from El Fuerte to Los Mochis in a private car they'd hired, Mother and I jumped at the chance to shave two hours off the trip. At ten o'clock that night, we gratefully descended El Chepe and waved good-bye to the Copper Canyon.

A day later, we were both recuperating at my favorite bed-and-breakfast in Tlaquepaque, a suburb of Guadalajara. I was nearly fully recovered, and Mother seemed relaxed, at last. I suspected she was looking forward to going home and resting up from her birthday trip, but my mother loves a good story and I knew she'd enjoy recounting this one to friends in the coming weeks and months.

In the chaos of the last few days, I'd completely forgotten about my "agenda."

But it didn't really seem to matter anymore. I think my mother felt a renewed confidence that her renegade youngest daughter still needed and appreciated her. And I realized that while she would always have difficulty demonstrating love and articulating her approval, I could always be certain of one thing: When I was down for the count, she was, and always had been, in my corner. What more could a grown woman ask of her nearly ninety-year-old mother?

That night at the Casa de las Flores, we lay in our beds like a couple of old friends, reminiscing about the past and sharing stories we'd never told each other. It was nearly midnight before we finally decided it was time to sleep. I got up to go to the bathroom and returned to bed.

"Night, Mom," I said.

"Good night," she replied, looking small and frail to me in her ancient, pale-blue nightgown. I reached over and turned out the bedside lamp.

Then, a moment later, she added: "Love ya, babe."

THE NEXT MORNING, after she left for the airport, I made a mental note to email Nick and tell him I'd met his friend Javier from Mazatlán. I wanted to tell him that my trip to the Copper Canyon had also been a bust, but that I thought I might get a story out of it anyway. I went downstairs to see if the inn's computer was free.

The first thing that popped up in my inbox was an email from Paul with BAD NEWS in the subject line. I felt irritated. To my husband, an incorrigible pessimist, bad news could be some-thing as benign as Nacho peeing on the living room carpet again. But this time it really was bad news. Nick was dead. He had died of heart failure, in a hospital in Athens, Greece, while on a writing assignment.

At first I could only stare at the screen in disbelief. Only slowly did the information sink in.

I emailed Paul back with a million questions. When I pressed the send key and the message "Your BAD NEWS has been sent" popped up on the screen, I burst into tears. Reflecting on the events of the past week I couldn't help but wonder — why Nick? Why not me? Why is it that one person can escape the hand of fate, but not another?

I TRUDGED BACK TOWARD MY ROOM and climbed the winding staircase. I lingered at the top, looking past the inn's gardens, which glistened in the morning sun. I looked past Tlaquepaque's bell towers, past Jalisco's agave-covered hillsides, to Mexico beyond. Like me, Nick Gallo loved this country. Maybe even more than his own.

As I stood there, taking comfort in a real and imagined landscape, I said a prayer for my friend. A plea to the Universe that his soul might find peace meandering along some undiscovered path in a Mexican paradise.

31 | *La Madrina*

B Y LATE 2008, finding steady work in San Miguel was becoming more difficult for our Mexican friends. My rentals at Casa Chepitos were also drying up. The Mexican economy, and especially San Miguel's, is inextricably tied to that of the United States. In the fall of 2008, when the American economy seemed on the verge of collapse, and mortgage lending had come to a near standstill, construction and real estate sales in San Miguel slowed with astounding swiftness. If the mortgage lending meltdown had been a punch in the gut to many people in the United States, it had KO'd our Mexican friends.

The majority of our neighbors on the callejón live hand-to-mouth, working in construction or at service jobs that begin and end on the whim of an owner or project supervisor. Only 25 percent of Mexico's working population has permanent, salaried jobs with benefits. Most people work for daily wages that are paid in cash. When work dries up, there's no unemployment insurance to fall back on. People literally go hungry if there is no work.

By early spring of 2009, the situation in San Miguel was becoming desperate. Many of our friends had been out of work for months and were having to find creative ways to make ends meet. I was shocked when I ran into a metal worker I knew. The man, who usually made intricately patterned lanterns for a living, was now selling jicama on street corners to get by.

"None of the shopkeepers are buying *faroles* right now," he said, looking demoralized. "I have to feed my family somehow."

Gracia's son Marcos and his cousin José had graduated from *preparatoria* (high school), but they could find only occasional odd jobs doing painting, plastering, or gardening work. They talked of going *al norte* to work with José's brother in Texas, but the coyotes now charged 25,000 pesos a person to cross, and that was beyond their reach.

Businesses throughout San Miguel were suffering. The Spanish language schools were in crisis. Many of them had reduced staff or hours or closed down completely. Once-lucrative galleries, boutiques, and tourist stands were struggling. Even San Miguel's most popular restaurants were languishing; many were nearly empty in the evenings.

JUAN AND LUPE, LIKE EVERYONE ELSE, fell prey to the bad economy. Juan was experienced, hardworking, and willing to do any kind of construction work, and still he couldn't find steady employment. He and Lupe were barely scraping by, and it was taking a toll on their dreams, especially their plan to marry. As Lupe's *madrina*, I felt obliged to ask her about their wedding plans.

"I want to get married for Gisela's sake, but we can't afford it," she said with a sigh. "Juan has so little work."

That night, I lay awake thinking about Lupe, and how, unlike most Mexican girls, she'd never had a *quinceañera*, the special party to honor her coming-of-age. There had been no rented *salon*, no fancy gown, no fiesta with drinking and dancing, no crowd of friends and family there to share the one special day that was all about celebrating *her*. The idea that her dream of a church wedding might also go by the wayside was unthinkable. Every girl deserves her day to shine, and I hated the idea that Lupe might never have her day. I thought long and hard about it that night, and debated with my conscience about what the right thing to do might be.

I considered the idea of offering to pay for the wedding myself. Hosting a simple Mexican wedding is something I could have afforded. A nice wedding in Mexico might cost a few thousand dollars, while the same wedding in Seattle would be upwards of $20,000. But my paying for the wedding didn't seem like the right thing to do. I was Lupe's friend, not her benefactor. Getting married wasn't essential to her security and well-being, like paying off the coyotes had been.

Around one o'clock in the morning, I finally came up with an idea I thought might work. It was loosely based on the old African proverb "It takes a village to raise a child." I figured that if a village could raise a child, why couldn't a callejón throw a wedding? The next day I discussed my idea with Lupe.

"As your *madrina*, I'm happy to chip in for the flowers and your dress," I said. "But maybe your family and Juan's and others in the callejón, could each provide something." I told her that way it would be more of a group effort. I envisioned a kind of giant potluck wedding.

Lupe took the idea and ran with it. She'd always been a great organizer, and when I returned in April for the Palm Sunday folk art market in Uruapan, she showed me the spiral notebook where she'd been making long lists of everyone who was willing to donate and what they were providing:

Her mom would supply the beer. Juan's family would prepare the dinner. Paola was buying the cake. In addition, Marcos and his girlfriend, Vicky; Lupe's cousins, aunts, and uncles; and other neighbors in the callejón had also committed to contributing something. But Lupe wanted me to pick the date. We looked at the calendar together and I picked Saturday, June 13, which we both prayed would arrive before the summer rains. We also made a date to go to Celaya, to shop for her wedding dress.

THE DRAB, WORKING-CLASS CITY of Celaya, Mexico, has little to recommend it to tourists. It's neither charming nor imbued with colonial history, like San Miguel or Guanajuato. The streets at the city's center are crowded and dirty and the outskirts clogged with American box stores. The familiar logos of Walmart, Costco, and Home Depot lining the highway outside town are what draw San Miguel's expatriate crowd to Celaya. The San Miguelenses themselves go there to attend technical schools, find work, or buy things, like wedding dresses, at significantly cheaper prices than in San Miguel.

Our search for Lupe's wedding gown began rather inauspiciously. I looked down at Cholo, wedged between Salvador and me on the front seat of the family's Ford Explorer, and realized we had a problem. Unlike my kids, who at age five would have whined and whimpered long before actually getting sick, Cholo had silently vomited into the lap of his soccer shorts. He sat quietly staring at the pool of slimy orange liquid filling his lap.

Luckily, his affliction turned out to be nothing more than a little car sickness. We cleaned him up with pockets-full of Kleenex, replaced his vomit-soaked shorts with an emergency pair bought at Costco (where we also found a dress for Gisela to wear in the wedding) and, in no time, we were back on the road.

As Salvador navigated narrow streets toward the center of town, I asked Cholo what he most wanted to do in Celaya.

"*Come nieve,*" he said. He wanted to eat ice cream.

"*¡Qué buena idea!*" roared Salvador. "You can throw that up on the way home!"

IT WAS LATE AFTERNOON by the time Salvador pulled the car to a stop on a corner of Celaya's tree-lined central plaza. Lupe, carrying Gisela, climbed out, and Gracia and I followed. We walked for several blocks, past taco stands, shoe stores, Mylar balloon vendors, and a *paletería de Michoacán*, to reach our destination: *la Calle de las Novias*. Loosely translated as Bridal Boulevard, the street was lined with shops offering everything a bride would need to celebrate the "once in a lifetime" occasion.

Old-fashioned floor-to-ceiling glass display windows lined the street, reminding me of ones I remembered from downtown Chicago in the 1950s. The displays brimmed with headless, armless mannequins sporting beaded bodices, trains of taffeta, flounces of chiffon, and great sweeps of satin. Strapless, spaghetti-strapped, and cap-sleeved costumes, stitched in pearls, seed beads, and sequins. Full-skirted fantasies.

In addition to the vast array of dresses, there was headgear worthy of Las Vegas showgirls, faux floral arrangements in every hue, lacy blue garters, little silver trays with silver coins, and other nuptial paraphernalia I couldn't imagine a possible use for.

In the first shop we entered, we were greeted by a Gloria Estefan wannabe with blonde-streaked hair, cutoff jeans, and four-inch heels. Gloria quickly sized Lupe up, grabbed a dress from the back, and shoved it at her. I could tell by the look on Lupe's face that she didn't like the dress. But that didn't dissuade the young woman.

"What have you got to lose?" she said. "Just try it!"

After a few minutes spent hassling with her, Lupe announced that we'd just begun our search, and we were off to the next bridal boutique.

We wandered down the street past a series of stores, each of them overflowing with dresses that had fitted, strapless bodices and ample skirts made from yards of cheap white polyester. But Lupe wanted an ivory-colored dress with cap sleeves, and I was hoping we could find a dress made of better-quality fabric than the cheesy polyester blends on display.

We found the largest selection of gowns at a store called Isabel's. A squadron of headless black mannequins in fancy dresses filled the store's four display windows. Lupe, Gracia, and I huddled together, pointing to the dresses we liked and discussing the merits of each. After a brief debate, Lupe tentatively selected one to try on. It was ivory satin and had the cap sleeves she liked. The tailored bodice had a tasteful embroidered design that was repeated at the bottom of an impressively full skirt. The three of us agreed: it was a very pretty dress. Gracia tracked down a salesclerk.

"That's the one," she said, pointing to the dress.

"I'd like it in ivory, please," Lupe added.

The saleswoman disappeared into the back of the store and, after a few minutes, returned with the dress in ivory for Lupe to try. In the tiny dressing room, it took all three of us to help her get into it. There's more fabric in a Mexican wedding dress than in the sails of the Niña, the Pinta, and the Santa Maria all together.

Once she was in the dress, it was obvious the bodice was too small. It might have fit the Lupe I'd known at age sixteen, but she'd put on weight since Gisela was born. She stood staring at the mirror in dismay, kneading her stomach as if that might make the newly acquired adipose tissue disappear, while the saleswoman strained to lace up the dress. When Lupe turned around to show us the back, Gracia noted that Lupe's T-shirt showed through the tightly stretched laces. Again we all agreed: the dress was too small. The saleswoman went in search of the next larger size while Gracia and I struggled to extract Lupe from acres of crinoline underskirts.

The saleswoman returned with the same dress in a larger size, only the new one was pure white. Not ivory like Lupe wanted. She tried it on anyway and it fit perfectly. Gracia and I stood back, eagerly oohing and aahing our approval of the lovely white dress. Lupe frowned and shook her head.

"I don't want a white dress," she said.

Gracia insisted that she liked the white dress. I did, too. The snowy white satin showed off Lupe's cappuccino-colored skin nicely. I told her I thought the dress looked pretty on her.

But when the furrow in Lupe's brow deepened, it occurred to

me what was bothering her. I remembered her telling me once that the color white symbolized the Virgin. She was reticent to wear white on her wedding day, not because she didn't like the color, but because it represented a purity she could no longer claim. With the manifestation of her sins toddling around the bridal reception in the pink-tulle party dress we'd just bought for her at Costco, it would be hard for Lupe not to feel like a hypocrite.

Her mother, who apparently didn't share her concern, persisted in promoting the white dress. Though Gracia is not one to break rules, especially those of the Catholic church, she's definitely willing to bend them to suit her needs. She and Lupe continued debating the issue for a few minutes. Then they looked at me. They wanted to know what *I* thought.

Being thrust into the role of moral arbitrator between mother and daughter was not something I'd signed on for. I had only agreed, as Lupe's *madrina*, to pay for the dress. While I stood there, searching for the right thing to say, I remembered a moment I'd shared with Gracia the summer before.

July 2008. We are standing in front of the bureau in Gracia's bedroom. She is looking for something — just what, I can't remember. She pulls out a box of old photos. Mixed among tattered black-and-white ones and a few school photos of her children, she finds one of her own wedding day.

"*Mira.*" Look, she says, handing it to me.

The cracked and faded color snapshot shows a doe-eyed Gracia in a white dress that fits tightly to her slim twenty-year-old waist. Salvador, looking uneasy, stands next to her. His hairstyle is vintage Beatles and he's wearing bell bottoms and a beige shirt with a giant collar. I turn the photograph over, read the date, and realize that Gracia and I have yet one more thing in common. Both of our firstborn children were conceived out of wedlock, at a time when it was considered disgraceful. Especially in conservative towns like San Miguel de Allende and Prairie Village, Kansas. Remembering the battle that ensued between my mother and me when I told her I was pregnant with his child but had no immediate plans to marry Paul, I wondered: Had there been angry words exchanged between Gracia and her parents when she'd confessed she was pregnant? Did she have qualms about wearing white on her own wedding day?

I LOOKED OVER AT HER AND LUPE, who were waiting for me to deliver a verdict.

"It's Lupe's wedding. I think she should have the dress she wants. Let's ask if we can order it in ivory."

It turned out we could order the dress in ivory, but the Easter-week discount would not apply. Gracia thought the full price of 3,500 pesos ridiculous and she began bartering with the saleswoman. Lupe signaled to me not to intervene.

"If we want to get it at a good price," she whispered, "you'll have to stay out of it." It's common knowledge that Mexicans pad prices for gringos.

Gracia bargained hard with the saleswoman, who eventually told her that she would have to consult the manager and disappeared. We waited for a while. I wandered down the street to buy water and some cookies for Gisela, who was getting fussy. Finally the woman returned.

"Sorry, but if we have to order the dress, the discount won't apply," she said.

Deflated, we left the shop and returned to the first one, where Gloria still lurked in the back. She eagerly stuffed Lupe into an ivory dress that was too short and too tight. Lupe looked miserable under the dim fluorescent light of the cramped dressing room. But Gracia was enthusiastic. "It's seven hundred pesos cheaper than the other one!" she crowed.

I began to wish I could wave a magic wand, like a more illustrious godmother, and make everybody happy. But not possessing her kind of powers, I did the only thing I could think of, and something I rarely do.

I ignored Lupe's advice.

Without a word, I left the shop and returned to Isabel's, where I found the saleswoman in conversation with the manager. She was still clutching the dress.

"Cual es el mejor precio por este vestido en beige?" I said, pointing to it and asking the manager in bumbling Spanish what her best price was for the dress in ivory. Having only withdrawn 3,000 pesos from my Lloyd's account, I wasn't bargaining just for the fun of it.

"I can't give you the discount if we have to order it," she insisted. "The underskirts alone are worth a hundred and seventy pesos. Plus there's the veil and the train, which we're throwing in for free."

We went back and forth, with me bargaining in broken, present-tense Spanish, while she looked down her slender Spanish nose at me. After a few minutes of getting nowhere, I looked her directly in the eye and switched into English.

"Listen. Do you want to make this sale or not?" I kept my gaze steady and gave her a moment to think about it. I'm not sure she understood a word I said, but she definitely got my point.

"Está bien, Señora," she said. We agreed on 3,000 pesos and I was relieved when she asked for only half down as a deposit.

I whipped out the required amount and slapped it down on the counter just as Gracia and Lupe returned with Gisela, our pink-tulle flower girl, in tow.

32 | *Outbreak*

LUPE HAD ARRANGED NEARLY ALL the wedding details. Since I was back in Seattle, she armed herself with a calling card and phoned weekly to update or consult me. The dress had arrived, the flowers were chosen, and the florist had her deposit; the mariachis had been retained; an extravagant four-tier wedding cake had been ordered from La Casita Feliz, the Happy House bakery on Calle Guadiana. Everything was going surprisingly smoothly, I thought, as Lupe chattered away at me, excited and happy. Then, in the midst all of the cheerful reports I was receiving, some upsetting news arrived that had the potential to derail our carefully laid plans.

I was on my computer one morning, searching for cheap flights back to Mexico in June, when Paul called to me from the other room, where he was also online, reading the *New York Times*.

"Hey, J, come here for a minute."

When I walked into the room, he scrolled down the page and pointed to the computer screen: "INFLUENZA OUTBREAK IN MEXICO," screamed the headline.

"Looks like we won't be going to San Miguel anytime soon," he announced.

"What do you mean we're not going to San Miguel?"

"They've discovered a new strain of a dangerous virus that has spread to Mexico. It's called H1N1, and it's more virulent than anything they've seen before. It attacks healthy young people.

We're not taking the kids down there." He made it sound as if the conversation were over.

"Well, I'm going to Mexico. I'm *not* going to miss the wedding." I was determined to be there for Lupe, despite my pessimistic husband.

Having had a doctor for a father, Paul began reading medical journals at age six. As a result, he tends to be somewhat of an alarmist when it comes to infectious diseases. He obsessively soaks fruits and vegetables — even bananas, melons, onions and garlic — in Microdyn when we're at Casa Chepitos.

I'm the one with the long history of food-borne illnesses. I've contracted salmonella three times in my life and had dysentery more times than I care to remember. But I have a tendency to dismiss things like flu epidemics as media hysteria.

"You're overreacting," I told my husband as he droned on about the perils of rogue viruses. I was certain that within a few days the hype over the flu bug would blow over and the media would be convulsing over some new and different issue.

But over the next couple of weeks, as President Calderón closed down schools, churches, museums, and government offices and halted almost all public services, it began to look doubtful that I would be returning to San Miguel any time soon. With photos of people in Mexico City wearing surgical masks splashed across every major newspaper, Paul wasn't the only person nervous about traveling there. Thousands of trips were canceled, to every part of Mexico — including tourist destinations like Puerto Vallarta, Cancún, Zihuatanejo, and San Miguel — places where there had been no confirmed cases of influenza. Tourism throughout the country came to a screeching halt, further damaging an already anemic economy.

But by the middle of May, when no full-blown plague materialized, schools and offices in Mexico City and the rest of the country began to reopen. People went out in public again, and thankfully, no large numbers of them fell ill with the new influenza that, by then, had been officially classified as a pandemic by the World Health Organization.

I emailed Miriam and Charlie, and they reported that while San Miguel looked and felt like a ghost town, health officials had yet to confirm a single case of the H1N1 virus in the area. I took my case up with Paul again.

"It's up to you if you want to go," he said, "but I still don't feel good about the kids going." We decided that he and Hannah would not come down for the wedding, but would come later if it seemed safe. I then talked it over with Will. Like me, he was determined to be at Lupe's wedding, so I booked tickets for the two of us. The upside was I found the cheapest fares to Mexico City I'd gotten in years. But the savings were canceled out when I hired a private car for the nearly three-hour drive from the airport to San Miguel. I wasn't going to risk being exposed to masses of potential flu carriers at Terminal Norte, Mexico City's megalithic, overcrowded bus station. Not even for Lupe.

OUR FLIGHT TO MEXICO, a few weeks after the country's worst influenza scare in decades, was not without incident. Will and I flew from Seattle to Los Angeles, and it was there in L.A. that the altercation around the H1N1 virus occurred. We arrived late and had to hurry to make our connection, and as we rushed to take our seats on the crowded plane, an angry American woman blocked our way. She was arguing with the flight attendant, insisting that a young Mexican boy be thrown off the plane because he had vomited. She was certain he was infected with the H1N1 virus.

"It's irresponsible of the airline to let him travel and infect the rest of us!" the woman shouted at the attendant. She refused to take her seat until the boy and his aunt had been escorted off the plane.

It turned out there was no room for my suitcase in the overhead compartment, so I took it back out to a waiting baggage handler on the jetway, where I found the teary-eyed and trembling boy huddled next to his aunt. They were waiting for a decision on whether they could travel with us or not.

"He have fear to fly; it what makes him sick," she said in broken English. "He never been in airplanes before."

"I'm so sorry this is happening to you," I said, shaking my head. It was the best response I could come up with. How do you explain, in only a few minutes and in a second language, how easily prejudice, when combined with fear and anxiety, can tip over into hysteria?

I never found out what happened to them. I only know that they did not fly to Mexico on that airplane.

After disembarking the plane at Mexico City's Benito Juárez airport, we were immediately accosted by three grave-looking officials in white lab coats carrying clipboards. They were stopping each passenger to ask a series of questions: Did we have a fever? Headache? Sore throat? Nasal discharge? Cough? Dizziness? Nausea? Since we could honestly answer no to all of the above, they allowed Will and me to pass. (A month later, Will would contract the H1N1 virus in Mexico, and unknowingly carry it to Belize, where he became very ill and was quarantined in a hotel room for four days. My husband was, unhappily, vindicated.)

It was a relief to find the driver from the shuttle service waiting for us after we were finally cleared by the posse from the Mexican Ministry of Health. Two hours and forty-five minutes later, as dusk was descending on the hills west of San Miguel, we pulled up to the mouth of Callejón de Chepito where we found Gracia and a small entourage of neighborhood boys waiting there to welcome us back and help with our bags.

33 | *The Godfather*

OUR FIRST MORNING BACK at Casa Chepitos, I was awakened by the avian symphony that performs regularly outside the window of our master bedroom. Amid the familiar trill of Señora Rosa's parakeets, the sweet song of Mexican finches, and the throaty warbles of turtledoves, I heard a birdsong I didn't recognize. The fellow was a real Pavarotti, and his heartfelt morning aria lovely. His range was astonishing, from tremulous high notes to low ones that ascended from the depths of his plumed breast. I went to the window, hoping to spot the feathered King of High Cs, but he was hidden among the jacaranda's foliage. His lovely song added to the feeling I had that morning —the same one I have each time I return to our Mexican home— it was good to be back.

Minutes later, the doorbell rang. It was Gracia, telling us that Lupe was coming in from the ranch in Santa Rosa and would be there around ten thirty. She urgently needed to talk with me, Gracia said.

Having no food in the house, Will and I decided to walk downtown for breakfast at the Café de la Parroquia on Jesus Street. I've learned from experience that time is fluid to my Mexican neighbors. When they say ten thirty, it could mean any time before noon. Or it might mean some time later. *Quien sabe?* Will and I were home from breakfast and our errands by twelve thirty, but we still waited most of the afternoon for Lupe to arrive. When she finally did, around three o'clock, she was flustered and red-faced from the heat and lugging Gisela uphill from *el centro*. As Gracia had said, Lupe did have a question for me.

"I wanted to see if Guillermo would be my *padrino*, since Paul isn't here," she said.

I was both surprised and amused that Lupe wanted Will, who is four months younger than her, to be her godfather. But I agreed to ask him.

"Since Dad isn't here, Lupe wants to know if you are willing to be her godfather in the wedding," I said to Will, who was busy blogging on the Internet.

"Sure, I'm happy to do it," he said, never looking up from the computer.

Will may have been perfectly nonchalant about it, but I wasn't. There were fewer than twenty-four hours until the wedding, and he'd brought no suitable clothing to wear as a member of a wedding party. I immediately dragged him back downtown to a bridal shop on the Plaza Cívica, and by an amazing stroke of good luck (most Mexican men are significantly shorter than my son), we found a dark-gray suit and a blue shirt that not only fit, but also looked great on him. I gave the saleswoman the required deposit and told her we'd be back in the morning to pick it up.

Like any bride the day before her big event, Lupe was stressed out from trying to keep track of so many details. But the question of how many chickens were needed for the *mole poblano* her in-laws were making seemed to be the most pressing issue on her mind. She spent the afternoon obsessing about the number of chickens she needed. Twenty or forty? Maybe thirty would do. She went back and forth, asking everyone's opinion. Finally, she settled on forty and called the order in.

"Forty chickens? Are they feeding the entire village of Santa Rosa?" I asked Gracia.

"The entire village will show up to eat, whether they're invited or not," she said.

Later that afternoon, Will joined Lupe, Marcos, and José as they piled into Paola's Ford F-150 for the chicken run. Gracia and I watched as they rumbled down the Cuesta de San José to gather and transport forty freshly plucked hens from the *pollería* on Mesones Street out to Santa Rosa. We then went back to her house to consult each other on our wedding attire.

She wanted me to help her choose between two possible outfits, and I was anxious to find out if she thought the dress I'd bought for the occasion was appropriate. As it turned out, both of us were probably pushing the envelope of what Emily Post would recommend the mother and godmother of the *novia* wear to the wedding.

There's something you need to understand here. I am not the dressing-up kind; I didn't even own a real dress. If I have to dress up, I usually choose from one of the vintage Japanese kimonos I've collected over the years.

I didn't think a kimono was quite right for a Mexican wedding, but I also thought being the only person there clothed in indigenous Mexican garb — my only other option — might seem a bit odd to my neighbors. So before leaving Seattle, I dragged Hannah downtown to Banana Republic to help me search for something suitable. When I overheard an older woman and her daughter speaking Spanish with Mexican accents, I begged their pardon and asked for their advice on what to wear to a Mexican wedding. The women didn't seem to mind at all, but Hannah, who at age fifteen found it excruciating when I struck up conversations with total strangers, watched in horror as I consulted them.

The older woman asked where in Mexico the wedding was to be held.

"San Miguel de Allende," I said.

"*¡Ah, que suerte, me encanta San Miguel de Allende!*" she exclaimed, clearly enamored of the town. She then asked what time of day the wedding was to be held, if it was a church wedding, and if we were invited to the reception. After answering her questions, she recommended a simple black cocktail dress.

"You can never go wrong with that," she said. I thanked her and bought a dress that fit her description: the only black cocktail dress I'd ever owned.

BACK IN GRACIA'S BEDROOM, she went to her closet and pulled out a beige three-piece suit and a scarlet skirt with white polka dots and a solid red short-sleeved jacket.

"Which do you think would be best?" she asked.

I demurred, guessing that in the States it would be considered a faux pas for the mother of the bride to wear a shockingly red outfit to her daughter's wedding. All the mothers I'd ever seen at weddings were dressed in pastels. But then I thought, *This is Mexico ... what do I know?* Clearly the beige suit was her second choice. I could tell she was dying to wear the red ensemble.

"I'd go with the red," I said.

I then described for her the simple black dress I'd bought and could tell by the look on her face that while a black cocktail dress might be *de rigueur* among Mexico's upper classes, Gracia found the idea of wearing black to a wedding a little morbid.

"I'm going to look like *una viuda negra*," I said. She laughed at the idea of me looking like a black widow.

The conversation digressed into undergarments and a discussion on the merits of girdles.

We lifted our shirts and compared the striations crisscrossing our flabby bellies, neither of which had ever been the same since the births of Lupe and Will. We both needed girdles to hold in our *panzas*. She proudly held up the one she'd borrowed for the occasion for me to admire.

THAT EVENING, I sat on the stoop in front of the store, watching a familiar Friday-night scene unfold in the alley. Marthín, Cholo, and a swarm of boys were kicking a soccer ball up and down. An occasional teenager on a motorcycle raced through, scattering their game. Paola's miniature poodle ran loose, barking at the motorcycles and soccer players until they chased him off. The corn-on-the-cob vendor wandered down the alley hollering "*¡Eloooo-te!*"

A group of *albañiles*, covered in calc and looking worn out from the week's construction work, gathered on the steps near me, drinking beer, eating peanuts, and spreading the shells everywhere. Everyone from our neighborhood seemed to be around that night, coming and going from the store in search of snacks, beer, or sodas, or looking for Lupe or Gracia. Only our dear neighbor Señora Rosa to the South was missing. She was in San Antonio, too sick and weak to make the trip back for Lupe's wedding.

Sitting there, I felt as if I were watching the final act of a comedic play, the kind where all the characters who have been running on and off stage throughout the evening converge for the big finale. If I were a director, this would be my *mise en scéne*. It was our callejón, the way I love it most.

As I took in the scene, I began thinking about how much had changed since we first arrived on Callejón de Chepito. In the past few years, we'd witnessed a mini baby boom on our alley. Teresa, Lupe, China, and Mario, all teenagers when we'd first moved in, were now young adults with babies of their own. Culito, a goofy kid with a perpetually runny nose, had grown a mustache and was now selling homemade donuts for a living. Marthín, only six when we'd first arrived, was a hulking thirteen-year-old, and Cholo, the baby, would soon be entering kindergarten. Marcos and José, eleven-year-olds when Will first played baseball with them, now sported goatees. Will himself had graduated from university and would start graduate school in the fall. José, Marcos, and Will leaned against the wall of Casa Chepitos, talking and joking with each other, the age difference no longer obvious.

Teresa's four-year-old daughter Ilse, a little girl as curly haired and dimpled as Shirley Temple, bounced up to me and began practicing her English. "Hello," she said, "My name is Ilse." She entertained the crowd gathered on the steps by launching into an English ditty she'd learned in preschool, and hopping from foot to foot in a little dance.

Lupe came over and sat down next to me. Gisela hovered about, whining and clinging to her mother. The two-year-old was tired and stressed from all the activity. Lupe seemed irritated with her daughter, which was unusual.

"Are you doing okay?" I asked.

"I'm really nervous about tomorrow," she said. "There will be so many people!"

I took her hand in mine and reassured her that everything was going to be fine.

"You and Juan will be surrounded by people who love you. Everyone there will be wishing the best for both of you. Nothing could be better than that."

But as it turned out, I was wrong. There was something better.

34 | *The Wedding*

T HE WEEK BEFORE THE WEDDING, I began to worry about having picked June 13 for Lupe's big day. Thirteen is a lucky number for me and Friday the thirteenth my lucky day. Friday, May 13, 1994, was the day a Korean social worker walked off a plane at Sea-Tac airport and placed four-month-old Hannah in my arms.

In June of 2009, however, I thought maybe the number thirteen wasn't going to be so lucky. In the days prior to leaving Seattle for Mexico, I'd checked the weather online and discovered thunderstorms were predicted all week. Each day I checked it again, but the stormy forecast never changed. I knew that if the predictions were correct, the dusty, unpaved courtyard in front of Lupe's house, where the reception was to be held, would quickly turn into a pit more suited for mud wrestling than a wedding reception.

As is often the case, my worrying was for naught. By a stroke of good luck, June 13 broke clear and sunny. In fact, when the thermometer hit thirty degrees centigrade at eleven in the morning, I worried that Lupe might melt like an expensive bar of chocolate under all those layers of crinoline and satin. But at least it wasn't going to rain.

The alley was bustling that morning. Will ran down to the market to buy a cheap pair of black shoes and to pick up his rented suit and I wandered over to Gracia's to see how things were going with the bridal preparations. Lupe's old bedroom, now the domain of her brothers Marcos and Marthín, had been turned into a makeshift beauty salon. A brood of wide-eyed little girls sat quietly on the beds, with their mouths hanging open, as Lupe's aunt performed a miracle of updos on her, Gracia, and Gisela.

Lupe, who was in the middle of being coiffed, called out to me.

"¡Hola Judith! Do you want Lola to do your hair, too?"

"No, gracias," I said. It was too hot to fuss with lacquering my unruly mane.

Gracia was already done up, and as Will said later that day, she looked *the bomb*. Her hair had been pulled back in a cluster of tight curls and she was wearing makeup that looked as if it were professionally applied by the women at the Estée Lauder counter at Nordstrom. In the eight years we'd been friends, I'd never seen her in makeup and with her hair all done up. I agreed with Will, Gracia looked pretty darn glamorous.

MID-AFTERNOON we gathered for photos at Remedios's house. Everyone was in full wedding regalia: Will, tall and handsome in his gray suit and blue shirt and tie; Lupe, the picture of elegance in her ivory satin gown with flowing skirts; Gracia's three sons, dressed in clean, collared shirts and freshly pressed jeans; and little Ilse in a powder-pink chiffon dress with her hair interwoven with tiny silk rosebuds. After the brief photo session, we headed out to the bright red SUV belonging to Esteban and Teresa for the ride to Santa Rosa. When Lupe nearly tripped on her skirts stepping out the front door, I asked Will to escort her to the car. He extended a bent arm, and she gracefully slipped her hand through it. As they walked arm in arm down the alley, I reached for my camera. The photo is still a favorite and a sweet reminder of how far they have both traveled, emotionally and physically, since that first day in front of Casa Chepitos in 2002.

THE REAR OF THE SUV was filled with floral bouquets and the hot air inside infused with the heady scent of wilting roses and oriental lilies. Since seven of us had to squeeze in, we decided that Lupe's hoop skirts would have to go. I helped her step out of the crinoline underskirts on the sidewalk next the car as Will hopped in up front with Esteban. After bundling the mesh underskirts into a giant ball, Lupe, plus Teresa, Ilse, another little girl, and me, crowded into the back seat for the thirty-minute ride to Santa Rosa.

Shortly after turning off the Querétaro highway and onto the road leading into Santa Rosa, Esteban pulled the car off to the side. He and Will and Teresa got out and began pulling floral arrangements out of the back. They attached enormous bouquets of white roses, oriental lilies, chrysanthemum, and baby's breath to the hood of the car with packaging tape. Smaller bouquets were taped to the windows and to both sides of the car. When they were done, Lupe's bridal chariot was covered in white flowers. Esteban steered us slowly down all four of Santa Rosa's simple, unpaved streets.

We parked opposite the village church. Its façade was whitewashed and the simple entryway painted sky blue — the color of the Virgin Mary. In the flagstone courtyard, a group of Lupe's and Juan's family and friends were gathered in the shade of the jacarandas.

Between the car and a school playground, I helped Lupe slip the underskirts on and Teresa smoothed the satin train and arranged the head piece and veil. Once we had her altogether again, Lupe looked lovely. As graceful and beautiful as any bride I'd ever seen. We then headed across the street toward the church and I spotted Juan standing under its arched entryway, dressed in a lavender shirt and a gray suit just like Will's. Lupe's soon-to-be husband looked small and scared, and suddenly very young.

Lupe had a few last-minute instructions for Will and me. She surprised us with the news that, as her *padrinos*, we were to sit in the place of honor in front of the altar, directly behind her and Juan. It was only then that I realized, unlike other weddings I'd attended, there were no bridesmaids or groomsmen at this one. It was the godparents who would stand up for the *novios*. Will and I were *it*.

"You'll be offered communion," Lupe said. She told us that after the priest offered us the host, we were to repeat, "*El cuerpo y la sangre de Cristo*." The body and blood of Christ. I repeated the line silently in Spanish several times, trying to commit it to memory.

Having been baptized and confirmed in the Episcopal church, I took communion every Sunday for years. Though Will was baptized at St. Mark's Episcopal Cathedral in Seattle, he had never been confirmed or attended church, except on the rare occasion. My children have mostly fallen under Paul's spiritual influence — who, as the popular Mexican saying goes, *es un ateo, gracias a Dios* (is an atheist, thanks to God). Still, Will seemed to be taking his new responsibilities seriously, nodding at Lupe's advice as if he knew exactly what she was talking about.

When a critical mass of friends and relatives had formed and the guitarist had finally been located, we proceeded into the church. Inside, it was pleasantly cool and ornately gilded for a small parish. Above the altar was a blue and white statue of the Virgin cradling baby Jesus. A cluster of golden cherubim hovered above them, but at the Virgin's feet there was a scary-looking papier-mâché devil's head that was painted black with bulging white eyes and huge bloody fangs. The Blessed Mother triumphing over evil.

A quartet of singers who had difficulty carrying a tune and the lone guitar player sat in a balcony above and serenaded Lupe and Juan as they walked down the aisle. Will and I followed closely behind, again per Lupe's instructions. The rest of their family and friends followed us. Parents and siblings gathered on their respective sides of the church, Lupe's on the left and Juan's on the right.

The officiating priest, Padre Lupito, had grown up around

the corner from the callejón, which practically made him family according to Gracia. The shaggy-haired *sacerdote* looked over-dressed in his ivory-colored woolen robes. Sweat rolled down his cheeks and into his graying beard as he launched into the sermon. He alternated between reciting lengthy reminders to the bride and groom about the responsibilities of marriage, and speed-reading the liturgy, as he swatted at flies and wiped sweat from his brow with his sleeve. I followed his Spanish well enough to genuflect at all the right moments, but halfway through the sermon, my knees began to ache and swell. The bare pine kneeler was torture on my bony knees. When we finally stood to take communion, I felt like shouting *Hallelujah!*

I lined up behind Lupe, Juan, and Will to receive communion, and was so awed by my son's impersonation of a devout Catholic taking communion that when it came my turn, I completely for-got my only required line of dialogue. When offered the host, I thanked the priest. In English.

We returned to our seats in order to pray and genuflect some more. When Padre Lupito finally posed the culminating ques-tion, "Do you, María Guadalupe, take Juan Jesús ... ," my aching knees were incredibly grateful.

AFTER THE WEDDING MASS WAS OVER, family members queued up in front of the altar to be photographed with the bride and groom. I noticed that no one, other than little Ilse with her child-star coyness, cracked the slightest smile during the photo session. Deadpan seems to be the standard expression in for-mal Mexican photographs, no matter what the occasion. Lupe, Juan, and the rest of their families wore the same poker faces as the nineteenth-century daguerreotypes of my starched-collared great-great-grandparents.

An uncle of Lupe's — a man who resembled the stone-faced men who rode with Pancho Villa in the Revolution of 1910 — was particularly stoic. To me, his unsmiling face seemed strangely out of sync with the happy occasion.

On the other hand, it occurred to me that the smiley American wedding entourages — with their expensive orthodontia and artificially whitened teeth — might look like a bunch of grinning hyenas to the Mexicans.

When every possible family member had been photographed with the newlyweds, we followed them out to the sun-baked courtyard where a band of mariachis in silver-studded black pants and jackets were playing songs I recognized from evenings spent in the *jardín*. Their lead singer, a young man who looked like Errol Flynn with his slicked-back hair and thin mustache, launched into an ardent version of "La Malagueña." I couldn't tell if it was the heat or the tenor's silky voice making me light-headed.

Family and friends swarmed Juan and Lupe as they exited the church. Everyone wanted their turn to embrace and congratulate them. This took a while since Gracia has eight brothers and sisters and Salvador has nine. Not all of their siblings had come, but I recognized Salvador's mother, and at least six of his brothers and sisters, and several of Gracia's. I too wanted to hug Lupe and wish her well, but I stood off to the side, in order to let family members congratulate her first.

The crowd around her had finally thinned out and I'd begun to move toward her, when Salvador suddenly appeared and placed his arms around his daughter. I felt like a voyeur, standing there watching. But I couldn't turn away. It was the first physical sign of affection I'd ever witnessed between them and I stood transfixed as Salvador pulled his daughter closer and whispered something into her ear. Their embrace grew more intense for a moment. Then, as suddenly as he had appeared, he was gone. Lupe turned toward me, and I saw her eyes filling with tears. When I held out my arms, she collapsed into them.

Months later, in a private conversation on the terrace at Casa Chepitos, I finally learned what Salvador had said to his daughter. But watching them embrace each other that day, I knew I was witnessing a moment of grace.

A moment when all that was hard between them softened; when years of contention and misunderstanding melted away; and forgiveness, in all its wisdom, had finally triumphed.

Part Four | *El País*

La amistad sincera es un alma repartida en dos cuerpos.

MEXICAN PROVERB

35 | *May Day 2010*

"¡**O**BAMA, ESCUCHA! ¡ESTAMOS EN LA LUCHA!" the crowd chants, and I chant along, imploring President Obama to listen up and take our fight seriously. It's May Day 2010, and I'm in Seattle marching down Jackson Street surrounded by a sea of Mexicans, with Guatemalans, Hondurans, and Nicaraguans scattered among them. Only a handful of other non-Latinos, like me, have shown up to march.

A half hour earlier, I'd asked Paul to drop me off at Judkins Park, so I could join what I'd assumed would be a small group of protesters demonstrating against Arizona's new anti-immigration laws. But a great swell of people was already flowing westward down Jackson Street by the time I arrived, and it grew larger by the minute as people with strollers and signs and Mexican flags funneled in from the side streets. From Twenty-Third Avenue clear down to Eighth Avenue in the International District, masses of people were marching in solidarity. Banners identifying home states in Mexico were held high and with evident pride. Zacatecas, Oaxaca, Guerrero, Michoacán. For nearly everyone there, English was clearly a second language.

A boy marching nearby, maybe eight or nine years old and wearing a Mexican soccer jersey, stares as I march along, chanting in Spanish.

"Why does she speak like us?" I hear him ask his father.

Porque ella tiene el corazón de una Mexicana, I want to tell him. It's what Gracia once said about me when someone in the callejón asked why I always sided with the Mexicans on immigration issues.

I strike up conversations with the people around me as we march along. A young man from Zacatecas proudly shows me his ID card from the King County Parks Department. He tells me he, too, crossed the border illegally but eventually managed, through great effort, to obtain a green card and a job as a gardener for the county.

"I can't believe how many Americans have come out to march," he says, pointing to the three or four white people visible in the crowd of marchers.

"Americans are brown-skinned too," I remind him, thinking not only of the many Latino Americans living in Seattle but also of my daughter, Hannah, and her friends who are Asians, Pacific Islanders, Ethiopians, and African Americans. He nods and chuckles at my increasingly truthful statement. The one some Americans are loath to acknowledge.

"*¡Un pueblo unido, jamás será vencido!*" He chants the phrase slowly so I can catch hold of it.

I do, and we march on, chanting in unison, reminding anyone who will listen that a people united can never be defeated. If only we Americans could ever truly achieve the united part.

The part even this country's founding fathers lacked the will to resolve.

Just beyond the Fairmont Olympic Hotel on Fourth Avenue, we pass an affluent-looking Latina who appears to be about my age. She is standing on the corner, dressed in a navy-blue business suit and high heels. As we file by, I notice tears rolling down her cheeks as she stands silently watching the marchers. I wonder, what is her story? How long has she lived in the United States? Twenty years? Forty? Did her parents or grandparents cross the border illegally?

It seems America has been good to her, at least financially. But what had it cost her and her family emotionally? Had it cost them the loss of country, identity, and language? Had it cost them a sense of belonging, of rootedness, and history? Was that the price they'd had to pay? The price so many immigrants, legal or illegal, pay. And I wonder if, after paying such a price, were her parents or grandparents then treated like criminals, or as dangerous, disingenuous, and untrustworthy? I imagine her tears would fill a lifeboat.

The march ends by the grassy slopes of the Olympic Sculpture Park and the crowd begins to disperse. When a young woman from Guerrero, pushing a three-month-old in a stroller, walks over and thanks me for marching with them, I too feel like crying.

IN THE YEAR following Lupe and Juan's wedding, a renewed anti-immigration sentiment swept the States, and the response in Washington, D.C., was more fractious than ever. At the same time, drug violence in Mexican border towns and in the state of Tamaulipas exploded, threatening to unravel the loose weave of the country's social fabric.

Yet life on Callejón de Chepito plodded along at the same relaxed pace. Children in school uniforms with books tucked into their backpacks wandered off to school each morning while their mothers gathered to gossip in the alley. On weekends young and old men alike continued to gather outside our front door, drinking until bleary-eyed, while lively *ranchera* music blared from Mario's speakers at Señora Rosa to the North's house.

Our travels around Mexico and life in San Miguel were mostly unchanged by the fury to the north, except for the negative effect the news coverage was having on San Miguel's economy. Fewer Mexicans were attempting to cross the border to work in the States, causing Salvador and other *albañiles* who lived on the callejón to complain about the men from poorer areas of Mexico who were flooding San Miguel's construction sites with their own cheaper labor. Tourism continued on a downward trend throughout Mexico, as the media spotlighted stories of violence between the drug cartels and government forces. Many of my American friends, even the more adventurous ones, were concerned about traveling in Mexico.

Expatriate friends in San Miguel were also experiencing the fallout from the bearish financial and construction markets. Miriam's husband, Charlie, had finally secured a work permit to sell real estate in Mexico, but business was slower than slow. It was almost nonexistent. Few people were arriving to build or buy new houses; more were trying to sell and get out. Ready for their experiment in life across the border to be over and done with.

Our experiment with life across the border, or a more full-time life across the border, was at last, only a few years away. Hannah would be off to college in the fall of 2012, leaving Paul and me free to live in Mexico for a greater part of the year.

But in the summer of 2009, only a few weeks after Lupe and Juan's wedding, we discovered something distressing: the lovely Casa Chepitos had a major structural defect. It seemed my dream of retiring to Mexico might crumble right before my eyes.

36 | *Escombro*

M Y BEAUTIFUL MEXICAN HOME, with its own cacophony of colorful folk art, sweeping views, and charming gardens, had delighted friends, family, and renters for years and was still the place I most loved coming home to. But Casa Chepitos had never been the Eden I'd originally imagined.

All the problems of owning a home in a distant and foreign country haunted me, as my mother predicted they would.

The challenges of managing a house from three thousand miles away began with having to change property managers three times in the first four years. Finding the right advertising sites and renters for the house had been more difficult than I initially thought, and would have been impossible without the Internet. I also soon discovered that managing the house's various utilities and financial accounts from afar was a nightmare.

Something was always in need of repair. Within a year of buying the house, the exterior paint began to peel, and we had to have the house repainted. The dishwasher drain often clogged up and the kitchen would flood. The second year, when temperatures in December dipped below freezing, the pipes burst in the master bath. The entire house flooded that time.

Every summer, during the rainy season, we were plagued by scorpions. Casa Chepitos seemed to be a preferred refuge for the small, brown, stinging arthropods. We found them everywhere — on the walls, on the spiral staircase, on the kitchen floor, in the sinks, in the showers, in our clothing. One night I pulled back the covers on my bed and found one nestled between the sheets. Needless to say, I didn't sleep much that night.

In addition, our electricity went out at random. Even when the rest of the callejón had power, we'd be sitting in the dark at Casa Chepitos. Once, when the lights went out, we discovered that every even-numbered breaker had power, while the odd-numbered ones didn't. The best electricians in town had no answer for why *that* was happening.

And while rentals were robust in the early years, the economic downturn and a surge of rental houses in the market (nearly every American who owns a home in San Miguel rents it out), reduced our rentals to a trickle by the late 2000s. My mother had been right in assuming that Casa Chepitos would be a burden to manage. Ultimately, it was a bust as a business proposition.

But none of this troubled me too much. I loved the house in spite of everything and only hoped it would continue to generate some income to help defray expenses until we could retire and manage it ourselves, which was less than three years away. Everything that had come before, however, was nothing compared with our latest problem, the one that had the potential to derail my dream of retiring in San Miguel.

IT BEGAN WITH a long diagonal crack in the southwest corner of the living room, next to the picture window that overlooks the Parroquia. While the house, being made of stucco, had always had small cracks here and there, this particular crack was seven feet long and nearly an inch wide in the middle. At the same time we found the crack, I noticed one day that I could see daylight where the beams that supported the ceiling in the master bedroom went through an exterior wall, and that the tiles in the shower of the master bath were spontaneously cracking and pulling away from the surface. Upon closer inspection, Paul and I found that both the bathroom and bedroom walls were separating from the exterior wall where they met at the corners. Taken all together, the appearance of all of these cracks and fissures pointed to one thing: Casa Chepitos was sinking, or at least shifting, toward its southwest corner. When Paul started in with his dire predictions of how the house was liable to soon fall down, it was hard to ignore him. The evidence seemed overwhelming.

As usual, I looked to Gracia for help and she again came to my rescue by sending over Salvador to consult with us.

"*La casa era construido encima de la escombro,*" he said, confirming our own diagnosis.

The house had been built on fill, and it was settling. But why was it settling ten years *after* it had been built? He suggested we inspect our twenty-foot-tall retaining wall, to see if it was failing.

We followed him around the corner, along the Cuesta de San José and down another callejón below, to the property that abuts ours to the west. It's where the barking dogs, bleating goats, and time-challenged roosters live.

"*Felipe Paz-Infante, a sus ordenes,*" the owner of the urban menagerie said with a little bow when Salvador introduced us.

Señor Paz-Infante was a scarecrow of a man in tattered trousers and a button-down shirt that hung limply from his narrow, hunched shoulders. He wore dusty *huaraches* on his feet. On numerous occasions I'd watched him from our terrace as he scratched in the dirt or pounded nails for hours into various remnants of lumber. But nothing ever seemed to sprout on his rocky, barren property, nor did anything come of his efforts at pounding and tapping. He appeared a rather hapless man, one who maybe wasn't quite all there. Salvador, by comparison, is a handsome, robust man with a quick wit, who was dressed that day in neatly pressed blue jeans, a clean white T-shirt, and brand-new Nikes. Next to his less fortunate compatriot, he looked like a descendant of Chichimec royalty.

It was interesting to see Casa Chepitos from below, and it consoled Paul and me to see that our retaining wall was still doing its job. But what I remember most about our encounter that day with our neighbor to the west was how impressed I was by the way Salvador treated him.

Mexican society — like India's — is very stratified. People in higher classes, especially those with lighter skins, are often condescending toward those of a lower class. People with darker skins or less education are, at times, severely mistreated and are often slighted or ignored. Though the two men's skins were the same medium brown, and Salvador had little formal education, he was clearly far closer to being middle-class than Señor Paz-Infante would ever be. But Salvador treated his neighbor with respect that day and spoke with him as an equal, something I hadn't expected. It made me admire Salvador even more, and also reflect on my own stubborn prejudices and assumptions.

TO FOLLOW UP on our quest to discover why the house was sinking, Salvador suggested we talk with someone who had worked on it. Since he and Gracia know practically everyone in San Miguel, it came as no surprise that Salvador played soccer on weekends with the man who had been the construction supervisor for Casa Chepitos. He agreed to bring the fellow by within the next few days so we could find out how the house had actually been constructed and what we were up against.

I was out with Hannah and her friend Tamara the day Salvador brought his teammate over to talk with Paul. Though Paul's Spanish and their English were limited, the three of them managed, with a few words and a lot of pantomiming, to discuss how the foundation of our three-story house had been constructed.

The *maestro de obra* for the construction of Casa Chepitos explained that three concrete pilings had been poured into the *escombro*, or fill dirt, that the back half of our house sits on. The footing that forms the perimeter of the house rests on them. But when Paul asked how large the pilings were and how deep they went, he discovered exactly what the problem was. The pilings

— according to the man's hand gestures — were no bigger than breadboxes.

Paul, Salvador, and the maestro were in agreement: the proper way to construct a piling for a house built on fill would have been to pour larger ones, down to the bedrock, which in our case was ten to fifteen feet below ground level. According to the maestro, the tiny pilings were specified on the architect's drawings. After I returned and the maestro was gone, Salvador looked at me with a glimmer of amusement and said, "You know the architect on this house was a woman, don't you?"

"I knew I could depend on you to bring that up!" I said, half wanting to laugh, and half to cry.

WE CALLED CHARLIE, who put us in touch with his contractor friend Norberto, who brought in a structural engineer to assess the situation. My vocabulary of Spanish construction terms grew exponentially over the next few weeks: *grieta, escombro, maestro, ingeniero estructural, construir, arreglar, echar los cimientos.* Words I'd hoped never to need.

The experts all came to the same conclusion: the supports for the foundation of our house were inadequate, and new pilings would have to be poured beneath the footing wall. The entire courtyard patio would have to be dug out, all of the plants and trees removed, and the house reinforced above, in order to dig fifteen-foot-deep holes to pour the new pilings. Norberto's estimate for the cost of all of this? About the same amount it would cost to send Hannah to a private college for a year, maybe two years of college at a state school. Since we were not a fount of cash, particularly with the recent tanking of the stock markets, we had to choose between educating our daughter and repairing the house. There was never any doubt of what our priority was. Though the house was clearly sinking, Paul and I both knew that saving for Hannah's education was more important than saving Casa Chepitos. The repairs would have to wait.

We hired Salvador to patch and paint the cracks and fissures, and repair the broken tiles and gaping holes, and held our breath, hoping that the house wouldn't fall down before we could afford to have the needed pilings poured. Throughout the ordeal, Gracia was the only one among us who remained persistently optimistic.

"The house just had a little settling to do," she said cheerfully, "I'm sure it's alright now!"

37 | *Fiesta*

WHENEVER SHE HAS SOMETHING with even the slightest hint of emotional resonance to ask or tell me, Gracia sends Lupe over as her emissary. Just as she did one day in late October 2009.

"My mom and I would like to host a luncheon for you and your friends. We want to thank you for everything you have done for us," Lupe said. She told me Gracia was planning to make *pollo en mole poblano* for my houseguests and me.

I was touched by their thoughtfulness and told Lupe that I would like to provide dessert. She then mentioned that we could also watch the video of her wedding, which I'd been hoping to see for months. It had taken her a while to save the money to pay off the videographer, and she'd just gotten the DVD out of hock.

We agreed that the luncheon and video showing would take place at Casa Chepitos. I had four friends from Seattle staying with me at the time, and Lupe also invited Wendy, another neighbor from the callejón. There wasn't room at Gracia's for such a crowd.

However, there was a little something that worried me. While I appreciated the idea of it, I was concerned about Gracia going to all the trouble of making Mexico's most popular festival dish, *mole poblano de Guajolote*. I knew, from the cooking classes I'd taken with Chef Felix at the Centro Bilingüe, that a good mole could take hours and dozens of ingredients to make.

In addition to three or four kinds of chiles, a traditional mole sauce includes at least seven different spices plus chocolate, garlic, onions, tomatoes, almonds, raisins, ground up tortillas, and more. For the wedding reception, Juan's mother and sisters had spent two days making mole over open fires in *cazuelas* (clay basins so large you could bathe babies in them). It was deliciously thick and rich and spicy. But I didn't feel Gracia should have to make such an effort for my sake, so I went over to discuss it with her. I found her at the back of the house, in her kitchen.

"You shouldn't trouble yourself with making mole — it's way too much work!" I said.

"Oh no, it's not any trouble at all," she said, reaching into the refrigerator and pulling out a large white plastic tub. The name *Emperador* was printed across it in bold blue letters.

"It's the best, much better than homemade," she assured me.

Yet another way that Gracia and I think alike. I'm always on the lookout for recipes that make it look as if I've gone to great effort, but in reality can be thrown together in a half hour or less.

AT EXACTLY TWO O'CLOCK the following day, Gracia arrived, dressed in the beige suit she'd passed on wearing to the wedding. She and Lupe began ferrying platters of cooked chicken, pots of rice and mole, a sieve full of salad greens, and a bag of sesame seeds across the alley.

I removed our everyday oil cloth and set the rustic pine table with brightly colored woven mats, bouquets of alstroemeria, and a scattering of votive candles. I gave Gracia eight of my best dinner plates, and she set to work assembling the plates of *pollo con mole* and sprinkling them with the sesame seed garnish. It was fun to watch her in yet another role in which she is so completely competent.

The elegantly plated food was delicious, but while my American friends ate the chicken with mole sauce, I noticed they pushed aside the leaves of romaine. Even though I had assured them that Lupe had assured me the lettuce had been thoroughly cleaned, they still wouldn't touch it.

After lunch we watched the video of the wedding and reception. Seeing people and scenes of the reception on our TV reminded me of how congenial that evening had been.

There was Salvador sauntering up to Gracia on the dance floor and shaking his hips in a sexy move, as she walked away in disgust. There was the sound of the chickens that had taken refuge in the pomegranate trees above, clucking their disapproval as the guests played raucous wedding games below. During the first one, Juan was tossed in the air over and over, like a scarecrow, by a mob of energetic young men, while Will raced around trying to make sure his head didn't hit the ground. In a game they call *la víbora*, a chain of dancing guests attempted to knock Lupe off a folding chair she stood on, while another group of us fended them off. I got knocked to my knees in an effort to keep her dress from flying over her head when she fell off the chair. Lupe's aunt Lola, a masseuse I've hired on occasion, pulled me out of the fray, "*¡Judith, está demasiado peligroso para ti!*" she said, worried I'd get hurt.

There were the two little girls who shadowed me half the night, holding my hands, stroking my blonde hair, and asking me a million questions about life in the States. And another blue-eyed, twelve-year-old siren — the Dancing Queen I called her — who for some unknown reason suddenly grabbed me by the hands and pulled me onto the unpaved dance floor. The girl jitterbugged and two-stepped, swinging and strutting as if we were participants in Santa Rosa's own *Dancing with the Stars*. She had all the moves, and I did my best to keep up, having once been quite the jitterbugger myself. But I don't think it was me she was so eager to impress. I believe it was the row of adolescent boys in the audience, their black hair hardened to pointy perfection with styling wax, whom she hoped to wow with her dancing prowess.

There was the lively debate between Paola and our neighbor

Jesús, in Lupe and Juan's kitchen, over whether Lucy Núñez, San Miguel's first female mayoral candidate, was qualified to govern.

"I have nothing against a woman being mayor!" Jesús exclaimed too loudly and one time too many to be believed.

Methinks thou dost protest too much — the popular misquote of the famous line in Hamlet — came to mind. But it was so late and I'd had so much beer, there was no way the words for it were going to come to me in Spanish. Instead I asked Jesús to keep his voice down, so he didn't wake the children who were asleep on Lupe's bed in the next room.

There was discovering, at midnight, that there were no more paper plates when the four-tiered wedding cake was brought out. No forks or spoons either. Lupe and her sister-in-law served up mammoth slices of the moist white cake on shreds of plastic bags or straight into bare hands. Afterward our hands and faces were covered in sugary icing and the ground was littered with pieces of dropped cake.

Finally, there was me, requesting the mariachis play the lively tune "Viva México." And also me, being the only person singing along with the men in black.

Women in Mexico, at least the ones I know, tend not to drink much. The exception seems to be at wedding receptions. Men in Mexico drink a lot, and weddings provide just one more excuse to break open the tequila. Needless to say, nearly all of us were tipsy by the end of the night, and a feeling of drunken bonhomie was shared by all. Before Will and I staggered back to the car with Teresa, Esteban, and a sleepy little Ilse, a relative of Lupe's I'd been chatting with for the last half hour pressed me to her generous bosom and insisted that I come visit her and her husband in Querétaro soon. "¡Sí, claro! Vendré," I promised her, "y muy pronto."

AFTER OUR LUNCHEON GROUP finished watching the video, my friend Kevin asked if she could take a photo of Gracia, Lupe, and me together. The two of them staged a brief protest but eventually we all trotted out to the courtyard to have our picture taken.

Back in Seattle, Kevin sent me an eight-by-ten-inch copy of the photo. Though it's in black and white and slightly blurry, it remains my favorite photo of the three of us. Not only because it reminds me of their generosity that day, but because just as Kevin was taking the shot, Lupe cracked a joke.

And for once, all three of us are smiling.

38 | *The Ride*

THE SAME SUMMER AS THE WEDDING, I took Hannah and a friend horseback riding at a hacienda on the outskirts of San Miguel. It was owned by an ex–Madison Avenue advertising executive who'd given up a high-profile life in New York City to come live in Mexico. Our outing that day included a visit to an eighteenth-century conversion chapel and a meandering ride on sleepy nags through tiny villages and emerald fields of *maíz*. But what I remember most about that day was neither the lovely pastoral views nor our languorous ride through cornfields.

It was something the man — who looked like Roy Rogers's sidekick, Cookie, in his worn leather hat and muddy Wellingtons — said while we were making small talk.

"You never really can be friends with the Mexicans," he announced, as we ambled along.

His bold, skeptical statement immediately drew my ire.

"I beg to differ," I replied. "There are many Mexicans I consider my friends."

"It's not what it seems," he said, as if he were an authority on cross-border relations. He continued, talking about his relationships with his workers and the Mexicans who lived in the villages surrounding his hacienda.

"I've done a lot for these people, trying to help them improve their lives, and do I ever get any appreciation or acknowledgment in return? Never."

I didn't know whether to feel angry with or sorry for this man who had traded his Versace suits for the costume of a cattle rustler from the Outback. His cynicism and self-referencing made me bristle. But on the other hand, he'd given up a successful life in New York to search for a new and different one in Mexico, only to discover that he didn't really know how to fit in. That couldn't have been easy for him or his ego.

We still had an hour-long ride ahead of us and an equally long car ride from town behind us, so instead of picking a fight with the man, I offered him *metta*, thoughts of loving-kindness prescribed by the Buddha, and went along for the ride.

BACK HOME AT CASA CHEPITOS that evening, I told Paul about the conversation I'd had with the cowboy out on the trail.

"You know how difficult it is for most Americans to befriend the Mexicans here," my husband said. "You make friends everywhere you go because you're so gregarious. But if you remember, it wasn't easy, even for you, at the beginning. For people who aren't as outgoing as you, or don't speak Spanish as well, it's hard to get a foot in the door here."

My husband empathizes with shy people, being somewhat shy himself. And, of course, he was right about it not being easy for Americans to make friends with the Mexicans in San Miguel. Being reminded of my own struggle to fit in and the feelings of isolation I'd felt our first years on the alley was what allowed me to have compassion for the man. But I didn't think shyness was the issue, and I told my husband so.

"Shyness is not his problem. It's more like he's hurt that the Mexicans don't acknowledge his attempts to help them, and they don't appreciate him. I think what he's really looking for is validation."

Thinking about him made me wonder about my own reasons for helping others: Am I motivated to help them as a way to feel better about myself?

Or am I somehow trying to atone for the prosperity I've been blessed with in this life?

As the discussion drew to a close, Paul said something pointed:

"If you give charity to people, then turn around and expect them to thank you, it's as if you're asking for part of it back."

Our conversation reminded me why — other than the cheese blintzes, potato latkes, chocolate matzoh, and Zabar's bagels — I like the Jewish part of the theosophical smorgasbord so much. In addition to all the delectable things I'm grateful to the Jews for, they've also provided me with a new perspective on the concept of charitable giving.

Contrary to the stereotype of Jews being tight-fisted, they are among the world's most generous philanthropists. Of the top fifty charitable donors listed in the *Chronicle of Philanthropy* in 2008, fifteen of them were Jewish. While Jews make up only 2 percent of the population in the United States, they provide nearly 30 percent of all charitable contributions. The tradition of giving has deep roots in Jewish culture, and providing for the poor is considered as much an obligation as it is a good deed. They even have a special name for it: *tzedakah*.

The word *tzedakah* is Hebrew for what, in English, we call charity. But the nature of *tzedakah* is very different. The word *charity* suggests acts of benevolence and generosity for the benefit of the poor and needy. It, intrinsically, includes some level of patronization. *Tzedakah*, on the other hand, is more accurately translated as "justice," "fairness," or "righteousness." In the true spirit of *tzedakah*, giving to the poor isn't a magnanimous act; it's an act of justice, the duty of those who are more fortunate. Orthodox Jews believe a beggar is doing the donor a favor by offering her the opportunity to perform *tzedakah*.

One day, I watched a man in San Miguel perform *tzedakah*, and it helped change the way I think about charity in Mexico. While waiting to pay for my latte at a café on Calle Reloj, a withered old woman shuffled in. She held out a shriveled, claw-like hand, and the café's owner automatically reached into his till and pulled out a ten-peso coin. As she shuffled out the door, mumbling a blessing for the man's soul, he turned to me and said in English:

"You know, we don't have Social Security here in Mexico, like you do in the States. This is all she has."

The experience was a sobering reminder that the poor, old, or sick in Mexico have no safety net. The responsibility to provide for them falls to their families — or to the more fortunate in Mexican society, if their families can't help them. I often think of the café owner's comment when I give money to the diabetic guy who sits on the sidewalk by the old gas pump with his pant leg rolled up to expose a great oozing wound that never heals; or the old woman with stumps for legs who propels herself through the market on her knuckles; or the blind man in the weathered cowboy hat and sunglasses who has been silently collecting coins in a tin cup on the corner of Mesones and Colegio for thirty years.

Learning about *tzedakah* also helped me find a new way to think about the eight-hundred-pound gorilla that wealthy expats in Mexico, like me, live with but rarely talk about: the enormous economic chasm between us and the majority of our Mexican neighbors. While there are no easy answers or quick fixes to the problem, after ten years of living off the largesse of Mexico, I have begun to think of the money and time I donate in San Miguel as *tzedakah*: not a charitable act but as an obligation I have to contribute to the social welfare of our poorest citizens. Like paying taxes. (Which are, by the way, quite low in Mexico.) My yearly contributions are about equal to what I feel I *should* be paying in property taxes there, and it is still only a drop in the vast ocean of need. What the country really needs is less corruption, more economic development, higher paying jobs, more opportunity, and the redistribution of Carlos Slim's wealth. But it's what I can do for now.

39 | *Bicentenario*

SOMETIME IN LATE 2008 OR EARLY 2009, I began noticing brown and white signs along the highways near San Miguel that said *Ruta 2010*. I assumed they had something to do with the bicentennial of Mexico's War for Independence, since it was coming up in mid-September 2010 and San Miguel, together with the neighboring town of Dolores Hidalgo, is considered the Cradle of Independence. But then I noticed the same signs in Michoacán and Guerrero and other states in Mexico. So I did a little Internet research and learned that the *Ruta 2010* signs referred to historical routes traveled by important revolutionary figures of both the War for Independence of 1810 and the Mexican Revolution of 1910.

In mid-February 2010, I was in a shuttle van full of Americans headed to San Miguel for a writers conference. Up front, next to the driver, was a woman with bleach-blonde hair dressed head to toe in crisp white linen. She'd been living in Mexico for fifteen years, she explained to us, and in San Miguel for the past twelve. As we drove by one of the *Ruta 2010* signs along the highway, she pointed to it and asked the driver:

"What are those signs that say Ruta 2010 for? They seem to keep popping up everywhere."

"They are there because of the bicentennial," he replied.

"Bicentennial of what?" she asked.

"The bicentennial of the War for Independence."

"What war for independence?"

I rolled my eyes at the woman sitting next to me, barely able to suppress a desire to groan.

I knew my attitude was more than a little snobbish — and that it went against everything I'd learned about the judging mind in our Buddhist study group. But I had a hard time believing anyone could live in Mexico for fifteen years and still somehow manage to miss the major details of its history. Like the two revolutions that had changed its whole course.

It's not uncommon for Americans to mistake Cinco de Mayo for Mexico's Independence Day. But the fifth of May — which for Mexican restaurants in the States is just another excuse to sell more margaritas — has nothing to do with Mexican independence. Cinco de Mayo celebrates Mexico's victory over the French during the Battle of Puebla in 1862. While it is a national holiday, it's not nearly as important as Mexico's Independence Day, which is in the middle of September.

El Grito de Dolores, the cry for independence that Padre Miguel Hidalgo y Costilla delivered to his congregation early on the morning of September 16, 1810, marked the beginning of the long and bloody battle that would become Mexico's War for Independence. Each year, late in the evening of September 15, a version of *el Grito* is invoked in the *zócalos* and plazas of towns and cities throughout the country. But in all the years I'd been traveling and living in Mexico, I'd never been there to celebrate the Independence. So, in early September of 2010, I returned to San Miguel with my friend Nora to celebrate two important events: the bicentennial and Gisela's third birthday and presentation to the Catholic church.

IT WAS MID-AFTERNOON when our plane landed in Mexico City. The driver we'd hired to pick us up was there waiting but confessed, as we loaded our luggage into his car, that he'd never driven in the *distrito federal* before. In short order we were circling Mexico City's *centro*, hopelessly lost. We navigated stop-and-go traffic through the city for two and a half hours before he found the exit onto Insurgentes Norte, which led to the highway to Querétaro and then on to San Miguel.

It was eight o'clock when we arrived home to Callejón de Chepito and found Gracia, Salvador, and Cholo sitting on the concrete bench out front. They were happy to see me, especially Cholo, who rushed up to give me a hug when I opened my arms.

"He's been chanting your name for two days," said Salvador in mock exasperation.

I smiled at Cholo and hugged him tight. To me, there's nothing sweeter than a child who has not yet grown too self-conscious to offer his affection.

A minute later, our neighbor Jesús walked down the alley. It was the first time I'd seen him since the mayoral elections were held. I pumped my fist in the air and shouted, "¡Lucy ganó!"

Jesús grinned, but added with more than a hint of disdain in his voice, "Yes, I'm afraid it's the women who control this town now."

Though she'd managed to get elected, nothing was going to be easy for San Miguel's first female mayor. Like President Obama, Lucy Núñez inherited more problems than any single human being could ever possibly deal with. There were claims that prior to leaving office, San Miguel's last mayor drained its coffers and left its public services in disarray. Rumors had circulated that when Lucy took office in February, there wasn't enough money to fill the gas tanks of the garbage trucks or police vans. I feared our first female mayor would sink under the weight of the mess she inherited, and that her gender would be unfairly pointed to as the reason.

Nora and I, who were both starving, dropped our bags inside the house and walked down to *el centro* for dinner at El Pegaso. We drank icy margaritas and dined on *sopa azteca* and shark tacos and were debating whether or not to split a piece of El Pegaso's signature raspberry pie when a golden burst exploded above the Presidencia. Shimmering sparks rained down outside the restaurant window and a sudden blare of trumpets issued forth from the *jardín*. That clinched it. We decided to pass on the pie that night and hurried out to join the pre-bicentennial party a block away.

On the cobblestone square between the *jardín* and the Parroquia, a large stage had been erected where a sixteen-piece band with guitars, drums, and a huge horn section was in full swing.

All the male band members were dressed in khaki suits and white shirts. The band's main vocalist, and only female member, had poured her voluptuous body into black jeans and matching tank top and was strutting around the stage in four-inch heels.

Their first number, a song made famous by Puerto Rican mambo master Tito Puente, had everyone's feet tapping, and soon a group of Mexican women, each possessing at least a sprinkling of gray hair, formed a circle and began swaying and twirling to the music. I smiled at them and moved my hips and snapped my fingers, and they waved me into their coven. I dropped the bag of leftovers I was carrying on the sidewalk and joined them.

Before long we were line dancing and taking turns demonstrating our salsa skills inside a circle, while the sidelined husbands gathered to watch. They looked a bit envious, I thought, as their wives danced around, so obviously having a good time without them.

At one point, a slender woman in a black turtleneck and thick black eyeglasses, with long silvery hair pulled back tightly, took a turn in the middle of our circle. The song was a samba and she appeared to be in a state of post-reproductive ecstasy as she swayed her narrow hips and swirled seductively in circles. Her imaginary dance partner was certainly far sexier than any real one could ever be. The rest of us smiled knowingly, nodded our heads in her direction, and called out "*¡Andale!*" and "*¡Hijole!*" as she pushed the boundaries of propriety.

After a half hour of dancing, Nora looked longingly toward home, and we turned to leave.

"Oh, don't go, we're just getting started!" said a woman who was a wicked salsa dancer disguised as a grandmother.

Having been up since four in the morning, Nora and I bowed out graciously. When I looked for the leftovers I'd dropped on the curb, I was amused to see some lucky boy already taking care of them for me.

On September 12, Paul forwarded me an article from the *New York Times* with the heading MEXICAN BICENTENNIAL FALLS SHORT ON FERVOR. In it, the author attempted to make the case that Mexicans are not, by nature, patriotic, and claimed they were not excited about the upcoming bicentennial celebrations. To substantiate his argument that Mexicans weren't patriotic, the reporter had quoted an expert: a student working the late shift at the Starbucks in Guanajuato. "Everything is very symbolic, far from reality, when Mexicans are not very patriotic," the young barista told the *Times* reporter.

It was not obvious to me, from the thousands of red, white, and green flags being displayed from the terraces of houses and apartments, and the balconies of restaurants, hotels, and government building throughout the country, that the Mexicans were not feeling patriotic.

It also wasn't obvious from the multitude of children sporting faces painted in the stripes of the flag; their parents' matching red, white, and green clothing; or San Miguel's *taxistas*, who had draped the hoods of their cabs with Mexican flags. Even Guanajuato's ranchers were cruising through town in their Ford F-250s, with Mexican flags flapping proudly from their tailgates.

San Miguel's narrow streets were decorated with enough green, red, and gold Mylar garlands to keep a factory of Chinese workers busy for a year. A portrait of Ignacio Allende and even more garlands and streamers adorned the face of the Presiden-cia, adjacent to the *jardín*, while across the way a nightly light show, projected on the façade of the Parroquia, attracted big crowds after dark.

Thousands of tourists were pouring into town, and they seemed in the mood to celebrate. A surplus of college-age kids from Mexico City flowed in and out of cafés, restaurants, and bars until all hours of the night. I'd never seen so many young *chilangas* marching in fashion lockstep: Aviator sunglasses and Aéropostale T-shirts now seemed to be hot, hot, hot among the youth of Mexico City; the Gap craze clearly over and done with.

Every day more people arrived in town. Hotels that had been empty for months were full again. Like they had during San Miguel's halcyon days in the mid-2000s, hotel clerks and waiters bustled about, happy to be busy again.

On my way home from *el centro* the day before Independence Day, I stopped to buy a Mexican flag from a vendor who was sell-ing them on the street. When I asked him how much they were, the man looked at me curiously, surprised that a gringa would want one.

"*¡Viva México!*" I said, handing him a hundred pesos. "*Sí, ¡viva México!*" he replied, laughing. Then I marched back up the hill with my Mexican flag and hung it from the terrace of Casa Chepitos, on the side facing the alley.

September 15, 2010. The big night. The night when, two hundred years after a cry for independence was delivered by a rebel priest from a tiny parish thirty miles north of San Miguel, President Felipe Calderón will deliver *el Grito de Dolores* to a half million people crammed into Mexico City's *zócalo*. Mayor Lucy Núñez will make history, too, as the first woman in San Miguel to issue the Cry for Independence. It will *feel* as though five hundred thousand people are crowded into the *jardín*, even if it's only a fraction of that.

Gracia, Cholo, Nora, and I gather at nine thirty to head down to *el centro* for the celebration. Lupe has opted not to come along. She wants to finish painting her kitchen in Santa Rosa before Gisela's birthday party on Sunday.

We're about to leave when Gracia points to the Mexican flag hanging from our terrace.

"Don't you want to bring your flag?" she asks.

I run upstairs to retrieve the flag and Cholo and I take turns waving it above our heads as we march down the Cuesta de San José. The crowd thickens when we reach the Plaza Cívica and we have to be careful not to poke people with the stick as we flow down Mesones Street toward the *jardín*.

"*¡Estamos al tiempo!*" Cholo shouts, excited that we've arrived in time to see the *desfile de los insurgentes*. He waves at the men dressed up as Padre Hidalgo — with his banner of the Virgin of Guadalupe — Ignacio Allende, Juan Aldama, and other members of their *Dragones de la Reina* mounted military unit as they trot down San Francicso Street. Behind them are a dozen more actors, wearing the loose white cotton pants and shirts and red bandanas of the Mexican *peón*. They wave fiery torches above their heads and shout as they march along:

"*¡Muerte a los gachupines!*" Death to the Spaniards! "*¡Viva la señora de Guadalupe!*" Long live our lady of Guadalupe!

We follow the procession of mock revolutionaries to the *jardín*, which is teeming with people. The crowd is even bigger than during Semana Santa, Easter week, when all of Mexico is on vacation. The four of us wind our way through the swarms and up the stairs into the *jardín*'s center. We find a spot in front of a series of *puestos*, carts selling snacks and soft drinks, on the southwest corner, and park ourselves in front of a heavy stainless steel cart where a *vendedora* is selling small plastic bags full of spicy *chicharrones* and homemade potato chips. From there, Gracia tells me, we'll have the best view. The balcony of Allende's house, where Lucy Núñez will give *el Grito*, is directly in front of us.

The only problem with our plan is that over the next hour, the number of people in the *jardín* continues to multiply — by two or three times. People push and shove their way into every square inch of space around us until we are squashed between the hordes and the potato chip vendor's cart. It's impossible for me to move forward or backward or bend over. I grip the flag tightly; there's no way I could bend over to pick it up if I dropped it.

As usual in Mexico, no effort is being made at crowd control, and people continue to cram into the *jardín*. An older woman leans hard against me, forcing my right hip into a soft drink cooler. I soon realize why she's pushing so hard. She's trying to create space around her granddaughter, who's panicking. The grandmother eventually convinces the potato chip vendor to allow her granddaughter to move around behind the cart where there's slightly more breathing room.

I'm worried too, about Cholo, who is buried beneath a profusion of elbows, thighs, and buttocks. He looks up at me with sleepy brown eyes, but doesn't say a word of protest. Nora, on the other hand, complains loudly. Like me, she's easily overwhelmed by crowds, so she heads for a spot farther away, under the laurel trees. But Gracia refuses to budge.

"We'll be able to see everything from right here," she insists. I have to wrestle my enochlophobia to the ground, but I stick with Gracia and Cholo.

ELEVEN O'CLOCK FINALLY ARRIVES and so does Mayor Nuñez. She stands on the second-floor balcony of Allende's house, waving an enormous Mexican flag, and passionately delivers *el Grito*. But her voice is drowned out by the raucous crowd. The only word I understand is *¡Viva!*, which the people around me are shouting over and over. I join in, but only half-heartedly, since it's impossible, given my anxiety level, to take a deep breath.

After Lucy finishes, the *castillo*, a giant wooden Erector-set-like contraption with fireworks strapped to it, is lit.

Mexicans are serious about fireworks. They shoot them off for weddings, baptisms, feast days, fiestas, and every other special event. This time around, the city's pyrotechnical squad has outdone itself. A man with a torch climbs around the enormous wooden frame, igniting the displays, and rockets burst like hand grenades; giant wheels of fire twirl and whirl and whiz; mortars explode in eardrum-bursting blasts. The profuse smoke and acrid smell of burning nitrates singes the inside of my nostrils and I'm certain what little hearing I have left from my rock concert days will be gone.

When it seems as if the clamor and chaos cannot possibly get worse, more fireworks explode from the roof of the Presidencia and fiery confetti begins raining down on us. A group of girls next to Gracia and me jump and scream and swat at the cinders hitting their bare arms and landing in their hair. Suddenly everyone around us is pushing and shoving, trying to avoid getting burned. Gracia and I are slammed against the potato chip cart, which lists sharply, threatening to topple and crush its owner and the little girl she's been sheltering.

The crowd begins yelling "*¡Whoa!*" in unison and I hear Gracia shout, "*¡No, no, no!*" I look over and see her trying to keep Cholo from being thrown to the ground. Remembering a newspaper article I read about ninety-three people being trampled to death at a soccer game in Sheffield, England, I become light-headed from hyperventilating and nauseated from anxiety.

For a brief second, I wonder: *Is this how my Mexican days are to end — trampled to death in the shadow of the Parroquia?* Then my survival instinct kicks in.

I throw down the flag I've been clutching all night and shove my way past a knot of screaming girls toward the square's outside wall. I figure we can escape the crowd by jumping over it. But as I squeeze past a soda vendor to get closer to the top, he yells, "You can't go over that wall, it's way too high!"

Just watch me, I think. I imagine lowering Cholo and Gracia

over the ten-foot wall, and then myself, which is, of course, totally irrational. I grab Cholo's hand and am pulling him toward it when Gracia yells, "*¡Judith, mira!*" She points to a tiny gap in the throng. I grip Cholo's hand tighter and push my way toward it. I keep pushing and pushing until the three of us are out of the *jardín* and standing safely on the corner of San Francisco and Hidalgo streets. Only then do I notice: Gracia's clutching my Mexican flag in her hand. I point to it, laughing.

"You saved the flag!"

"*¡Claro que sí!*" Of course, she says. "You paid good money for this."

The people in the streets begin shouting "*¡Viva! ¡Viva!*" again, and we join in.

"*¡Viva México!*" Gracia and I shout in unison.

El Grito de Dolores
Long Live the Heroes that gave us our Fatherland!
Long Live Hidalgo!
Long Live Morelos!
Long Live Josefa Ortiz de Dominguez!
Long Live Allende!
Long Live Aldama and Matamoros!
Long Live National Independence!
Long Live the Independence Bicentennial!
Long Live the Centennial of the Revolution!
Long Live Mexico! Long Live Mexico! Long Live Mexico!

40 | *La Presentación*

PADRE LUPITO IS LATE. The mass celebrating Gisela's presentation to the Catholic church was supposed to have started an hour ago. I'm sitting on a low stone wall in the courtyard of the same parish church where Lupe and Juan were married, with a small group of their family and friends. We are waiting for the priest to arrive. Waiting is an art form in Mexico, one that I am only now beginning to appreciate.

"On Sundays *el Padre* travels from ranch to ranch delivering blessings and saying mass," Lupe's sister-in-law explains. Apparently, if the food is good or the drink abundant at one ranch, he sometimes lingers longer than he should. As Lupe moves from group to group visiting with her guests, I notice she keeps an anxious eye on the road. At one point she asks someone for Padre Lupito's cell phone number. He doesn't answer.

Three-year-old Gisela, who will be formally presented to the Catholic church today, looks like a miniature debutante in her white satin gown embroidered with streams of fuchsia-colored flowers. The heels of her tiny white pumps make a tiny clicking sound on the flagstones as she wanders about, playing with cousins and having her picture taken. Nora trails her with the diligence of a professional wedding photographer, making her pose with each group of cousins, aunts, and uncles. Gisela coos in delight when she sees her own image on the digital screen.

I get so much joy out of watching the antics of the innocent toddler that I forget for a moment that she is the source of a vitriolic debate two thousand miles to the north. It's hard to fathom how the Fourteenth Amendment rights (which guarantee citizenship to all persons born in the United States) of this little girl have ended up being the focus of the acrimonious and divisive debate going on in the United States Congress, and on blogs generated by people associated with the Aryan Nation.

"Anchor babies," "taco babies," "illegal burritos" are some of the names hate groups in the United States call children like Gisela on their websites. Their mothers are called much worse things.

When the white SUV carrying Padre Lupito and his mother, and driven by his altar boy, finally arrives, Lupe exclaims under her breath, "*¡Gracias a Dios!*" The mass goes smoothly. Gisela sits quietly in her chair in front of the altar. Amazingly, her young mind seems to understand the sanctity of the occasion. It helps that Padre Lupito delivers the liturgy and prayers at warp speed, like he did for the wedding. Once again, I understand next to nothing. I do, however, catch the Lord's Prayer at the end.

Afterward, everyone files down Santa Rosa's dusty streets to Lupe and Juan's house where hundreds of pink and white balloons festoon blue tarps that have been draped over the courtyard to keep the sun and any potential rain off the guests. Beneath the tarps are rows of long folding tables and dozens of chairs. Vases of white chrysanthemums and pink carnations dot tables covered with hand-embroidered tablecloths.

We're treated to barbecued chicken with pasta and plenty of hot, handmade tortillas. Instead of beer, tall glasses of homemade pulque are served. *Tuna*, the fruit of the nopal cactus, has been added to the pulque, making the potent alcohol look like health-rendering beet and wheatgrass juice. I've heard that the pulque made at local ranches is some of Mexico's best, but I notice Gracia isn't touching the stuff, so I don't either.

Five-year-old Ilse, Teresa and Esteban's precocious daughter, spends twenty minutes recounting the story of the Little Mermaid for me. I listen intently — where else am I going to learn important Spanish words like *príncipe*, *bruja del mar*, *pulpo*, *langostino*, and *sirenita*?

The story of *La Sirenita* has been prompted by the cake Lupe picked out at La Casita Feliz. It's decorated with pink icing-sugar and a very accurate, very blonde rendition of *la Bella Durmiente*. As Remedios and I sit discussing the historical significance of the Virgin of Guadalupe in Mexican culture, we're each served slices of cake with one of Sleeping Beauty's smiling blue eyes peering at us from the frosting.

THE SKY GROWS DARK and random pellets of rain begin to fall. Gracia anxiously rounds up those of us who rode out to the ranch with her and herds us toward the Explorer.

"I don't like Marthín driving after dark," she says. Earlier, I offered to drive, but apparently Gracia has about as much confidence in my driving skills as she does my sweeping skills.

When no one else does, I volunteer to ride up front with Marthín, who will be fifteen in November. Another successful graduate of Lupe's Driving School, he is, in fact, a good driver. But on the way home, as the car reaches sixty-five miles per hour, and rain and darkness threaten to obscure our view, I gently suggest he might want to turn on his lights and employ the windshield wipers.

When I turn around to say something to Gracia, I notice she is white-knuckled from gripping the seat. When I mention it, she replies: "I'm only nervous when he drives on the highway."

I look over at Marthín, nearly as long and lanky as Will was at age sixteen.

"I have confidence in you," I say. Somehow, saying it aloud helps shore up my own confidence, as we speed along the unlit, rain-slicked road toward home.

41 | *Gratitude*

ONE EVENING DURING the bicentennial week, Patrice came over to Casa Chepitos for dinner. She brought her friend Lulu, and Nora was still there too. Though dinner was only simple bistro-style fare — a ragout of vegetables cooked in garlic and olive oil over penne, with stewed mission figs and tea cookies for dessert — the evening was one I would not soon forget. The four of us drank plenty of wine and talked nonstop for three and a half hours about our businesses and the economy, our passions and the things that sustained us, our lives spent abroad in Mexico, Europe, and the Far East. Lulu entertained us with a story about meeting Véra Nabokov, the wife of Vladimir Nabokov.

The beauty of the evening was that all four of us were old enough to hold AARP cards, yet never once did we digress into the usual self-effacing talk of fading beauty or failing health. Nor did we bring up the subject of men, the shortage of available ones in San Miguel, or the problems we had with the ones who inhabited our lives.

At the end of the evening, the conversation, as it often does among my expat friends, turned to the United States' broken immigration policy, especially as it pertained to our Mexican friends. Our discussion inspired Patrice to repeat the toast she'd made at a bicentennial dinner two nights before:

"Let us honor the greatness of Mexico and its people: their spiritual nobility, artistic genius, respect for traditions, authentic family values, and valor in the face of adversity. And we, especially, should be grateful for their generous immigration policy, which enables so many of us foreigners to live here in peace and prosperity."

It was sobering for each of us sitting around the table at Casa Chepitos that night to reflect on how easy the Mexican government makes it for us to travel back and forth across the border, while U.S. immigration officals often stymie Mexicans, even when they are entering the United States legally.

GRATITUDE TURNED OUT to be the theme of the week, because the next day I had a conversation with Lupe that was rooted in that very sentiment. With Gisela and Cholo seated between us, we'd taken the *urbano* down Ancha San Antonio to La Casita Feliz in Colonia Guadiana to order a cake for Gisela's third birthday party. Afterward, we decided to walk the kids over to the playground at the Parque Juárez. On the way, I told Lupe about an intense dream I'd had the night before.

In it, she, Juan, Gisela, and I were attempting to cross the border together. It was clear I was playing the role of coyote, and that it was my responsibility to get them across safely. It was a long and complicated dream, with shadowy landscapes, lurking *migra*, and an old Jeep Cherokee that I'd commandeered to drive them to safety. I remembered zipping Gisela into a duffel bag and praying she wouldn't cry out. The dream was so real that when I awoke from it my heart was racing.

Lupe listened intently as I described the dream and then asked:

"Did we make it across safely?"

"I don't know. I woke up before the dream was over."

She was quiet for a moment. Then Gracia's familiar Mona Lisa smile crossed her lips.

"You know, my mom still tells me I should never have gone *al norte*, but I'm glad I did."

"Why's that?"

"Because going there taught me that Mexico is where I belong, and I had to learn that for myself. Juan and I may not have much, but we've got each other. We've got Gisela, and our families, and our health, and we have enough to get by on. I have a lot to be grateful to God for."

I looked at her and smiled, impressed by how wise she had grown in the last eight years.

OF THE MANY TIMES I've flown into Del Bajío International Airport in León, only once was it cloudy. In fact it was so cloudy that night, the pilots seemed to have miscalculated how close the runway was, and the plane hit the ground with such an unnerving force that the Mexican passengers all began crossing themselves. Some were still at it, long after we'd landed safely and were taxiing to the gate.

While waiting for the luggage to arrive, I was talking with an American woman who had also noticed the Mexicans crossing themselves.

"What I don't understand is why they crossed themselves *after* we'd already landed safely. It was obvious by then that we weren't going to die," she said.

Though her comment amused me, I attempted to answer her seriously, with the bit of knowledge I have of *persignarse*, the Mexican practice of touching forehead, heart, and both shoulders, left to right, in the sign of the cross, and then kissing their right thumb twice.

"I think in this case, crossing themselves was intended as a gesture of gratitude. Not as an insurance policy against death that they hoped God would provide."

Recently I read an article about *persignarse* written by a woman named Judy King, who lives in Ajijic on Lake Chapala, near Guadalajara. In it she provided this poignant description: "The Sign of the Cross is a refuge in moments of grief, fear, need, and danger. It is a symbol of joy, thanksgiving, hope, and gratitude.

This rich gesture helps [Mexicans] maintain continual contact with God."

THERE IS NOWHERE ON EARTH I feel closer to the divine — whether you call it God or Yahweh, Krishna or Allah, or nothing at all — than up on the terrace of Casa Chepitos. It is where I go to seek solace and find inspiration, to read, to meditate, and to ruminate on the world. It is there that I find peace from both internal and external problems.

It's a place where I've celebrated happy times. Like the night of July 8, 2008, when San Miguel de Allende was named a United Nations World Heritage site. Being selected was a great honor for our city, and it was celebrated with the customary speeches, plenty of pyrotechnics, and symphonic music. I watched the dramatic fireworks display from the terrace and listened to a flood of inspirational music so loud it could be heard all the way up in Atascadero. I remember being lulled to sleep by grandiloquent melodies that climaxed sometime around midnight.

The terrace is also a place where I've sought refuge when the unfairness of life feels unbearable. Like the night I was alone at Casa Chepitos and received news that a former City People's employee, a brilliant young man whom we all adored, had thrown himself in front of a freight train, leaving behind his distraught partner — our store manager — and their six-month-old son. As I leaned against the terrace's waist-high wall that night, ranting at rain-choked clouds and sobbing as if one of my own had been lost, my neighbors stared up at me in stunned silence.

ON A RECENT EVENING, under happier circumstances, I was up on the terrace again, watching the sunset and enjoying a cool evening breeze. As the sun began to sink behind the distant mountains, the light-blue sky turned turquoise and the grassy green pastures beyond the city deepened to a shadowy forest. The pewter waters of the Presa de Allende gleamed mirror-like in the early evening light, and ribbons of clouds to the west turned from salmon pink to blood-orange red as the sun continued its descent. I've enjoyed that familiar view many times, but that evening I saw something I'd never seen in my nine years at Casa Chepitos.

The final rays of sunlight, filtered through clouds from the west, struck the dome of the San Francisco church at a certain angle and streamed back out through its three long windows and the cupola above, making the tiled dome appear as if it were illuminated by some mysterious inner light, like that in a Renaissance painting. At that exact moment, the bells of the Parroquia's *campanario* began to toll. Intoxicated by the radiant vision and the sonorous *bong* of church bells, a feeling of gratitude spread through me like a soothing golden liquid. Gratitude for my lovely terrace. Gratitude for its incandescent view. Gratitude that I was present, at that exact moment, to enjoy it. And above all—gratitude for the Mexican life I'd stumbled into.

Epilogue

The problem with the world is that
we draw our family circle too small.

MOTHER TERESA

OCTOBER 2012. I'M SITTING IN A WINDOWLESS basement room in San Miguel's San Antonio church. It must be ninety degrees in the tiny, low-ceilinged room, and it's so tightly packed with people there's barely room to walk. In my prayers, I urge *la Guadalupe* to make sure fire doesn't break out down here. We'd never get out alive.

Young mothers and fathers, wearing their Sunday best, hold infants dressed in snow-white gowns or rompers. The parents, along with godparents, grandparents, and other family members, sit shoulder-to-shoulder on wobbly folding chairs listening to a man pontificate on the blessedness of baptism. He's dressed in a green plaid cotton shirt and khaki work pants, and it takes me a while to figure out that he's actually a priest. His lecture goes off on many tangents: from the duties of godparents, to the sanctity of marriage, the blessedness of the Virgin Mary, and how good kids are turning bad these days. When my children were baptized, I was required to attend baptism classes every week for four weeks. Mexican Catholics seem to cram that month-long class into one, interminable, morning session.

I've returned to San Miguel this month to celebrate the baptism of Lupe's second daughter, Juana, who was born in July of last year. The one-year-old, who is my godchild, is a perfect blend of her father and mother and grandmother. She has Juan's moon-shaped face, Lupe's beautiful light-brown skin, and Gracia's big brown eyes, along with her spirited temperament. Though Lupe was anxious to have Juana baptized as soon as possible, she didn't have the money for the fiesta at first. When she'd finally saved enough, she then had to wait patiently until I could break loose from my job in Seattle to be there.

The babies grow restless as the priest drones on. One of them awakes from a nap howling and wakes others, who also begin to fuss. Toddlers squirm and wiggle, desperate to be untethered from their parents. Fretful mothers offer bottles and blankets and bounce their babies so vigorously I fear for the infants' jostled brains. All of it to no avail. The *sacerdote*, oblivious to the chaos around him, continues to talk over the howl of bawling babies.

WHEN THE PRIEST GOES ON for more than an hour, I turn to Lupe and say, "*Ave Maria, llena de gracia*, pray for us that this priest does not go on for another hour." She giggles quietly. Luckily, my goddaughter, who Gracia describes as *traviesa* (troublesome), sleeps through the entire thing.

Finally, the priest begins calling out the names of the parents and handing them cards that we carry upstairs and into the main church for the actual baptism.

Compared to the agony of the basement, I feel as though we've ascended into heaven entering the church's open, airy sanctuary. I've visited San Antonio's church only once before, and that was in 1974. Today it's the centerpiece of one of the fastest-growing barrios in San Miguel. In the early '70s, it stood in the middle of a barren field like a lonely sentinel. I remember it as being a simple and dimly lit church without the decorative gilding or the bright, freshly painted nave it has now.

What struck me most on my first visit was the church's miracle board with its hundreds of tiny silver *milagros* and scraps of paper with scribbled prayers pinned to it. Prayers of thanks. Appeals to God. Petitions to the Virgin of Guadalupe. Simple notes announcing the death of a loved one. I read them all.

We sit patiently, waiting for our turn to proceed to the font where the babies will be sprinkled with holy water. Four or five photographers roam the aisles snapping pictures of the "baptees" and their parents. (Yet another way to eke out a living in Mexico.) When it's Juanita's turn, I follow Juan as he carries her, rosy-cheeked and refreshed from her nap, up to the ornately carved font where a posse of white-robed priests are pushing people through the line like bouncers at a popular nightclub.

"Who is presenting this child, Juana Judith, to be baptized in the holy Catholic church?" a priest asks. I choke up hearing my own name, touched that Lupe has chosen to name her daughter after me. I fight to keep my composure in front of the stern-faced priest who is now staring at me, awaiting my response.

"I am," I finally blurt out.

Juanita Judith fusses, but only a bit, as he pours holy water over her head and says the blessing.

"In the name of the Father, the Son, and the Holy Ghost," he says.

And the Blessed Virgin Mary, I silently add.

The only mishap of the day is when the special baptism candle I'm charged with carrying will not stay lit. A photographer grabs it from me and uses his penknife to whittle away the wax to create a longer wick, but still the flame goes out. Juan is troubled by this. He thinks it's a bad omen for his daughter. But I don't agree. I think it's just a cheap candle made in China that has a faulty wick, and that my namesake, the troublesome Juana Judith, is going to live a long and blessed life.

Acknowledgments

FIRST, AND FOREMOST, I want to express my gratitude to Gracia Rodriguez and Lupe Cordova for welcoming me into their homes and their hearts, and for allowing me to share their stories. Being part of their lives has expanded mine in so many ways, I only hope the converse is true.

I am also deeply grateful to the coterie of talented editors who helped midwife this book into the world: Kyra Freestar, Jennifer Hager, Beth Jusino, Eleanor Licata and, most of all, Barbara Sjoholm, whose insightful edits helped give shape to an amorphous mess.

I want to thank my first writer's group, Erika Giles, David Bauman and Lisa Weil, for their patient critiques of my very shitty first drafts; and The Shipping Group, especially Mary Oak and Waverly Fitzgerald, who cheered me on when things seemed hopeless. *Mil gracias* to Muriel Bevilaqua Logan and Patrice Wynne, *mis compañeras de viajes*. I am especially grateful to Muriel for her Spanish edits and for sharing her knowledge of Mexico, and to Gordon for driving.

A huge thanks to my husband, Paul Atlas, and our children, Will and Hannah Atlas, for allowing me to drag them down to Mexico year after year. And for putting up with a wife and mother who was often M.I.A. while writing this book.

Last, but certainly not least, I want to thank my mother, Lucile Gille, for being the one steady beacon in her children's often tumultuous lives. For this, and everything else she has done for us, we are, and always will be, eternally grateful.

About the Author

JUDITH GILLE is the founder of City People's Mercantile and City People's Garden Store in Seattle, but her passion is writing about Mexican art and culture and immigration issues. Her work has appeared in the *Los Angeles Times*, *The Dallas Morning News*, the *Florida Sun-Sentinel*, in magazines, online literary journals, and several anthologies. She currently divides her time between Seattle and San Miguel de Allende.

CPSIA information can be obtained at www.ICGtesting.com
Printed in the USA
BVOW07s0113180913

331436BV00001B/1/P

9 780578 124698